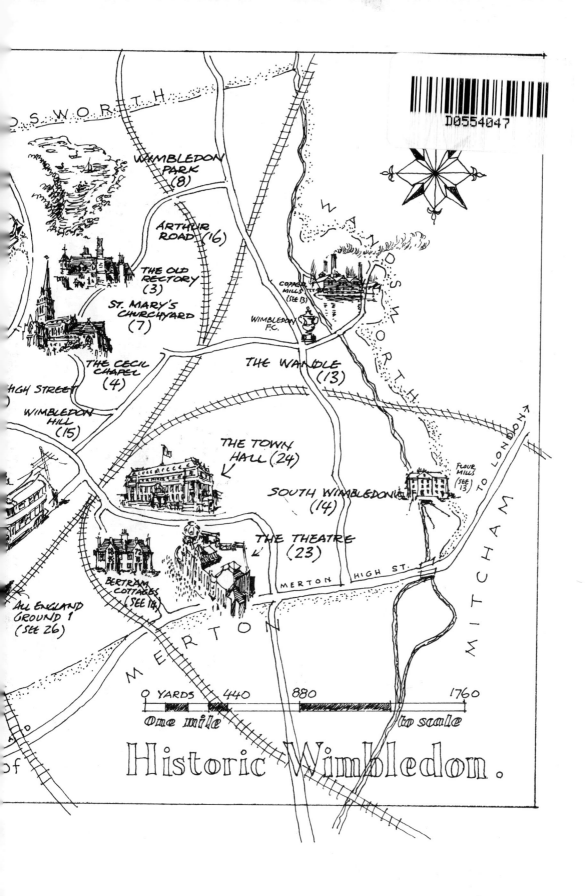

WANDSWORTH

WIMBLEDON PARK (8)

ARTHUR ROAD (16)

THE OLD RECTORY (3)

ST. MARY'S CHURCHYARD (7)

COPPER MILLS (SEE B)

WIMBLEDON F.C.

WANDSWORTH

THE CECIL CHAPEL (4)

THE WANDLE (13)

HIGH STREET

WIMBLEDON HILL (15)

THE TOWN HALL (24)

SOUTH WIMBLEDON (14)

FLOUR MILLS (SEE 13)

TO LONDON

THE THEATRE (23)

BERTRAM COTTAGES (SEE 14)

MERTON HIGH ST.

ALL ENGLAND GROUND 1 (SEE 26)

MERTON

MITCHAM

0 YARDS   440   880   1760

One mile   to scale

Historic Wimbledon.

Historic
WIMBLEDON

Historic WIMBLEDON

CAESAR'S CAMP TO CENTRE COURT

Richard Milward

THE WINDRUSH PRESS · GLOUCESTERSHIRE

and

Fielders OF WIMBLEDON

First published in Great Britain by
The Windrush Press and Fielders of Wimbledon,
Windrush House,
Main Street,
Adlestrop, Moreton-in-Marsh,
Gloucestershire

Fielders Bookshop
54 Wimbledon Hill Road
Wimbledon
London SW19 7PA

First published 1989
Reprinted 1989

British Library Cataloguing in Publication Data
Milward, R.J. (Richard John), *1924–*
    Historic Wimbledon: Caesar's Camp to
    Centre Court.
    1. London. Merton, (London Borough).
    Wimbledon, history
    I. Title
    942.1'93

    ISBN 0 900075 16 3

Production by Landmark Production Consultants
Typeset by DP Photosetting, Aylesbury, Bucks
Printed and bound in Great Britain by
The Bath Press, Avon

Contents

VICTORIAN WIMBLEDON

WIMBLEDON IN THE TWENTIETH CENTURY

LIST OF MAPS

Preface

Wimbledon has a fascinating history. The site of a major prehistoric hill-fort, it has successively been part of a prosperous manor owned by the Archbishops of Canterbury, the home of three leading families, the Cecils, Churchills and Spencers, and a centre of society attracting politicians like Pitt and Wilberforce, and aristocrats like the Duke and Duchess of Cannizaro. In Victorian times it was transformed into a railway suburb, which grew at amazing speed, and became famous first for rifle-shooting and then for lawn tennis. Amid all the changes, the ordinary inhabitants continued their daily lives in the High Street, in the fields around the village and later in the new roads off the Broadway or Worple Road. And since becoming part of the London Borough of Merton in 1965, history continues to be made in Wimbledon's struggle to maintain its identity. Yet, so far, only one full local history has been written — nearly 125 years ago by a local parson, Revd William Bartlett. Since then so much has happened that it would need a formidable amount of research to do the subject justice.

Historic Wimbledon is an attempt to fill the gap. It has been written to show to both residents and interested outsiders (perhaps even to our councillors and developers) the wealth of history and tradition that lie within the parish boundaries. It aims to provide a novel approach to the past — neither a straight narrative, nor an account of different aspects of that past, but a history of all the important places and buildings that survive from the past, along with the lives of people closely associated with them. Twenty-six topics have been selected for lengthy treatment, together with nearly fifty other connected places of interest which have been given brief accounts at the end of each chapter. The topics are arranged in chronological order, so that the book can be read as a partial history. But there is little on the poor and virtually nothing on the Second World War (which has already been well covered in Norman Plastow's *Safe as Houses*).

The book is the result of twenty-five years' intermittent research. It relies heavily on the work of many others, both those who have written the books and articles listed at the end, and those who have generously shared their own researches. Among them I must give a special word of thanks to my friends in the Wimbledon Society Local History Group. At our monthly meetings they regularly provide useful information and ideas on Wimbledon's past which have been of incalculable help in writing this book. I am also grateful to my brother John and to Bill Stanton for reading the chapters in draft and making helpful comments; to Evelyn Jowett and Norman Plastow for their help with the Wimbledon Society photographs; and to John Wallace for providing the excellent maps and drawings. Above all, I must thank Richard Heath of Fielders, his wife Gillian, and Victoria Huxley of the Windrush Press for their constant help and encouragement in both the writing and the production of the book.

In *Historic Wimbledon* I have tried to correct many legends about Wimbledon's past. In the process I may easily have created a few new ones myself, so I would be grateful for any corrections or additions that could improve a future history of Wimbledon.

Richard Milward
May 1989

Early Wimbledon

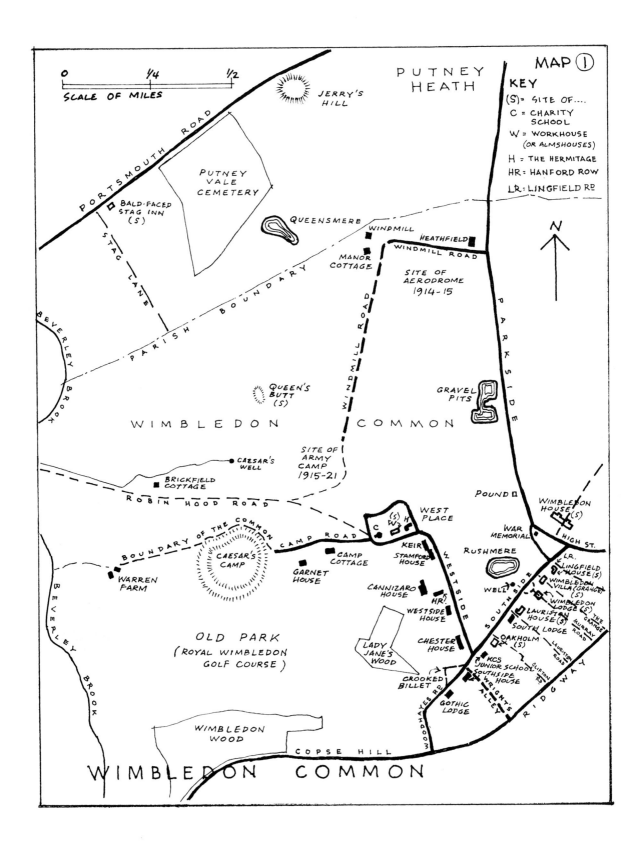

— 1 —

Caesar's Camp

Sir Thomas Jackson, a distinguished architect, once described his contemporaries as "this destroying generation [who] have robbed [our children] of so much that would have been interesting". He was referring to developers, who already existed in late Victorian and Edwardian Wimbledon. In the 1880s he had prevented them from pulling down Eagle House, a fine early seventeenth century building in the High Street, by making it his home. But he then had to watch powerless as they destroyed

Aerial view of the Camp taken about 1923.

1

two neighbouring eighteenth century mansions, Wimbledon House, Parkside and Belvedere House. Had he settled in Wimbledon a little earlier, he would have been equally shocked at their destruction of one of the village's few genuinely ancient sites, Caesar's Camp.

The position of the Camp on the south-western edge of the Common is magnificent. Though not on the highest part of the plateau and with only limited views to the north and west, it commands a fine panorama to the south across the

John Samuel Sawbridge-Erle-Drax M.P., owner of the Camp when the ramparts were levelled in 1875.

valley towards Epsom Downs. One hundred and twenty years ago its ramparts were still ten to twenty feet high and its ditch on average twelve feet deep. Yet now these are little more than minor obstacles to the Royal Wimbledon golfers and the Camp's true glory as a prehistoric hill-fort is almost impossible to imagine.

The destruction was the responsibility of a Victorian landowner, John Samuel Sawbridge-Erle-Drax M.P. (1800–1887). Through marriage he had inherited not merely a big estate in Dorset, but a large area in Wimbledon between Beverley Brook and Westside, once known as The Old Park. He seems to have shown little interest in his Wimbledon property until the town began to be developed. Then in 1870 he leased several of his fields south of the Common, including the old Camp, to a Mr Dixon who planned to build houses there. Dixon did put up three large houses in Camp Road, including a fine mansion now known as Garnet House, the home in the 1890s of a distinguished electrical engineer, John Hopkinson. But when he proposed to build more houses on the Camp itself, he met strong opposition.

CAESAR'S CAMP

Among the critics was Sir Henry Peek M.P. who lived at Wimbledon House, Parkside and who only a few years before had led the fight against Earl Spencer's scheme to enclose the Common. Peek and his friends raised a fund and offered to buy the Camp, but Drax refused to sell. Finally, in 1875, Dixon started building. He had bricks and scaffolding sent to the site, cut down the trees growing on the Camp, levelled its ramparts and filled in the ditch. At the last minute the Commons' Conservators stepped in. These men, who had recently been given the responsibility of looking after the Common, realised that for Dixon to get his materials and workers to the site, he would have to use Camp Road, just inside their Common. They therefore went to court and asked the Master of the Rolls to ban the use of the road for any other than "agricultural purposes". They won their case, but by then it was too late to save the Camp. The place was now hardly recognisable as a hill-fort and in 1907 it became part of the Royal Wimbledon golf course.

Caesar's Camp, however, still remains a place of great historical interest. Many theories have been put forward as to who were its builders. They range from claims that it was constructed by Neolithic men, Celts of the late Bronze or Iron Ages, Romans or Romanised Britons, to older ideas that the Saxons or even the Danes were responsible. Unfortunately, the Camp has never been thoroughly excavated. In 1937 a single ditch was dug across the site from east to west by the Metropolitan Water Board, supervised by two archaeologists, F. Cottrill and A. W. G. Lowther. They discovered a small pit with the remains of some coarse Iron Age pots and bowls and so dated the Camp approximately to the third century B.C. Their conclusions, however, have recently been questioned and the building of the Camp has now been pushed back to a period of transition from the Bronze to the Iron Age, namely the eighth to the sixth centuries B.C.

Whenever it was built, the Camp was found by the archaeologists to have had quite formidable defences. The single ditch had been about thirty feet wide and probably twelve feet deep. The one rampart had had timber revetments on both its inner and outer sides and, with a wooden palisade on top to protect the defenders, had probably been about twenty feet high. Underneath the mass of earth used for these ramparts, the archaeologists even found the original layer of turf. The defences were almost circular and enclosed a large area of about twelve acres, with only one gate

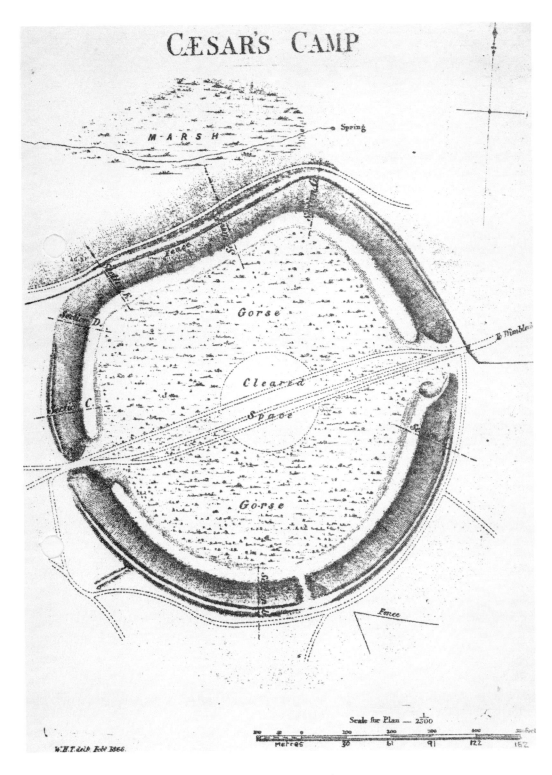

CÆSAR'S CAMP

MARSH

Spring

Gorse

Cleared

Space

To Wimbledon

Gorse

Fence

Scale for Plan — $\frac{1}{2500}$

Metres

W.H.T. delt. Feby 1866.

4

on the west towards Coombe Hill and with its best water supply, a spring, just outside the ramparts to the north-west.

The purpose of such a camp still remains a mystery. A. W. G. Lowther thought it was one of a string of hill-forts constructed in south-east England about 250 B.C. to meet the threat of invasion from northern France by a Celtic tribe using the latest weapon, fighting chariots. More recently, Prof. Barry Cunliffe claimed that it was the headquarters of a "warrior aristocrat", while Dr Cook thought it was more a place of refuge from attack for local tribesmen and their animals. The latest view, put forward by Viscountess Hanworth, sees it as a centre for trade, a place like St George's Hill, Weybridge, and Coombe Hill to which goods and animals were brought from the Thames and then distributed inland.

Whatever its use, the Camp seems to have been lived in for only a short time. The archaeologists found very few signs of occupation inside the defences, while these defences themselves seem never to have been reused as the timbers had not been repaired. They certainly show no sign of ever being attacked, not even by Julius Caesar.

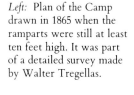

Left: Plan of the Camp drawn in 1865 when the ramparts were still at least ten feet high. It was part of a detailed survey made by Walter Tregellas.

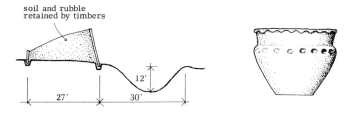

soil and rubble retained by timbers

12'

27'   30'

Far Left: Section through ramparts. *Left:* Iron Age pot.

The Roman general's name seems first to have been given to the hill-fort by a nineteenth century map-seller and publisher, G. F. Cruchley. The words "Caesar's Camp" (along with "Caesar's Well") appear on his "New and Improved Map of the Environs of London", published in 1824. Until then the Camp had been given a variety of names. To the people of Wimbledon it had been known simply as "The Rounds". To the Elizabethan historian, William Camden, it was "a circular fortification called Bensbury". To an early seventeenth century surveyor it was "an old fort called Benchebery fort".

Whatever Mr Cruchley thought, however, Julius Caesar almost certainly never visited Wimbledon. Although he has four other Camps named after him (at Aldershot, Bromley, Easthampstead and Keston), he probably had nothing to do with any of them. Indeed he had little reason to go anywhere near Wimbledon. His route was not along our Ridgway, but further east and so he is more likely to have crossed the Thames at Westminster or Chelsea, than at Kingston or Brentford.

CAESAR'S WELL

The Well is the best known of the springs on the western edge of the Common. It lies in a hollow ringed with pines, five hundred yards to the north of Caesar's Camp. Round it is a circle of large granite blocks, put there in 1872 by Sir Henry Peek M.P. who had just helped to save the Common from enclosure. Water no longer comes from the Well, but from a stand-pipe a few yards away which taps the spring

The earliest photograph of Caesar's Well, taken before 1860. It shows the well, encased in brick since 1829, still in use, and without its later ring of pines.

eighteen feet down. Its flow never stops, even in very dry summers such as that of 1976, although it was then reduced to a third of its normal rate.

The spring was used from earliest times as shown by the discovery nearby of Neolithic arrowheads and knives. But, like the Camp, it was never visited by Julius Caesar. In the eighteenth century it was known as Robin Hood Well and its water was so pure that it was thought to have special medicinal qualities. In 1829 it was encased in brick and a surveyor, Robert Vazie, was sent by a London aqueduct company to see if the water from "Wimbledon Springs" could be brought to the Chelsea area by aqueduct over the Thames. Fortunately the plan was dropped.

THE RIDGWAY

This road, running from the southern end of the High Street along the edge of the plateau to join Coombe Lane as "the highway to Kingston", is certainly old. Both Revd William Bartlett, Wimbledon's first historian, and Walter Johnson, who wrote about the Common, were sure it was Roman. Bartlett thought it a branch of Watling Street; Johnson claimed it was part of an otherwise unknown Roman road that ran from the Sussex coast to Kingston and Weybridge. A far more ingenious theory was put forward by Alan Elliot in an issue of the Wimbledon Society Newsletter. He maintained that the Ridgway could have been part of a Neolithic salt route, linking a farming community at Kingston (which recent excavations have proved certainly existed) to the nearest supply of salt, the marshes in the Thames estuary near Greenwich. The road, he claimed, followed the line of a series of gravel deposits: over Coombe Hill, along the Wimbledon plateau and a finger of gravel beyond St Mary's Church, then across the Wandle, up to a new layer of gravel by Clapham and on to Greenwich.

In fact there is no hard archaeological evidence that early man ever passed this way. No Neolithic arrowhead, Iron Age sword, or Roman coin have yet been found along the road. Its main use clearly was to link the village to the nearest market at Kingston and it must therefore have been used by many generations of Wimbledonians.

Rushmere Green

Caesar's Camp is at one extremity of a large, irregular plateau which extends more than three miles between the hills at Wimbledon and Putney. To the south the plateau overlooks a wide sweep of country as far as the North Downs; on the other three sides it looks down on river valleys, the Thames to the north, the Wandle to the east and Beverley Brook to the west. Its soil, gravel and sand over a thick layer of clay, is of little use for farming, but as it supports only light vegetation, it is ideal for hunting and grazing. Its large pond, known as 'Rushmore' in Tudor times, was an invaluable source of rushes, widely used in early huts and cottages.

For many centuries only a handful of men and women recognised these advantages. Their few relics — Mesolithic stone knives, a Neolithic flint arrowhead, a bronze axe and a probable Bronze Age barrow — have been found on the western side of the plateau. But nowhere is there any sign of a genuine "Prehistoric" settlement, apart from Caesar's Camp. The Romans and early Saxons seem to have taken even less interest in the plateau. A few coins and a fragment of a vase are all that have been found from the Roman period, while the early Saxons appear to have left nothing at all.

A place called "Wunemannedun" near the Thames is mentioned in a late Saxon charter, but its site is unknown and it is not named in William the Conqueror's Domesday Book. Its existence as a true community can only be dated from the early thirteenth century when it appears in documents as "Wimeldon", "Wimmeldun" or "Wymbaldone". Unfortunately, recent attempts by archaeologists to find any trace of it, first in the High Street and then near St Mary's Church, proved abortive. Like Medieval Putney, it may not have been a coherent village, but a collection of scattered settlements or farms, situated below the hill as well as on the plateau. If it was a village, the plateau seems the more likely site as it had one great advantage, a good water supply thanks to the natural springs and to the ease of sinking shallow wells in the gravel.

The chief evidence for life at Wimbledon in the Middle Ages comes from documents in the Library of the Archbishops of Canterbury at Lambeth Palace. They show that the Archbishops owned a lot of land in south-east England, including the manor of Mortlake. This was one of the largest manors in England and comprised the fields and villages of Putney, Roehampton, East Sheen and Wimbledon, as well as Mortlake itself, where the Archbishops had a manor house. At Wimbledon they had a grange or farmhouse and by it a stable, granary, sheepfold and "cowhouse", all enclosed by a wall. In the farm lived the Archbishops' full-time servants: a carter,

RUSHMORE GREEN

8

ploughman, shepherd, cowherd and dairymaid. In the granary were stored the wheat, oats, rye and barley grown in the four large arable fields. In the sheepfold were kept over five hundred sheep which grazed on the Common, while the cowhouse was needed more for the twenty-two oxen used to pull the ploughs than for the relatively small number of cows.

The Archbishops rarely ventured nearer Wimbledon than the manor house at Mortlake. The only one who certainly visited the village was Archbishop Peckham, a distinguished Franciscan, theologian, author, poet and church reformer. In 1286 he came to St Mary's Church and ordained to the priesthood two local men, Adam and "John, called Payn". One of Peckham's immediate successors, Walter Reynolds, had previously been Rector of St Mary's, but it is doubtful whether he ever visited Wimbledon either as Rector or Archbishop, although he died at Mortlake in 1327. He was tutor and chief adviser to the very unpopular King Edward II. Perhaps, as a result, his corn "lying in a grange at Wymeldon" was burnt by a large crowd, while later "evildoers felled the trees and hunted the deer" in several of his parks and woods, including Wimbledon. The park was almost certainly a large area, fenced off from the "common waste" and known in the seventeenth century as the Old Park, which then extended from Westside to Beverley Brook and included Caesar's Camp.

The Common was thus larger in the Middle Ages than it is today. It was treated not as a place for a pleasant walk or a training run, but as an essential part of the daily struggle for existence. Its land may have been technically "waste" as the soil was too poor for regular cultivation, but its lush grass, especially on Rushmere Green near the

Rushmere in 1908, with mothers, nannies and their charges out for a walk. In the background is the Green, with newly built houses to the left and the Georgian Holly Cottage, the white building, to the right of centre.

An aerial view of Rushmere and the south-eastern end of the Common, taken in the early 1920s. Beyond lies the Green and the High Street.

village, provided excellent pasture for animals, while its larger trees and bushes further from the village were a source of wood for the home. Its gravel was used to fill in ruts on the roads and its loam was spread on the arable fields.

Legally it was owned by the Archbishop as lord of the manor, but over the centuries his tenants had gained "rights of common". Everyone who farmed a "virgate" or fifteen acres was allowed to graze five "plough beasts" or oxen, two cows, twenty-five sheep and two pigs, so long as they had rings in their noses. They could also take for their own use "estovers" or branches of trees over eight feet high, as "housebote", "ploughbote" and "cartbote" (i.e. for the repair of their cottages and implements), and brushwood — "thorns, brambles, briars, ferns, furze and the like" — for use as "firebote" or fuel, and "hedgebote" for repair of their hedges.

The tenants' use of these rights had to be carefully supervised as the Common could only support a limited number of animals. These animals too were liable to stray into the common fields (any that did so were promptly placed in the village pound). There was also a danger that enterprising tenants might try to sell wood to outsiders. Therefore three or four times a year the Archbishop's Steward held a special Manor Court, with the chief tenants acting as a jury. Matters affecting village life were settled there: use of the common fields as well as the common waste, petty offences, repair of roads and ditches, enforcement of rules about the quality of bread and ale,

10

and the banning of "unlawful games". The decisions of the Court were recorded in Latin on long rolls of parchment and kept carefully in the parish chest.

The Wimbledon Court Rolls only survive from 1461. The earlier records were either destroyed in the Peasants' Revolt of 1381 or simply disappeared. But the Rolls from the last seventy-five years of the Archbishops' tenure of the manor give a good idea of why Rushmere Green and the rest of the Common were so important to the inhabitants and what the chief hazards were in using it:

Having "eight pigs unrung, overturning the pasture of the Common, to the common nuisance" (1461); keeping "three cows and four calves on the Common, though having no right to do so" (1463); an outsider from Ham cutting "three cart-loads of wood on the Common" (1467); setting fire "intentionally to many oaks and saplings on the Common" (1478); pasturing "mangy horses" (1488); stopping up "the common footway leading from Wymbledon Common to the common fields" (1492; probably the passage now known as Wright's Alley); taking "any wood or furze from the Common" by any baker or brewer (1521); digging "the land of the lord [probably near the later Brickfield Cottage] and making 430,000 stones called bricks" (1528); gathering "apples called crabs growing in the Common and selling them so that the tenants cannot have the apples according to their rate as from ancient times they were accustomed" (1529).

Only seven years after this judgment, the Archbishops lost the right to hold any more such Courts. In 1536 Thomas Cranmer was forced to surrender his manor to the new supreme Head of the English Church, King Henry VIII.

THE POUND

An essential part of every well-regulated Common was a wooden enclosure for keeping stray animals — or those with no right to graze there. Wimbledon is one of the few places that still has a pound, on the eastern edge of the Common, a little north of the Green. Although the present enclosure is probably rather smaller and certainly less secure than its predecessors, photographs show that it was used as late as the start of the present century to hold a straying horse, and, in 1940, to hide a concealed pill-box to halt any Germans who dared to land on the Common.

The earliest record of the position of "Wimbledon Pounde" is in a survey of the manor made in 1617. It was then at the junction of Church Road and the High Street, opposite the Dog and Fox. It was moved early in the eighteenth century to the top of the Village Green, not far from its present position. It was looked after by a pinder or pound-keeper, who had the duty of catching any animals that strayed off the Common, and "impounding" them until they were claimed by the owner who naturally had to pay a fine. He also had to support the "supervisors of the Common" (known from 1727 as "Common Keepers"), one of whose duties was to "drive" the Common from time to time and find cattle with no right to be there. He did not, however, have to keep the pound in repair; that was the responsibility of the lord, or in 1727 "the lady of the manor", Sarah Duchess of Marlborough who was asked by

The Pound, securely padlocked with a horse inside, watched by two small boys. The photograph was taken in July 1912.

the Manor Court to see to its repair as it was "in the greatest decay".

Local records rarely make explicit mention of the impounding of animals. The most notable occasion was in 1588 when one after another five stray horses "came into the manor", clearly a result of the general upheaval caused by preparations to meet the Armada. They were impounded, put in the care of different villagers and when they were not claimed became the property of the manor bailiff who sold them at a good profit.

Two hundred years later the chief concern was over "hogs and swine found feeding in lanes or byways". In 1796 the Beadle reported that he had impounded ten pigs belonging to Mr Hatchett (who lived in a small cottage near Claremont House), but that "someone had broken down part of the pound and let the pigs out". Mr Hatchett must have been responsible, as he had to repair the pound and pay the Beadle "for his trouble". Pigs were still a nuisance thirty years later. In 1827 the local magistrates, in session at the Horn, Wandsworth, and learning that "divers swine are permitted to stray about the parish", damaging fences, ditches and even the roads, ordered that they must be impounded.

WRIGHT'S ALLEY

This ancient right of way between the Common and the fields below the Ridgway is named after an early nineteenth century resident of Southside House, Robert Wright, Esq. He lived in the part of the house nearest to the alley from about 1800 until his death at the age of eighty-four in 1832. He was a gentleman from Suffolk, of "independent means", and obviously made a deep impression on his

Wright's Alley, with its swing-gate entrance, taken in May 1913.

contemporaries. Not merely did his name stick to the alley, but a tablet was put up inside the parish church to his memory, recording that he was "esteemed and respected by all who knew his worth, while his pious resignation under the infirmities of increasing years was a blessed example to those who witnessed it". His unmarried daughter continued living in the house, looked after by six servants, until her death in 1851.

The real origin of the alley is lost in the mists of time. Its first mention is in the Manor Court Roll of 1492. In the 1617 survey it is alluded to as a "lane leading out of the Common to the common field", through land called "Ward hawes", now the playing fields of King's College School and the origin of the name Woodhayes Road. Along with all other rights of way in the parish, it is not marked on John Rocque's map of 1745, but it is there on all later detailed maps of Wimbledon.

Its exit on the Ridgway almost opposite the top of the Downs, another old right of way, suggests that it was once a route not just to the immediate fields, but from Wimbledon to Merton Common. It therefore had to be preserved when the railway was being constructed in 1838, hence the narrow Lower Downs tunnel.

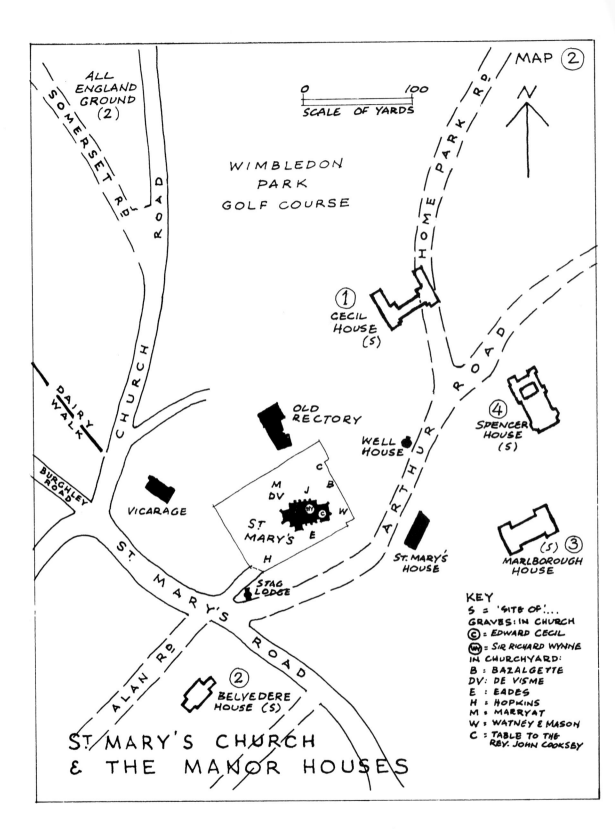

MAP ②

N

ALL ENGLAND GROUND (2)

SOMERSET RD.

CHURCH ROAD

HOME PARK RD.

0   100
SCALE OF YARDS

WIMBLEDON PARK GOLF COURSE

① CECIL HOUSE (S)

ARTHUR ROAD

④ SPENCER HOUSE (S)

DAIRY WALK

OLD RECTORY

WELL HOUSE

BURGHLEY ROAD

VICARAGE

C
M   J   B
DV
ST. MARY'S   W
E

ST. MARY'S HOUSE

(S) ③ MARLBOROUGH HOUSE

H

STAG LODGE

ST. MARY'S ROAD

ALAN RD.

② BELVEDERE HOUSE (S)

KEY
S = 'SITE OF'...
GRAVES: IN CHURCH
ⓒ = EDWARD CECIL
Ⓦ = SIR RICHARD WYNNE
IN CHURCHYARD:
B : BAZALGETTE
DV: DE VISME
E : EADES
H : HOPKINS
M : MARRYAT
W : WATNEY & MASON
C : TABLE TO THE REV. JOHN COOKSBY

ST. MARY'S CHURCH & THE MANOR HOUSES

14

3

The Old Rectory

Only ten years after dispossessing Archbishop Cranmer of his manor of Mortlake, Henry very nearly died at Wimbledon. While staying at his new Palace, Oatlands near Weybridge, late in 1546, he was taken seriously ill with some undefined fever. He could not be treated properly in Surrey, so his doctors advised an immediate return to London.

Slowly the King journeyed along the uneven roads. He stopped first in Wolsey's old Palace by the Mole at Esher, then at his own new Palace of Nonsuch at Ewell. Here he had to rest for a week, while Thomas Alsop, his apothecary, supplied a stream of remedies to control the fever. At last he was fit to travel again, but could not manage the ten mile journey to Whitehall without a break. It was therefore decided to make a further stop half-way at the royal manor of Wimbledon.

Henry's stay here lasted barely two days and only one reference to it survives, in the State Papers. This, however, takes the form of a very interesting account of "materials supplied" by Thomas Alsop:

> "1546. December 20. Perfumes for Wymbyton [to make the sick-room bearable].
> Juleep [a sweet drink to help down medicine].
> Aqua majorane cum musco [a stimulant].
> A Succat [fruit, preserved in ginger].
> December 21. Manus Christi powder [soothing powder].
> Juleep.
> Aqua cum musco ad nares [water flavoured with musk, for the nose]."

Helped by this treatment, Henry was just capable of travelling again on 22 December. By nightfall he was back in his palace at Whitehall, very sick and in no condition to enjoy Christmas. Just over a month later, on 28 January 1547, he was dead.

The first and last visit by the King would have caused a great stir in the village. Unfortunately there is no record of where he stayed. The logical place was at the manor grange which then belonged to his sixth and last wife, Catherine Parr, but it was hardly fit to receive a King. Far more suitable was a large two-storeyed brick building just to the north of St. Mary's Church, known then as "the Parsonage House" and now as the Old Rectory.

It is still an impressive building, a fit stopping-place for a sick monarch. Sadly, the

Aerial view of St Mary's Church and the surrounding buildings, taken about 1920. It shows the Old Rectory in the bottom left hand corner and the Manor grounds (but not the house) beyond. In the background are fields along Lake Road.

red-tiled roof and Tudor turrets are the only parts of the house that can normally be seen, peeping above the hedge at the side of the churchyard, so few people realise that the Rectory is Wimbledon's oldest building and has played a crucial part in its history.

Built about 1500 the Rectory probably occupied the site of a previous house. Its original owners were almost certainly the last pre-Reformation rectors of St Mary's, who unlike many of their predecessors lived in the parish. They were wealthy, particularly the last rector, Thomas Mylling. At his death in 1540 he left a large sum in legacies to friends and to at least eight servants. His successor, now a mere vicar, had to hand over the house to the King who leased it to Sir Robert Tyrwhitt, Steward of the royal manor of Wimbledon. Tyrwhitt, an experienced official who had done well out of the dissolution of the monasteries, had the job of looking after the mortally sick King.

In 1546 the Rectory was much larger than it is today. In the centre was the dining hall, long rather than high with thick walls. At one end was a "withdrawing room" and a parlour. Opposite were the kitchens, pantry, larder, meat room, buttery and

16

dairy. Near the hall were two spiral staircases which led to the bedrooms and to the servants' garrets in the roof. Outside across a yard were extensive outbuildings: a brewhouse, bakehouse, washhouse, granary, barn, stable, mew (for hawks) and henhouse. Beyond was a large garden and orchard with two dovecots, a summer house and a fig-walk which still survives.

Not long after Henry's death, Tyrwhitt passed on the sixty year lease of this imposing house to an even more important friend, Sir William Cecil. Though only in his early thirties, Cecil was already a Secretary of State in Edward VI's Privy Council and a wealthy landowner in Lincolnshire. In 1550 he needed a country mansion not too far from London, to which he could retreat when pressure of work became overwhelming. For this purpose the Rectory at "Wymbledon" was ideal. Three years later, however, when Mary Tudor became Queen, he fell from favour and left office.

The next five years, 1553 to 1558, he spent mostly at the Rectory. He lived there with his second wife Mildred, one of the most learned women in England, their unmarried sisters, his eldest son Thomas a small boy of eleven in 1553, and two other boys — one Cecil's ward, the other an orphan — who were there to keep Thomas company. They were waited on by over twenty servants dressed in blue livery.

Sir William kept careful records of all expenses at the Rectory and so provides an intimate picture of life there in the 1550s. He had very definite ideas about food and stored an impressive array of "provisions necessary" for his large "howshold". At Christmas 1553 he even drew up detailed menus for each meal. For a Sunday dinner, then eaten about midday, he provided a wide choice of meat:

"First Course: Brawn and mustard; Boiled meat stewed; Boiled beef; Chewetts or pie; Veal or pig; Roast capon [chicken].
Second Course: Wild fowl or coney [rabbit]; Lark or pigeon; Tart."

Not a single vegetable appeared on the list, but there were large quantities of wine and home-brewed beer to help wash the meat down.

On great occasions like Christmas, the Cecil family probably ate with all their servants in the large hall. They decorated the high table with silver cups, bowls and plates, a silver spice box, and silver "salts" and pepper-boxes. They wore their best "apparell": Sir William a long black satin gown, furred with squirrel; Lady Mildred a gown of cloth of silver, bought from the effects of "my lady Anne of Cleves" (who died in 1557). During the meal they were entertained by musicians playing lutes and virginals. In the afternoon they got some exercise hunting deer in the manor park. In the evening they consumed another large meal and then Sir William retired to his study to read one of his many volumes of the classics.

This relaxed life came to an abrupt end in November 1558. On the death of Mary Tudor, Cecil returned to office as chief adviser to her half-sister, Elizabeth I. He now had far less chance of slipping away to Wimbledon, even at weekends, and soon decided to concentrate his attention on his main country house, Burghley in Lincolnshire. So in 1564 he handed over the lease of the Rectory to a friend, William Bowyer.

The Cecil family, however, had certainly not given up their connections with

THE OLD RECTORY

The Old Rectory, drawn from St Mary's Churchyard by Henry Warren about 1818. It then had many fewer windows and no south wing.

The Old Rectory today, with its modern porch and wings added in the nineteenth century.

Wimbledon. Only nine years later Sir William's eldest son, Thomas, now a young man of thirty-three, married with a large family and recently knighted by the Queen after distinguishing himself in a tournament at Kenilworth, decided to return to his old home. In March 1575 he took over the lease of "the parsonage howse, barnes, stables, orchardes, gardynes and all other howses and buildyngs to the same parsonage belongyn". Only six months later he was trying to persuade his father, now Lord Burghley, his formidable stepmother and his stepsister, Lady Oxford, to visit him. In 1576 he bought the Archbishops' old manor house at Mortlake and soon began a grand new manor house in the latest Elizabethan style. He had it perfectly sited to the east of the Rectory, on the slope of the hill looking north across a "New Park" towards Putney.

"Wimbledon's greatest ornament", according to the Elizabethan historian, William Camden, was finished in Armada year, 1588. It was constructed of "excellent good brick" and rose two storeys to a gabled roof. Its interior was rich, with a "fair and large hall" used for banquets or great social occasions, state rooms with elaborate fireplaces and panelled walls, and upstairs a "great gallery", a "fair dining room" and a "great chamber". To the south of the house lay twenty acres of

The Elizabethan Manor House, built by Sir Thomas Cecil in 1588. His previous home, the Rectory, lies just beyond the entrance to the right through which the coach has come. This drawing was made by Henry Winstanley in 1678.

19

magnificent gardens, rising in a series of terraces up the slope of the hill. On the north side "a cascade" of more terraces and steps led down to the park, well-stocked with deer.

Once Sir Thomas moved into this palatial residence, the Rectory was almost literally overshadowed. It was referred to as an "outhouse", while through its grounds ran the final stage of the main drive from the London road. Along the drive came some very distinguished guests, above all the Queen and her chief courtiers on several occasions in the 1590s, followed by King James I who rewarded Sir Thomas by making him Earl of Exeter in 1605. For the rest of the seventeenth century the Rectory seems to have been used to accommodate the servants of the great guests at the manor house. By 1720 it had sunk further to the status of the "Old Laundry House". At some stage in the eighteenth century half was pulled down and the rest used as a farmhouse. In 1882 it was well restored by Samuel Willson. Since then it has been added to by successive owners and is now in fine condition, although recently part of its grounds have been used to build town houses — and the legend of its secret tunnel has been exposed.

SECRET TUNNELS
(By Norman Plastow F.R.I.B.A.)

Tunnels have a certain fascination and for many years there have been stories of tunnels in connection with the Old Rectory and the 1588 Manor House which, if they were all true, would involve a complete warren of underground passages, not only in the Arthur Road and Church Road areas, but extending as far as Merton Priory! In fact only two tunnels have been proved to exist: one which runs from Park House

The tunnel linking the Marlborough and Spencer Manor Houses, photographed in 1908.

School across the Ricards Lodge playing fields and another said to run from the Wimbledon Park golf course to the Old Rectory. The first of these has been well documented. It was last opened at the time Park House School was built and the cellars of Wimbledon Park House were exposed. This is a large and well constructed tunnel of arched brickwork, six feet wide by nearly eight feet high and a hundred and fifty feet long. Its purpose was to link the Duchess of Marlborough's house (built in 1735) to the nearby servants' building. Such an arrangement was quite common at the time and enabled the servants to reach the main house without spoiling the landscape by being seen crossing the lawns. The idea that these tunnels were built as secret escape routes in times of trouble cannot be supported. They were such large works of engineering that they could not have remained secret.

The other tunnel, associated with the Old Rectory, has also been explored, but has never been traced to its source. It measures only two feet wide by three feet, six inches high. A survey carried out in 1948 placed the end of the tunnel somewhere under the garden of the Well House in Arthur Road. In 1984 the tunnel was explored by two members of the Chelsea Spelaeological Society. What they found below the garden of number 124 Home Park Road, was a brick chamber over ten feet deep from which a tunnel ran approximately east and west. The tunnel has a brick floor and walls with an arched top. The brickwork is no earlier than the eighteenth century and any historical link with the Rectory or the 1588 Manor House is therefore ruled out. After travelling about two hundred and seventy feet, the west tunnel terminates under a bush on the golf course. In the other direction it ends after about a hundred feet under the houses in Home Park Road at which point it is blocked. If continued it would run under the triangular green where Home Park Road and Arthur Road meet and then across Arthur Road to the site of the servants' wing of the Duchess of

The fig walk in the garden of the Old Rectory.

Marlborough's house, which was later incorporated into the Spencers' Manor House, built in 1801.

The tunnel was probably used to drain the site of the Spencers' Manor House. When the cellars were excavated it was noted that the building was surrounded by brick surface drains leading to a deep sump from which a small tunnel ran to the south-west. This was probably the other end of the tunnel. The soil here is clay and there are many underground springs. In fact there is still a trickle of clear water running through the long tunnel to the golf course.

THE FIG WALK

Only two fig walks are said to exist in England; one is at Wimbledon in the Old Rectory garden. It consists of two lines of fig trees and their shoots planted on both sides of a path, trained on a frame to meet overhead and producing a tunnel of green, well over fifty yards long.

It is said to have been planted in the 1550s by Sir William Cecil. This is possible as Sir William certainly loved gardens, but fig trees are not mentioned in any of his papers written when living at the Rectory. Another source claims that Princess Elizabeth and Robert Dudley, later the Earl of Leicester, first met in the fig walk in 1549; a small stone sarcophagus is said to mark the spot. In fact, the meeting took place eight miles away and five years later, in 1554, when both were held in the Tower by Mary Tudor.

4

The Cecil Chapel

The Old Rectory remains the least known of Wimbledon's historic buildings, yet just over the wall stands probably the best known, the Parish Church of St Mary the Virgin. Every year its two hundred foot spire appears at the beginning or end of television transmissions from the Lawn Tennis Championships, dominating the courts from the hill above Church Road. To all appearances it seems an enduring link with Wimbledon's past.

St Mary's Church before it was rebuilt in 1788. The drawing is crude, but it shows the Cecil Chapel with its four small square windows to the right of the chancel.

Sir Edward Cecil,
Viscount Wimbledon.

In fact the present church is just under one hundred and fifty years old. The nave, tower and spire date from 1843, the restored chancel from 1860. They are the work of one of the most famous of all Victorian architects, Sir George Gilbert Scott, and his friend and partner, William Moffat.

Scott's church is probably the fourth, and certainly the most distinguished looking, to stand on the site. The first was built in late Saxon times, possibly as a minster by missionary priests spreading Christianity. It served a wide area to the north and was mentioned in the Domesday Book of 1087 as the church of the manor of Mortlake. In the late thirteenth century it was completely rebuilt in stone, possibly by Walter Reynolds, a wealthy rector who later became Archbishop of Canterbury under Edward II. It was still small, but it now had a wooden belfry and spire. Parts of the medieval chancel survive in the core of the present building and one of its windows was rediscovered when the Warrior Chapel was being built in 1920.

Just beyond this Warrior Chapel, which is dedicated to the young men of Wimbledon who were killed in the two World Wars, is a much older chapel added to the side of the chancel three centuries earlier. Known as the Cecil Chapel, it was built by the owner of the manor house, Sir Edward Cecil, who had succeeded his father, the Earl of Exeter, as lord of the manor in 1623. He meant it as a mortuary chapel for himself and his family. It was designed in the late Gothic style and was lit by a large perpendicular window in the south wall and by six little windows, commemorating his two wives and four daughters (he had yet to marry for a third time).

Sir Edward Cecil was a professional soldier who had distinguished himself in the Netherlands as a brave cavalry commander. He was also a courtier, on friendly terms with James I's son, Prince Charles, and his favourite, the Duke of Buckingham. Within two years of becoming lord of the manor, he had been created Baron Putney and Viscount Wimbledon, and been appointed commander-in-chief of an expedition to attack southern Spain. From the start he was doubtful of success. He managed to catch the Spaniards by surprise and land his army just south of Cadiz, but his attempt to capture the port ended in chaos and Sir Edward returned to Plymouth to meet a very hostile reception. Already nicknamed "Viscount Sitstill" by the sailors, he was accused of showing lack of leadership and became the butt of innumerable popular ballads. However, he was saved from ruin by his patron Buckingham and was soon restored to royal favour. He was made a member of the King's Council of War and became Lord-Lieutenant of Surrey.

In 1628, shortly after his promotion, he suffered two new disasters. First, on 18 November, his manor house at Wimbledon was rocked by a huge explosion and the servants' quarters disappeared. According to a contemporary, the cause was "the mistaking of some maids, who instead of a barrel of soap opened a barrel of gunpowder which lay in the cellar, and let a spark of the candle fall in". Then, the very next day his London house in the Strand was completely gutted by fire. As a result, all Cecil's "evidences and papers" were destroyed and sadly few records survive of his life at Wimbledon. Indeed, one of the few sources of information left is the Parish Register of births, marriages and deaths.

The Register records that in August 1623 "Sir Edward Cecyll, Knight" gave away in marriage Albinia, the eldest of his four daughters, to a wealthy Lincolnshire

THE CECIL
CHAPEL

landowner, "Mr Christopher Wray Esquire". Then, six years later there is a special entry for the christening (sadly followed soon after by the burial) of a grandson born to his third daughter, Elizabeth, wife of Lord Willoughby of Parham. In 1631 it notes another death in the family, that of his second wife. His first wife, mother of his daughters, had died in Holland long before he became lord of the manor. The second, who was childless, died in London, but was brought to Wimbledon by night, "with

The interior of the Cecil Chapel, photographed in 1921 when armour was still displayed on its walls. The window behind the tomb of Viscount Wimbledon contains the earliest stained-glass in the Church – a fifteenth century figure of St George. The plaques and coats of arms in the little windows commemorate Cecil's four daughters.

a train of twenty carriages drawn with six horses apiece, and with torches without number". She was the first member of the family to be buried in the new Cecil Chapel.

Sir Edward, however, had still not given up hope of having a son and heir to inherit his titles and estates. So in 1635 at the age of sixty-three he married Sophia, daughter of Sir Edward Zouch of Woking. His action was said to have caused "surprise" as the bride was only seventeen, but it produced the desired result. The Parish Register records that on 31 December 1636 "Allgernoune Cecill" was christened in St Mary's. Within a year, however, the little boy was dead and the poor father heartbroken. His health had been failing and this death proved the final blow. On 16 November 1638 he too died at his manor house. In his will he left strict instructions that his corpse "be not opened or mangled as many are" and that it should "have no vault, but to be deep buried in the earth as may be".

Over his grave in the Cecil Chapel his daughters placed a large black marble altar tomb. Unlike his father's massive tomb in Westminster Abbey, it has no effigy, only an inscription listing his achievements and his "assured hope in his Saviour Christ to rise again to glory everlasting". Above the tomb is suspended a viscount's coronet. On the walls are inscribed the names of his three married daughters and their husbands, along with the fourth, "Dorothy Cecill unmaryed as yet". In fact, she never married. In her will she asked: "If I die near Wimbledon, that is to say within half a day's journey, that then my body may be carried privately by night and laid by my father's tomb." Unfortunately, she died in 1652 while on a visit to France and so had to be buried there.

On Sir Edward's death, without a son to succeed him, his Wimbledon estate had to be left to his widow and the four daughters. The young widow (who remarried a few years later and did not die until 1691) inherited the manor house and park. She had no desire to continue living in Wimbledon and put them up for sale. They were bought by King Charles I for his wife Henrietta Maria. But she had barely finished renovating the house and remodelling the gardens when Civil War broke out and she had to leave them in the care of her treasurer, Sir Richard Wynn. At its end, the royal manor was confiscated by Parliament, shortly after Wynn's death, and was sold to Cromwell's ablest general, John Lambert. At the Restoration of Charles II he too lost the house and park, and they passed to two leading politicians, first George Digby, Earl of Bristol, and then in 1677 to Thomas Osborne, Earl of Danby. Finally, in 1717 they were bought by a Huguenot businessman, Sir Theodore Janssen, who found the house in need of such major repairs that sadly he decided to pull it down and use the bricks to build a new manor house on a fresh site west of the church (between the present Alan and Highbury Roads). So after just over a century as a home the great Cecil house disappeared.

Yet its building proved to be one of the great turning-points in Wimbledon's history. It transformed the village from a relative backwater into one of the social centres of Elizabethan and Stuart England. It changed the lives of many of the inhabitants called on to provision and repair it, or work in the gardens. Above all, it brought the place into contact with government officials and City merchants who soon realised, like William, Thomas and Edward Cecil, that Wimbledon was ideal as a country retreat.

THE WYNN GRAVESTONE

Let into the floor by the entrance to the chancel, and so not far from the Cecil Chapel, is the memorial to Sir Richard Wynn. It is a large black stone slab and originally covered his grave inside the chancel. Its Latin inscription, roughly translated, reads: "Here lies Richard Wynn of Gwydir in the county of Caernarvon, Knight and Baronet, Treasurer and Councillor to the Honourable Princess, Queen Henrietta Maria, and descended from an old and illustrious family of North Wales. He died 19 July 1649, aged 61."

Sir Richard Wynn, Keeper of the Queen's Manor of Wimbledon, 1642–1649.

The chancel of St Mary's. Wynn's gravestone lies under the mat in front of the gates.

The Wynns were a wealthy and influential family. Sir Richard, born in Armada year and trained in law at Lincoln's Inn, became a Gentleman of the Privy Chamber to Prince Charles in 1618 and accompanied him to Madrid five years later. Soon after Charles became King, Wynn was made Treasurer to his French wife, Henrietta Maria, and so was responsible for looking after her estates, to which Wimbledon was added in 1639. When Civil War broke out in 1642 he was asked, as a respected

Member of Parliament, to stay in the London area and look after the Queen's interests. So he took over as keeper of Her Majesty's house and manor of Wimbledon.

Over the next seven years he kept careful accounts of all expenditure. His four big ledgers still survive and they show in meticulous detail how he looked after a house and park "under siege". He had to keep the buildings in repair, the gardens cared for and the animals safe in the park. But all the time his main concern was the war and its many unpleasant consequences: prices went up; most of the servants had to be discharged; thefts from the park became more frequent; above all, there was a constant threat from roaming bands of Parliamentary soldiers. They "threw over" the palings round the park, stole fish from the ponds, killed the "genny [Guinea] hens", demanded billets in the house and even broke in and stole some of his wife's property. All he could do was to employ "divers men" to guard the house, others to "watch in the park two nights for the safeguarding of the deer" — and keep two bloodhounds. In 1647, after the New Model Army had won the war and set up its headquarters at Putney, he secured "a protection for the preservation of the park and house" from its Commander, General Fairfax, but even this did little good.

The unending strain took its toll of Sir Richard's health. Worn out by seven years of worry and uncertainty, he did not long survive his King. On 19 July 1649, less than six months after Charles's execution in Whitehall, he died in the manor house and at his special request was buried in St Mary's. His younger brother described the occasion in a letter:

> "Sir. We have yesterday interred the body of our dear brother, according to his desire in Wimbledon Chapel. Most or all of our countrymen were there. His loss is very much bemoaned. The surgeon found his heart sound and his lungs, but his liver was spotted and his gall clean spent, which was the disease that took him."

Sir Richard Wynn's gravestone is thus in a very real sense a war memorial.

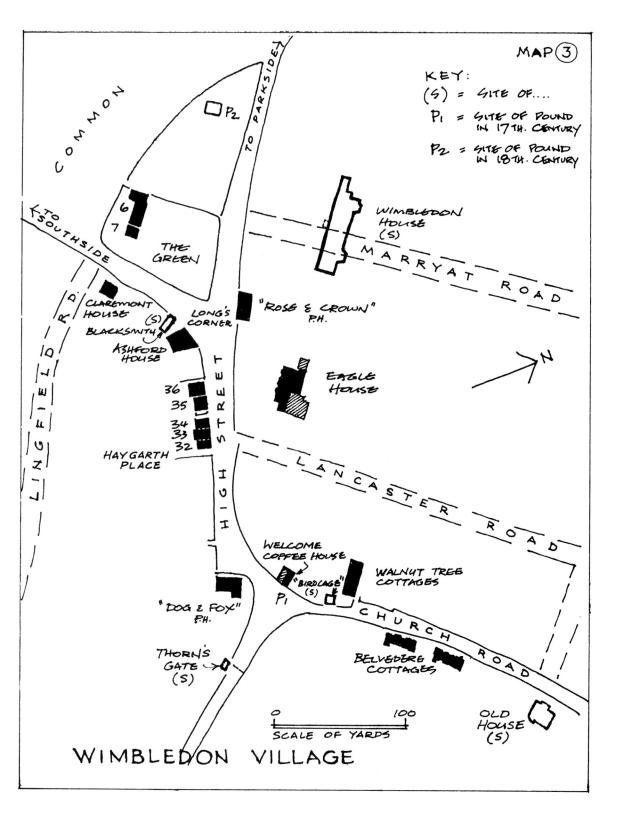

MAP ③

KEY:
(s) = SITE OF....
P1 = SITE OF POUND IN 17TH. CENTURY
P2 = SITE OF POUND IN 18TH. CENTURY

COMMON

TO PARKSIDE

P2

THE GREEN

6
7

WIMBLEDON HOUSE (S)

MARRYAT ROAD

TO SOUTHSIDE

L I N G F I E L D   R D.

CLAREMONT HOUSE (S)
BLACKSMITH
ASHFORD HOUSE

LONG'S CORNER

"ROSE & CROWN" P.H.

N

EAGLE HOUSE

36
35
34
33
32

HAYGARTH PLACE

H I G H   S T R E E T

LANCASTER ROAD

WELCOME COFFEE HOUSE

"BIRDCAGE" (S)

P1

WALNUT TREE COTTAGES

"DOG & FOX" P.H.

CHURCH ROAD

THORN'S GATE (S)

BELVEDERE COTTAGES

OLD HOUSE (S)

0   100
SCALE OF YARDS

WIMBLEDON VILLAGE

31

Eagle House

One City merchant who followed the example of the Cecils and built a country house in Wimbledon was Robert Bell. His family had owned land there since the early sixteenth century, but both his grandfather and father had made their way in the City before returning and settling in the village as prosperous yeomen. Robert was born in the family home at the top of the High Street in July 1564. As the youngest of four children, he benefited from the manor's unusual law of inheritance known as "Borough English" and inherited all the family land when his father died in 1575. For many years, however, it made little difference to him as his mother continued to live in the family home until she died in 1602.

So, like his father, Robert was sent to London and apprenticed to his uncle, Richard Walter, Master of the Girdlers' Company. He was taught how to make the fashionable girdles with elaborate fastenings that were the source of the Company's profits. He was probably also given a good general education. He certainly spoke French well, wrote a vigorous letter and quickly became a successful businessman. He bought a house in Leadenhall Street, married Alice Colston, daughter of a wealthy Colchester merchant, and rose to be Deputy Alderman in the City and, in 1611, Master of the Girdlers' Company.

The best proof of his wealth and standing, however, lies in the way he broadened his business ventures. He became interested in overseas trade and in 1600 his name appears among the 215 founders of "The Society of Adventurers for the discovery of the trade for the East Indies", or East India Company. At first he merely invested two hundred pounds along with his brother-in-law, John Potter, but when he realised the possible profits to be made, he followed it with further sums in later voyages amounting to over two thousand, six hundred pounds. From the start he played an important part in the Company's affairs, being a member of the managing committee with his own agent or "factor" in Amsterdam. He was commissioned to buy trade goods, including elephants' teeth from France. He negotiated with the Privy Council over the Company's strained relations with the Dutch, especially after the massacre of English merchants on the island of Amboyna in the East Indies, "wherein", he claimed, "the honour of our country lies bleeding". He even led deputations to the King and in 1614 visited James I at Whitehall to "procure letters from His Majesty to the Emperor of China and the King of Japan". Later he met Charles I at Hampton Court. His growing reputation is clearly shown by a report in 1618 that "Master Bell, the merchant, was made a Gentleman of the Privy Chamber".

Such a successful man of affairs needed a country house to show his importance and to enable him to escape from London whenever he wanted. So in 1613 he returned to his birthplace, took over two cottages next to the family home and on the site erected a "fayre new howse", the building now known as Eagle House, with a large garden and orchard. The walls of the house were of solid brick, about two feet thick; the corners of the building and of the lower windows were of stone; the main timbers were oak.

The entrance was up a short flight of steps and through a nail-studded oak door under carved cyphers of Robert and his wife Alice. Inside was the great hall, which extended the entire width of the house. Its walls were covered with panelling or tapestry; on one side a high chimney piece reached up to a fine plaster ceiling; directly opposite the door was a large window looking out onto the garden. The hall was used by the Bells for their meals, prepared in the kitchens below. Up a great oak staircase on the first floor was the "withdrawing-room" with an even finer ceiling. Above were the family bedrooms and the servants' attics between the gables. It was clearly a fitting home for a prosperous City merchant.

How often Robert Bell stayed in the house is uncertain. Not long after it was built, a letter-writer reported that he was "not always to be found keeping much in the country". But by the 1630s he certainly needed a country retreat. In 1630 he was removed from the East India Company Committee after a vote. The next year he was found trying to smuggle twenty tons of white wine, "not of the best", on one of

Eagle House today, used as offices. The Bell's "withdrawing-room" is over the front door. To the right is part of the extra building added by Revd Thomas Lancaster in 1789 to house his school. The stone eagle over the central gable was placed there in 1860.

the Company's ships to India. But these troubles were just a prelude to his final decline which started in 1634.

In that year, at the age of seventy, Bell was appointed Master of the Girdlers' Company for the second time. So "as a remembrance of his love", he presented the Company with a fine Lahore carpet, "seven yards long and three and a half broad, with his own and the Girdlers' arms thereon". It was handmade in wool of many colours and shows Bell's very appropriate arms: an eagle with bales of goods stamped R. B. The carpet still survives in a large glass frame in the Company's hall in London. (A small reproduction can be seen in the Wimbledon Society Museum.)

Bell's gift, however, led to serious trouble with the East India Company Committee which accused him of failing to pay for the carpet. He replied that the money had been sent to an agent in India who had since died, but his explanation was not believed and seventy bags of his pepper were confiscated by the Committee. Shortly afterwards he withdrew from the Company, "on account of the many losses that have lately befallen me, and for other reasons".

Back view of Eagle House and its garden, taken about 1900.

34

Part of the plaster ceiling of the "withdrawing-room" with the coats of arms of Robert Bell and his wife, Alice. Robert's includes an eagle and the fleur-de-lys. The photograph was taken in 1905.

Among the other reasons must have been illness. In his will he specially mentioned "my maid servant Katherine Harp who hath been with me some years and hath taken great pains with me in my sickness". Through these last trying years his one consolation seems to have been religion. The phrasing of his will suggests that he was a Puritan who put his trust in "the precious blood of Christ Jesus who hath paid whatsoever was due for my sins and will receive my soul into his glory and peace". He died in March 1640 and was buried in St Mary's Churchyard. He had no children

EAGLE HOUSE

and so left his house to his "dearly beloved and faithful wife". Alice soon let the house and moved back to Colchester where she died seven years after her husband.

The Puritan atmosphere established under the Bells was maintained for at least the next thirty years. In 1647 the house was bought by Sir Richard Betenson, a supporter of Parliament in the Civil War and a leading member of the Surrey Committee which ran the county for Parliament from the Crane Inn, Kingston. Despite his eminence, Betenson is a more shadowy figure than Robert Bell and little is known of his life or personality. Like so many gentlemen of the time, he was willing to serve whatever government was in power: Parliament in the 1640s, Cromwell in the 1650s and Charles II (who rewarded him with a Baronetcy) in the 1660s. His occupation of Eagle House is notable for the fact that, like Sir Richard Wynn at the Manor House, he had to billet men from the New Model Army, though he at least got compensation "for three soldiers who did not pay their quarters" in June 1649. He was also probably responsible for building the original Rose and Crown Inn next to his house. Yet he does not appear to have been very popular in the village. He was twice accused of "throwing his rubbish on the highway to the common annoyance" and "stopping up the common sewer", the large open drain that ran in front of the houses in the High Street. Shortly afterwards, in 1658, he handed over the house to his son Richard on his marriage to a granddaughter of Sir Edward Cecil, Albinia Wray. The couple lived there until early in 1666 when they leased the house to a friend and probably went abroad. Richard certainly died at Montpelier in southern France eleven years later. His body was brought home and "decently, quietly and privately buried in the upper corner of the chancel at Wimbledon" (in other words, in the Cecil Chapel).

The friend who took up the lease was a lady described as "remarkable for her learning, piety and benevolence". She was Lady Mary Armyne, widow of a leading Lincolnshire M.P. who had been a member of Cromwell's Council of State. She was a noted Puritan who spent hours every day reading religious books, meditating and praying, and chose her servants for their "godliness". She gave large sums in charity, especially to Puritan ministers expelled from their parishes after the Restoration and to missionaries sent to convert the Indians in North America. From the roof of her new home she would have had a grandstand view of the spectacular Great Fire of London in September 1666. From the front windows she would have seen both the bustle of the High Street where the first shops had recently opened and beyond them the growing number of houses lining the Common.

After she died at the age of eighty in 1676, no noteworthy personality seems to have lived at the house, apart from William Grenville, Speaker of the House of Commons and close ally of William Pitt, who leased it in the 1780s. Then towards the end of the eighteenth century it was transformed into a private school. One of the headmasters, Dr Huntingford, gave the house its modern name. He had earlier run a school at Eagle House, Hammersmith. When he moved to Wimbledon in 1860, he brought an ornamental eagle with him, put it onto the central gable and there it has stayed ever since.

THE ROSE AND CROWN

In the Wimbledon Society Museum there is a copy of a unique trade token (struck because of a shortage of small change). On the front are the words: "T. E. Heburne; In Wimbleton [16]59"; on the back is the drawing of a rose. The token in fact is proof that the Rose and Crown in the High Street is over three hundred years old. Documents from later in the seventeenth century show that the Inn was first called "The Sign of the Rose", that it had stables and a garden, that it was run by Thomas Heburne, a married man with five children, and that it was owned by the Betensons.

It seems likely, therefore, that the Inn was established some time in the late 1640s or 1650s, probably by Sir Richard Betenson. It certainly did not exist in 1617 and almost certainly not thirty years later when Betenson bought Eagle House. Its name too is significant: just "the Rose", at a time when Crowns were out of favour. The present name "Rose and Crown" first appeared in the eighteenth century.

Georgian Wimbledon

The High Street

Eagle House was still a "fair new house" when in 1617 the first detailed account was written of "Wimbledon Street" as the High Street was then known. It appeared in a survey of Wimbledon Manor made by Ralph Treswell for Thomas Cecil, Earl of Exeter.

He recorded few buildings on the same side of the road as Robert Bell's home. The only places of interest were a bowling alley near the site of the present Rose and Crown inn and the pound for straying animals at the corner with Church Road. Opposite, however, there was a line of small houses or cottages, starting at "My Lords Arms", the main inn on the site of the modern Dog and Fox, and ending at "Long's Corner" facing Eagle House. Some were probably farmhouses, half-

The earliest known photograph of the High Street, taken about 1875. Several of the houses and shops on the right hand side were then at least 100 years old; they are still standing. The vehicle in the middle of the road is the original London omnibus with a door and step at the back.

Number 35 High Street, probably built about 1760. It was first a baker's shop, then a draper's. From the 1860s until 1987 it was a doctor's surgery. Now it is an estate agent's.

timbered with three rooms on the ground floor (a "hall" for eating, a kitchen and a parlour) and three "chambers" above, bedrooms reached by a steep stair-ladder. Behind each house was a barn for storing hay and corn, a shed for farm implements, a stable for the animals, an orchard and a small "backside" or garden. Such properties were the homes of the leading inhabitants, men like William Steadman and Lancelot Thackstone. Between them were much smaller, very primitive cottages, only one storey high, where the poorer farm labourers lived. At Long's Corner there was the smithy, run by John Linton, who shod the horses, repaired the ploughs and cart wheels, and made farm implements.

The High Street in 1617 was clearly a place of much activity and the centre of local life. But as yet there were no shops. These first appeared fifty years later, just after the Restoration: a butcher's run by Phanuel Maybank (whose gravestone survives, set into the wall of St Mary's vestry) and a barber's.

In the next century as the population grew, the original properties were split up.

Extra cottages were squeezed in, while the homes of the richer inhabitants were rebuilt in brick. This meant a more crowded High Street, with posts in front of the houses to protect them and the pedestrians from the increasing number of carts. Its appearance is shown on the first detailed map of the village, a "Sketch of the Town of Wimbledon", drawn for Earl Spencer in 1776, which marks every house and shop, and in a key gives the names and occupations of every inhabitant. From the present Haygarth Place, the site of John Paterson's farmhouse, in an arc to Claremont House (by the modern Lingfield Road), shops already line the road, some in buildings which still survive. In the present number 32 was a tailor, in 33 a glazier and plumber, in 34 a butcher, in 35 a baker and in 36 a builder. Next door was a doctor, probably the first to live in the High Street, and beyond, in the newly built Ashford House (not then split into shops), there was an apothecary. Finally, beyond the smithy and some labourers' cottages, came Claremont with a general store attached to it.

The man who ran this store was Charles Newson Pigott. He settled at Claremont in 1756, lived there for forty years and, when he died at the age of eighty-nine, was said to have been "the oldest inhabitant of this village". At his store, helped by his third wife, Mary, he sold a wide variety of goods: butter and cheese, snuff and soap, nutmeg and ginger, starch and "blew" for laundering, clogs and mops, candles and tape — and articles he called "neting needels" and "specticalls". Charles Pigott played his part in helping to run the parish; he acted as Churchwarden, Overseer of the Poor and Surveyor of the Highways. Like his three brothers, he was also a member of the Mercers' Company in the City and became their Warden in 1777. Yet in none of the parish records is there any hint of the kind of man he was.

Another leading personality in the Georgian High Street was Samuel Mason, the landlord of the Rose and Crown for over twenty years (1770–1792). A carpenter by trade who also acted as undertaker, he helped to make the Rose and Crown "a genteel inn" and the leading public house in the village. Its dining-room was often used for meetings of the Vestry (leading ratepayers who governed the village), for the Whitsun banquet of the local Friendly Society and for the Archdeacon's visitation dinner. For such an occasion, Mason could provide a huge meal with dishes of beef and veal, lamb and ham, puddings and tarts, bread, butter and cheese, wine, sugar and lemons, porter, brandy and tobacco — and could round it off with the village's first printed bill. In 1780 the inn became the starting place for the "Wimbledon Machine", the first public short-stage coach travelling to London every Monday, Wednesday and Friday, and taking two hours to reach Charing Cross.

Samuel Mason ended his life as landlord, not of a pub, but of a new estate on The Green. His wife, the only daughter of Daniel Watney (the founder of the famous family), inherited four cottages in the Crooked Billet. With the help of their rents, Samuel managed in 1782 to buy The Green with two substantial Georgian houses (now numbers 6 and 7) already on it. He then took out two big mortgages on the estate and built five more houses and shops there. He leased them to wealthy inhabitants, including the vicar, Herbert Randolph, or rented them furnished to visitors making a short stay. In one of the shops facing down the High Street he set up his younger son Thomas as "grocer and general merchant". By the time he died in 1810, the family fortunes had been made. For the next century they prospered on the proceeds of the "Mason Estate".

THE HIGH STREET

Ashford House before the ground floor was converted into shops in 1908. The building on its right is the smithy.

On the opposite side of the High Street stood Ashford House, then a fine Georgian mansion. Its early history remains shrouded in mystery, but in 1784 it was bought by a young apothecary from Herefordshire, John Sanford. The rumour spread that he was the illegitimate son of a wealthy gentleman who lived at Ayshford in Somerset. Whatever the truth, the young man soon proved himself a very competent apothecary and was often described as "Doctor" or even "Surgeon". He was notable for his work among the poor, above all in insisting on general inoculation against the killer disease of the eighteenth century, smallpox. For ordinary illnesses, his normal remedies were "mixtures", "powders" and "draughts", as well as pills, castor oil and the great stand-by, bleeding. He drove everywhere in his coach and continued in practice to a very advanced age. His family thought him "a bit of a martinet", though kindly and affectionate. When he died in 1855 at the age of ninety-two, he was buried (like many of his patients) in St Mary's Churchyard.

THE DOG AND FOX

This inn is certainly the oldest in the village, yet its present name only dates from the middle eighteenth century. An inn on the site is first mentioned in the survey of 1617. It was then known as "The Sign of My Lord's Arms, an Inn by Wimbledon Pound". It had eight rooms, "four above, four below", along with two butteries, two barns and a stable, and was run by the widow of the last innkeeper.

44

The Dog and Fox Inn about 1860, from a water-colour.

The London and Brighton coach at the Dog and Fox in 1892. This was probably a special trip as the door of the coach has "Wimbledon" on it.

The name "Dog and Fox" is first mentioned in a parish document in 1758. Until then the inn had been referred to as "Edward Winchester's", after the man who ran it for thirty-five years, from 1748 to 1783. Meetings of the Vestry regularly took place there and Winchester attended them equally regularly. His successor, John Thorn, could not have been very satisfactory; he was soon relegated to the job of minding the gate across the road just to the south of the inn, which prevented animals straying too far from the Common. James Steel, a carpenter, who took over in 1786, was much more successful. His great moment was in 1797 when, with Napoleon threatening invasion, he helped to organise meetings at the Dog and Fox to set up a force of Volunteers, or Home Guard. He joined the Volunteer Horse himself and allowed a Sergeant from the Regular Army to use the ground behind the inn to instruct other Volunteers "every Monday, Wednesday, Friday and Saturday from 10 a.m. to 12 noon and 3 p.m. to 5 p.m. in their military discipline".

From the low, white, two-storeyed inn his customers had a grandstand view of the Fair held every year on the Monday after Lady Day, 25 March. The line of booths and stalls, along with a theatre and menagerie, extended from the Dog and Fox to the Rose and Crown. The wealthier inhabitants strongly disapproved of it. The second Earl Spencer claimed that it brought to the village "all sorts of London blackguards". Mrs Marryat said it had "a bad moral effect on the people". Finally in 1840 the Vestry suppressed it on the ground that it was "disorderly".

Claremont House, photographed in 1913.

CLAREMONT

The house was probably built in 1650 by Thomas Hilliard, "citizen and mercer of London", who had just retired to Wimbledon. The next year he set up a charity, based on rent from the house, to help "four poor, aged widows" in the parish. When he died in 1674 he left the house "to my loving wife Anne" and after her death to their only son Nicholas, so long as he promised in writing to stop "all actions, claims and law suits" against his mother. He must have done so as he was living there in 1690.

For the first half of the eighteenth century the house passed through various hands until Charles Pigott settled there in 1756. All the occupiers duly paid the money to the widows — until 1801 when Pigott's widow refused to do so any longer. The Churchwardens did not think it worth trying to enforce the claim and so the charity disappeared.

7

St Mary's Churchyard

It is possible to get closer in spirit to the men and women of Georgian Wimbledon in St Mary's Churchyard than anywhere else in the village. Well over three thousand of them lie buried here, literally on top of their Saxon, Medieval, Tudor and Stuart ancestors who filled the graveyard in previous ages. Indeed, until Gap Road cemetery was opened in 1882, all Wimbledonians (and some outsiders) were buried in this

The earliest known photograph of St Mary's, taken in 1862 just after the chancel had been restored by Sir George Gilbert Scott. It shows the old tithe barn in which services had been held in the early 1840s, while the nave was being rebuilt. Shortly after this photograph was taken, the barn was demolished.

The north-eastern part of the Churchyard, taken in 1927. Near the Church are the larger eighteenth century tombs including that of Sir Theodore Janssen.

relatively small plot. Over the centuries the level of the ground has steadily risen, as can be seen from the Cecil manor house gateway in the east wall whose step is well below the modern ground level. Few headstones have survived from before 1714, so the graves seen now are almost entirely Georgian and Victorian (twenty-six of them have recently been placed on a list of buildings of special architectural or historic interest).

The Georgian headstones often show the last resting place of whole families who formed the backbone of village life in the eighteenth and early nineteenth centuries:

49

the Watneys, Masons, Jennings, Terrys, Crofts, Everatts, Patersons and Withems. All handed on their trade or shop or farm from father to son to grandson. All played some part helping to run village affairs. All seem to have carried on their businesses reputably and profitably. Several were regularly employed on repairing the church; members of three of the families even rebuilt it in the late 1780s. Their marriages were celebrated there; all had their children christened there; most seem to have gone to morning service there Sunday after Sunday, although there was no longer any strict obligation on them to attend; all were buried there. Yet there is no means of telling how many of them were pious Anglicans.

One family who certainly did not class as pious Anglicans were the Hopkins. They lie buried in a large vault topped by a rather battered stone monument just to the right of the gateway into the churchyard. Their founder John Hopkins, "familiarly known as Vulture Hopkins", was a skilful London financier who invested his fortune in Wimbledon property. In the early 1720s he bought Wimbledon House, Parkside with its hundred acre grounds, as well as a number of houses in the village and a lot of land along Southside, the Ridgway, Worple Lane and the Broadway. He boasted that he was the richest businessman in London and earned the comment: "He lived worthless, but died worth £300,000." Yet with all his love of money, he seems to have been a sincere Nonconformist and when he died childless in 1732, he left a large sum for "poor dissenting ministers and their widows". It took over forty years to sort out the complications of his will, but finally in 1774 the large estate passed to a distant relative, Benjamin Bond, who thereupon changed his surname to Bond-Hopkins. He too was a Nonconformist. According to the vicar, "he professes himself a Presbyterian and keeps a chaplain who holds services in a private chapel in the house on Sundays". Yet when he died in 1794 he too was buried in the family vault, as was

Wimbledon House, Parkside, from an engraving of about 1815. The central block is the oldest part; the pillared entrance and the wings were probably added later. In the left hand wing was a conservatory and billiard room. Beyond are some of the fine trees in the garden.

Mrs Charlotte Marryat who lived at Wimbledon House from 1815 to 1854.

his only daughter Caroline who inherited the large estates in Wimbledon, although not the house. She lived with her husband, Richard Mansel Phillips, in the different houses she owned along Southside. After her death in 1850, her children and grandchildren gradually sold the family land to developers.

Another derelict tomb, this time of brick with a plain stone top, situated north of the church, covers the remains of Vulture Hopkins's greatest rival, Sir Theodore Janssen. He was a Huguenot refugee, yet became a leading City merchant and financier, a Director of the Bank of England and of the South Sea Company. He too settled in Wimbledon, first buying Wimbledon House, Parkside in 1710 and then seven years later the Cecil manor house, which he replaced with a smaller Georgian mansion (later known as Belvedere House) to the west of the church. He certainly attended services there and thought the vicar, Edward Collins, "a good preacher and tolerable good man". But he strongly disapproved of Mrs Collins, whom he suspected of being a Jacobite, and of her large, unruly family, as well as of the vicar's spate of begging letters asking for an increased stipend and a house of his own. Within a few years, however, Janssen had lost all his property as a result of the collapse of his South Sea Company. He retired to a house in Church Road and lived there or in Hanover Square in complete seclusion until he died in 1748 aged ninety. On his tomb there was placed a short inscription (now illegible): "Once Lord of this Manor".

Not far from Janssen is a third tomb which also looks in need of repair, a large stone sarcophagus, decorated with a coat of arms, but with no inscription. It covers a vault which, when opened in 1905, was found to contain the remains of eight members of the Marryat family, though not of its most famous member, the novelist Captain Frederick Marryat. His father was a merchant and banker like Janssen, and like Bond-Hopkins the owner of Wimbledon House, Parkside which he bought in 1815. His mother, a rich American from Boston, was a keen gardener who developed the grounds of their house into one of the finest gardens near London. When Joseph, an M.P. and Chairman of Lloyds, dropped dead at his office in the City in 1824, she took control not merely of the house, but also of the moral character of the village. More than anyone else, she was responsible for the suppression of the annual fair in the High Street. She then held her own "grand fancy fair", which went on for several days in the grounds of her house, to raise funds to build and endow almshouses in Camp Road. She did not die until 1854 aged eighty-one and was described by one inhabitant as being "as much thought of at Wimbledon as the Queen at Windsor".

Very appropriately the grave of the Marryat's *bête noire*, William Eades, is about as far from their tomb as was possible at St Mary's — right over the other side of the church, near the modern Fellowship House. The Eades family had lived in the High Street since the early years of the eighteenth century. One was a shoemaker; another, William's father, was a grocer. William inherited the grocer's shop in the early 1780s and made it prosper. During the Napoleonic Wars he served in the Volunteer Cavalry, a Home Guard on horseback, raised in 1797 to protect Wimbledon against French invasion. By 1815 he owned two houses and over a hundred acres of land, including a field just off the Ridgway which contained a patch of brick-earth. There in the next few years he built fifteen cottages which he leased to poor labourers and appropriately named Brickfield Cottages (now Oldfield Road).

William Eades was a prosperous Wimbledonian, but he was also a very unpopular one. In 1818 on his own authority as Overseer of the Poor, fearing an outbreak of disease, he had some extra rooms built onto the overcrowded workhouse in Camp Road. The Vestry, however, with Joseph Marryat in the van, refused to pay for them as they felt that the Poor Rate was getting out of control. William was outraged and took the Vestry to court. Marryat then proposed that a select Vestry be set up, effectively depriving Eades of all say in village affairs. This was agreed to, but in the end, after a lot of unnecessary expense and bad feeling, a compromise was reached.

With Marryat's death in 1824, the select Vestry lapsed and Eades returned to the old open Vestry. But he was soon in trouble again. At the end of a meeting in 1826, he followed a fellow Vestryman out, "with the most violent and abusive expressions, tending manifestly to the breach of the peace". To prevent the same thing happening again, the village constable was ordered to stay at the door, "to protect such members as may require it".

There is no record of his services ever being needed. But the members of the Vestry were doubtless relieved when Eades died in 1836 and was laid to rest in the family grave.

CHURCH ROAD

"The Way to the church, an ancient winding country lane", was the scene of innumerable funeral processions. But it was not the only route from the village to St Mary's. On eighteenth century maps a "footway" is marked, starting at the junction of Church Road and the High Street (on the site of the modern bank building) and following the line of Alan Road to end directly opposite St Mary's. It was, however, "a long and dirty walk", according to the vicar in 1758 and only thirteen years later it was blocked with the Vestry's consent by Samuel Rush, the owner of Belvedere House.

The corner of Church Road and the High Street, painted by Major General Poulton about 1880 from his house in Homefield Road. In the foreground is the hedge of the Dog and Fox garden. To the right is the high wall of the Belvedere estate. To the left are shops, including The Welcome, a temperance coffee tavern and reading room.

ST. MARY'S
CHURCHYARD

Most of the land along the south side of Church Road was occupied by the grounds of Belvedere House (built as the second manor house in 1720 by Sir Theodore Janssen and only pulled down in 1900; the massive wall of its kitchen garden is still standing along Belvedere Avenue). The only other house of any importance on this side of Church Road was the so-called "Old House". It was probably built in 1690 by John Breholt, another Huguenot refugee and London merchant. It had a fine garden, complete with "grapery", mushroom house and summer house, as well as a large yard, surrounded by a coach house, stables, brewhouse, hen house and "house of easement". It was not pulled down until the 1960s, when town houses were built around Old House Close.

In the eighteenth century there were also a few cottages, a builder's yard and the Swan Inn on the south side nearer the High Street. In 1864 the builder's yard was used as the site for thirty "artisan's dwellings" for workers on the Belvedere estate. They were built in Victorian Gothic style by the vicar of Downend, Gloucestershire, Revd Alfred Peache, whose father, James Courthope Peache, a timber merchant of Belvedere Road, Lambeth, had bought the estate in 1834. Belvedere Cottages still grace Church Road, although their entrance gate has long disappeared.

Opposite the cottages is a line of small shops, and a pub. The shops first appear on a map of 1776, with two of them occupied by barbers. Beyond is a small alley opening onto Walnut Tree Cottages. These cottages were built in 1836 by John Bishop, a grocer in the High Street, with the help of a large loan. But their rents did not make his fortune; indeed, when he died in 1850 he still owed all the money he had borrowed fourteen years before. Perhaps he had not chosen the ideal site. Just by his new cottages was "the Birdcage", a small windowless building with a hole in the door, covered by bars, where prisoners were kept when first arrested. Nearby were the parish stocks, which periodically had to be rebuilt, and the watch-house where the parish watchman sheltered before going on his night rounds.

At the top of this north side of Church Road, where it merges into the High Street, are two tile-hung shops, one an estate agent, the other an Indian Restaurant. They are said to be "among the earliest buildings in Wimbledon, dating from the late seventeenth century". Unfortunately, a late eighteenth century map shows only a row of small shops and houses here, "recently built by Mr Rose", a farmer employed by Earl Spencer.

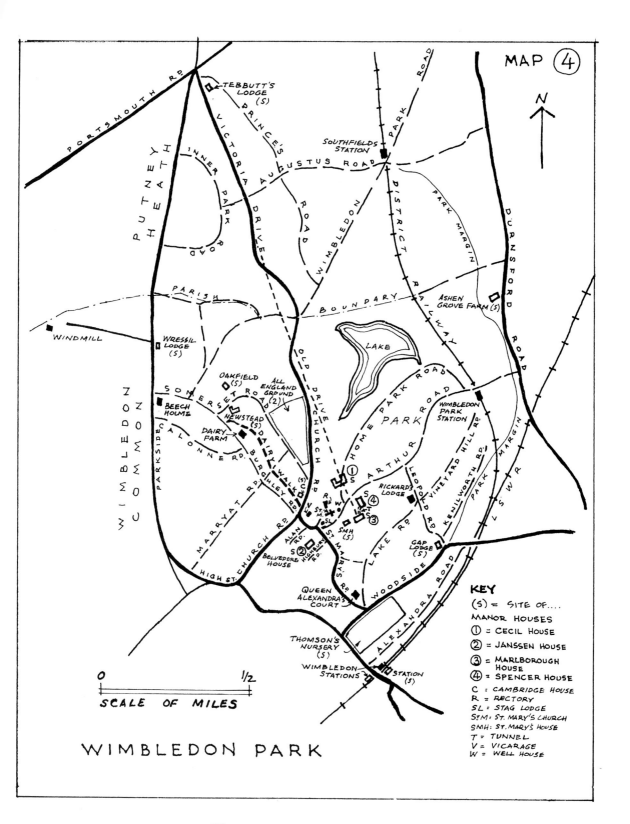

MAP ④

N

KEY

(S) = SITE OF....
MANOR HOUSES
① = CECIL HOUSE
② = JANSSEN HOUSE
③ = MARLBOROUGH HOUSE
④ = SPENCER HOUSE
C = CAMBRIDGE HOUSE
R = RECTORY
SL = STAG LODGE
S.M. = ST. MARY'S CHURCH
SMH = ST. MARY'S HOUSE
T = TUNNEL
V = VICARAGE
W = WELL HOUSE

SCALE OF MILES
0   ½

WIMBLEDON PARK

8

Wimbledon Park

St Mary's Churchyard overlooks Wimbledon Park and the sites of its four manor houses. In 1748 the Park and the third manor house, a fine new Georgian mansion built by Sarah, Duchess of Marlborough, were inherited by a small boy of eleven, John Spencer. Until he was eighteen the estate had to be managed by trustees who did their work so well that they almost doubled the size of the park to over 1,200 acres.

In 1755 John married a lively, attractive lady, Georgiana Poyntz. They had one son, George, and four daughters, two of whom, Georgiana, Duchess of Devonshire and Henrietta, Countess of Bessborough, became famous leaders of Whig society in the 1780s. Their father was barred from holding public office by Sarah's will, but he was able to support the Whig cause in the House of Lords as he was made first a Viscount and, in 1765, an Earl by King George III. He was said to be "generous and amiable", but suffered badly from gout and had to pay frequent visits to Bath and to Spa in Belgium for his health. Nonetheless he loved fox-hunting when fit and, when confined to the family home, Althorp in Northamptonshire, he spent his time building up his large library. He also collected paintings and commissioned his friend Sir Joshua Reynolds to produce a fine series of family portraits.

The Earl and Countess made frequent visits to their estate at Wimbledon. The large Georgian house, built of grey brick, with four stone columns on the front, had been planned by Sarah with her own gout in mind. The ground floor had been sunk into a large hollow or "saucer" so that she could enter at first floor level without going up steps. When staying in the house, she lived entirely on that floor and had her bedroom, dining-room and library all close together. The Earl naturally approved of the lack of steps to climb, but as soon as he moved in he changed the rooms around and had the house completely redecorated by a brilliant young architect, James "Athenian" Stuart.

He then began an even greater change, the improvement of his large park. Early in 1765 he commissioned the famous gardener, "Capability" Brown, to landscape it. Over the next three years Brown transformed the park with a new winding drive from the Portsmouth Road (the route followed by the modern Victoria Drive and Church Road) and a new entrance lodge, looked after at the end of the century by Mr and Mrs Tebutt. He cut down the long avenues of trees, thinned out the woods and produced less formal clumps, given names like Hall's Cover, Horse Close Wood and Evergreen Oak Clump. Above all, he drained swampy areas by linking two old fish ponds into a large thirty acre lake, with a boat house at one end.

Not content with improving the house and park, the Earl had a large "Hothouse" and kitchen garden laid out at the bottom of Wimbledon Hill (just below the modern Woodside and over the site of the Public Library). He employed a farmer, James Rose, to transport over 300,000 bricks from a kiln on the Common and then three local craftsmen, William Jennings, Samuel Mason and Thomas Withem, made the walls and the gates, as well as cases for peaches and other exotic fruit.

The general effect of all the Earl's changes was dramatic. "The ground about Lord Spencer's place at Wimbledon is perhaps as beautiful as anything near London", reported one newspaper in the 1780s. "Nature has done much for it; and Brown made of it much more." Another visitor, Hannah More, completely agreed. In 1780 she wrote to a friend: "I did not think there could have been so beautiful a place within seven miles of London. The park has much variety of ground. I enjoyed the violets and the birds more than all the marechal powder and the music of this foolish town [London]."

In 1783 this fine estate, along with a new town house in St James's Street and the old family home at Althorp, was inherited by George Spencer, a young man of twenty-five. The second Earl had appropriately been born at Wimbledon Park House in September 1758 and a month later had been christened at St Mary's. Like his sisters, he seems to have been brought up mainly at "the Nursery" in Wimbledon. He soon grew to love the place. When only twelve he referred to the park in summer as "the prettiest place in the world". The year after becoming Earl, and now married to a beautiful, but strong willed, Anglo-Irish lady Lavinia Bingham, he spent a lot of the summer at the house with his wife and baby son. In successive letters to his mother, he wrote: "I have just returned from a rather wet and very unsuccessful fishing party on the great water [the Lake]. Wimbledon as usual at this time of the year looks beautiful." Then a fortnight later: "I got up just after nine. The Duke of Devonshire [his brother-in-law] had already arrived and had breakfast with us. The evening was wet, so we played cribbage, whist and Pope Joan [a popular card game]." Finally, early in July: "The first real summer day since we have been here. I enjoyed it by lounging about in the morning and reading "Cook's Last Voyage" by an open window. We had a large party to dinner [about 3 p.m.]. The Duke of Devonshire had given us a turtle, which was the foundation of the feast. It went off very well. After dinner we played bowls till it was quite dark."

Nine months later, on Easter Monday 1785, the Marlborough manor house was reduced to ruins. "The accident was occasioned", according to one report, "by the carelessness of some of the women servants who left some linen too near the fire in the laundry." The Earl was away when the fire started and was shocked when he saw the ruins: "I had really no conception of so complete a demolition of everything combustible in a house. The fire began to be known of a little after six in the evening, and by eight it had become impossible for anybody to get into the house, so that it is really quite wonderful that [the servants and people from the village] should have saved what they did. But towards the latter end of the fire, the mob broke into the wine-cellar and many of them got excessively drunk." With the house left a mere shell, the Earl had the walls pulled down and the site grassed over. (It is now part of the playing fields of Ricard's Lodge School.)

For the next sixteen years, whenever they visited Wimbledon, the Spencer family

WIMBLEDON PARK

George, second Earl
Spencer (1758–1834). He
built Wimbledon's fourth
and last manor house.

stayed in the old servants' quarters to the north-east of the mansion. The Earl could
not yet afford to build a new manor house as he was committed to a complete
renovation of Althorp and was spending large sums of money on making a unique
collection of early printed books. Then for most of the 1790s he was First Lord of the
Admiralty during the dangerous war with Revolutionary France. He gave up almost
all relaxation, even his favourite sport, shooting, and concentrated on the crucial
struggle for control of the Mediterranean, singling out Nelson for command over
more senior Admirals.

In 1798, shortly after Nelson's great victory at the Nile, the Earl decided that he needed a new country house near London and now had the means to pay for it. First, he had the water supply improved by considerably deepening the well under its domed house near the church. He then commissioned Henry Holland, who had just finished renovating Althorp, to build a new manor house around the existing servants' quarters.

The new house was ready by the autumn of 1801. It was not so impressive as the

The Spencer Manor House, from an engraving of about 1820. The portico and drawing-room on the south front gave a fine view across to the North Downs.

A photograph of the house taken in 1908 from almost the same position as the engraving. By then a large conservatory had been added to the left of the drawing-room

Cecil or Marlborough houses, but it had a fine colonnade on the south front. Behind lay ornate drawing-rooms, library, billiard and smoking-rooms, and round the house were fine gardens and a large lawn. Countess Lavinia was delighted: "Here we are so comfortable. The bedrooms are incomparable. My dressing-room is really beautiful. The whole house is perfectly dry and doesn't smell of paint — except the billiard room.... The portico will be completed in little more than a fortnight."

Every July for the next few years the house and grounds were the scene of a great garden party, which the Spencers called "a breakfast" (apparently to ensure that it ended before nightfall). It started in the afternoon and was graced by up to 1,500 guests. The Earl described that of 1807 in a very matter of fact way: "Our breakfast went off remarkably well. It turned out a very fine day and the better for not being too hot. It was very simple and had nothing to recommend it but the beauty of the place and plenty of victuals for everybody." His eldest daughter, Sarah, gave a more lively account. "It was the prettiest scene I ever saw. The numbers of people dressed in brilliant colours wandering about under the trees and on the lawn and in the portico, the sound of the different bands of music, the extreme beauty of the place which had put on its best looks, the profusion of roses and pinks in every part of the house, and the sincere pleasure one saw in every countenance made it quite delightful."

The Spencer box pew in St Mary's Church, drawn in 1810. The double-decker pulpit is shown to the right.

Apart from such grand occasions, the house was used by the family for a few weeks in spring, midsummer and early autumn as a place to relax and breathe fresh country air after the fogs and smells of London. The normal life there was described by Sarah in a letter of April 1803: "We breakfast and have prayers as usual. Then Papa goes out riding or to settle his farming accounts; and we females walk, though Harriet [a cousin] and I do little else but play and sing. She plays the harp and I the piano almost all day."

The Spencer family clearly loved Wimbledon Park, but they seem to have mixed little with the people who lived in the village, except at church. Almost every Sunday when they were in residence, the Earl, his wife, and their children would take their places in a large private gallery in the chancel of the new St Mary's. There they would listen to one of Revd Herbert Randolph's "long and heavy sermons", unless they were saved, as the Earl once was, by "an unfortunate fit of sleepiness which made me too late for church".

Over one matter, however, the Earl aroused strong local feeling — an attempt to enclose the Common. In 1803 he had a notice fixed to the church door telling parishioners that he was applying to Parliament for a bill "for dividing, allotting and enclosing the Commons, Heaths and Wastes", and that he was doing so because of "the depredations committed on the Common to the injury of his manorial rights". He did nothing for four years. Then without further warning the Bill was read twice in the Commons. The inhabitants were furious. At a meeting of fifty-nine "proprietors of land" the Bill was opposed "in toto" and the vicar was deputed to tell Earl Spencer so. Judiciously he bowed to the opposition and agreed to withdraw the Bill as it was "detrimental to the people of Wimbledon".

Otherwise life for the Spencer family in their large park continued uninterrupted until the mid 1820s. Then Lady Spencer, who had once loved staying there, took a dislike to the place after her husband had been seriously ill at the house and she herself "had not known a day's uninterrupted comfort during my residence here". So early in 1827 they leased the house and grounds to the Duke of Somerset, and never stayed there again. Nineteen years later the fourth Earl sold the house and park to John Augustus Beaumont, and ever since the only interest the Spencers have taken in Wimbledon Park is as lords of the manor.

SPENCER WELL HOUSE

The domed Well House in Arthur Road, not far from St Mary's Church, is the only building put up by the Spencers in Wimbledon that still survives. It covers a well originally dug to a depth of only thirty to forty feet, but enough to provide water for the Marlborough house.

In 1798 Earl Spencer decided to have it deepened to supply the new house he was planning. Over the next fifteen months the workmen went steadily downwards until at a depth of 563 feet they at last struck water, which shot up over 100 feet with such force that the men were nearly drowned. A pump, operated by a horse, was then installed to raise the water to a reservoir at the top of the house.

Unfortunately, the well was not properly constructed. Sand began to seep in and it slowly silted up. It was still in operation in 1815, but Countess Spencer warned her husband that, due to the brickwork, "it is gradually sinking as if something has given way in the foundation". But nothing effective seems to have been done to "stop the further progress of the mischief" and it soon had to be abandoned. The house was then used as a garden store and the well concreted over.

By 1970 the dome was in danger of collapse. It was saved by Norman Plastow F.R.I.B.A. and the house transformed into a delightful residence.

The Artesian Well,
Arthur Road, about 1910.

9

William Wilberforce School

The Spencers were generous to local charities, above all the Free School on the Common. The real founder of this school, John Cooksey, an eighteenth century vicar, is commemorated by an octagonal tablet let into the east wall of St Mary's Churchyard. Its Latin inscription, roughly translated, reads: "An M. A. of Merton College Oxford and a Fellow of the Royal Society, he was a diligent minister of this flock for nearly forty years. He died on 26 January 1777, aged 70."

Cooksey has a claim to be remembered in Wimbledon because of the very practical help he provided for many poor children. In 1739 when he became vicar, he found that at least twenty boys and girls were dependent on the Vestry for providing both their clothes and a form of children's allowance to enable them to go "into service". He also discovered that the money left by Dorothy Cecil in her will made in 1651 to apprentice children from large, poor families had long been "misappropriated" by the trustees, among them Vulture Hopkins. So he secured the appointment of new trustees, including himself, and as a result numerous boys were "bound apprentice" to "masters" in Wimbledon, Kingston and even in London.

John Cooksey also saw the urgent need to help poorer children to read and write. Earlier in the century there had been two charity schools in the village, but by the 1740s they seem to have closed. So he got the Dorothy Cecil Charity to pay schoolmasters to teach boys from the workhouse. Then in 1757 he persuaded the Vestry to set up a committee of leading gentlemen to plan and build a school and secured Earl Spencer's permission to enclose two acres of the Common, by the modern Camp Road. There an octagonal schoolhouse (the present William Wilberforce School) was built with money raised from the local gentry. The school opened the next year, but the masters were constantly complaining that they had not been paid. By 1770 the school seems to have ground to a halt.

In June 1773 therefore Cooksey set up another committee, with William Wilberforce, uncle of the great reformer, as treasurer. Cooksey argued that "the daily appearance of numerous poor children in the parish, destitute of the means of acquiring an orderly education" made some action essential. This time he made sure that an adequate income was raised by appealing for a promise of annual subscriptions from the wealthy families living in the area. His appeal was a success and "The Wimbledon Free School" was refounded in the repaired octagonal building.

Joseph Andrews from Bermondsey and his wife Sarah were appointed the first schoolmaster and mistress. Their joint salary was fifty pounds a year with house and garden rent free, but they had to keep the house in repair and provide coal to heat the

WILLIAM
WILBERFORCE SCHOOL

The "Charity School on Wimbledon Common", drawn in 1810 by William Porden. This octagonal building is now the centre-piece of the modern William Wilberforce School.

school in winter. They were responsible for teaching fifty boys and girls, selected by the subscribers. Only those "with some degree of instruction" were admitted and their curriculum was very limited: "the rudiments of reading and writing, so that they may be able to read the Bible or any other religious book, and to understand any common written paper or direction in writing, whereby it is hoped they may be more likely to become good Christians and useful members of the community, but by no means be put above handicraft labour". Hence, for the first five years no arithmetic was taught and then it was only to be "the first four rules, as far as concerns pounds, shillings and pence".

Andrews and his wife worked themselves and their young pupils hard. Lessons started at 8 a.m. and went on until noon. Then, after a two hour break for lunch at home, they restarted at 2 p.m. and finally ended at 5 p.m. a long seven hour day (an hour shorter in winter). School went on every day from Monday to Friday and there were relatively few holidays: only a week at Christmas, Easter and Whitsun, as well as periodic days off for Shrove Tuesday, Maundy Thursday and Good Friday, Guy Fawkes Day, the birthdays of King George III, Queen Charlotte and the Prince of Wales, and the anniversaries of Charles I's execution and Charles II's Restoration. Soon an extra summer holiday had to be allowed, "some of the parents having desired their children may have leave of absence for a few days, it being harvest time".

The school seems at the second attempt to have been a success. The Andrews were clearly good teachers and the number of children quickly rose from 50 to 76.

Absenteeism, however, was a constant problem. Another was abusive parents, furious that their children were corrected. The most extreme case happened in 1784 when Mr Andrews complained about a brother and sister who had been sent to school "with the itch upon them and in a very dirty and nasty condition". The mother appeared and "in a violent and outrageous manner" insulted the master and threatened to beat him "till he could not stand". Even when a doctor certified that Andrews was in the right, she refused to apologise and "behaved in a rude manner".

Perhaps the matter that disturbed the vicar (now Herbert Randolph) and his committee most was that "many of the children neglect coming to church on a

William Wilberforce (1759–1833) lived for a time at Lauriston House on Southside. His uncle, also William, was Treasurer of the appeal to help refound "The Wimbledon Free School".

Sunday". So in 1786 they started a virtual Sunday School. All the children who normally came during the week were expected to attend at the schoolhouse half an hour before the service started, and were then to go in procession to St Mary's. In the afternoon, during the winter, they had to return to the school for two more hours of Bible study, Catechism and "Psalmody". Those who attended regularly were given tickets, redeemable for a penny, but if they "behaved improperly" in church they lost them.

An incentive for hard work was also offered: a prize Bible, "handsomely bound, gilt and lettered". It was given to boys and girls in the two senior classes who showed "diligence and good progress" in reading and writing. Later, prayer books were given as well. The winners received their prizes in church at the end of Sunday morning service and the proud parents often saw several of their children gain Bibles.

The boys and girls stayed at the Free School until they were about eleven or twelve; only a few continued to thirteen. Some left early and were found jobs with farmers "to relieve their parents of the burden of their maintenance". Others seem to have wanted to stay on longer and had to be told that once they gained their Bible they had "received their education in the school" and should leave. Most, however, needed some help in finding a job. In 1778 the Committee complained that pupils after leaving "generally lie unemployed for some time and fall into habits of idleness". They therefore started an apprenticeship scheme of their own. One of the first to benefit, John Blincowe, was taken on by John Watney, "baker and farmer", who lived on Southside, and became a successful baker in the Crooked Billet.

Boys like John Blincowe owed a lot to Joseph Andrews. Throughout his fifteen years in charge of the school, he showed himself to be capable and hardworking. He obviously insisted on discipline and succeeded in awakening the abilities of at least some of his pupils. Then in the summer of 1788, still in harness, he died. He was buried in St Mary's Churchyard, but no monument was put up to his memory.

After Andrews's sudden death, the school suffered several years of uncertainty under incompetent masters and mistresses. But it had now been established on sound foundations and soon settled down again. In 1813 it was linked to the National Society for the Education of the Poor in the Principles of the Established Church and so became known as the National School. In the late nineteenth century the name was changed again to the Central School, later becoming the Old Central. In the 1960s the Church of England built a new primary school in Lake Road and the octagonal building was taken over by Merton Education Committee. It was partly rebuilt and reopened as William Wilberforce School for handicapped children. It thus has the proud record of being used for over two hundred years as a centre for the education of the boys and girls of Wimbledon.

CAMP ROAD

As late as 1865 this road to Caesar's Camp was known as Workhouse Lane. A Workhouse had in fact been set up by the Vestry on the edge of the Common, six years before the octagonal school was built next to it in 1758. It was designed to house about fifty "impotent poor" — old men, elderly widows and even young children — and they were meant to be kept "with proper economy". The regime was strict: no smoking, no drinking gin, no swearing or quarrelling, early rising for some form of work. But at least the inmates were assured of three meals a day.

The Workhouse was emptied of its residents by the Poor Law Amendment Act of 1834. This created Unions of parishes with a single Workhouse — at Kingston for the Wimbledon area. So the parish Workhouse was demolished and in its place Victorian Almshouses were put up with the help of large donations, especially from Earl Spencer and from Mrs Marryat's "grand fancy fair". They remained in use until recently and have now been replaced by modern buildings.

WEST PLACE

Further small plots on the Common to the east of the Workhouse were sold by Earl Spencer in the early 1760s and 1780s. They were bought by John Paterson, a farmer, James Adams, a blacksmith and John Watney, a baker and farmer, who then put up a number of small cottages along a track which has since been given the name West Place.

In the early nineteenth century many of the cottages were bought or rebuilt by William Croft. He was a builder and timber merchant who had his yard at the south end of West Place and a saw pit on the Common opposite. His son George probably built the large early Victorian house, known as the Hermitage, as a family home.

Several cottages in the middle of West Place were built in the 1840s by Daniel Mason, grandson of Samuel Mason who developed The Green. He became prosperous on their rents and began calling himself "land and estate agent", probably the first to do so in Wimbledon.

West Place in the early 1890s, showing the saw-pit, clothes-lines and sheep returning home. This photograph is the only one known of animals on the Common.

10

Cannizaro Park

During the last years of George III's reign, Westside House, facing the Common to the south of the Free School, was the home of the Melvilles. Robert Dundas, second Viscount Melville, like his father, was First Lord of the Admiralty, but held the office for longer, from 1812 to 1827. His wife Anne had her favourite son in the navy, so they were soon on "the most intimate terms" with Lavinia, Countess Spencer, who had two sons, Robert and Frederick ("Bob" and "Fritz"), also in the navy and was naturally anxious to ensure they were posted to the right ships.

At the end of October 1813 Lavinia wrote to her husband that she had had a long visit from Lady Melville, "a most talkative Scottish lady, but seemed quiet and sensible". They discussed their sons' doings and she was able to thank Lord Melville "for his goodness about our dear boy". Later she paid a return visit, though, she insisted, only a "short" one. Lord and Lady Melville responded by "tramping across the Common" for another long talk and "we parted as thick as puddings". The last visit seems to have been in June 1822, just before the Melvilles left Wimbledon, when Lavinia reported: "I have just ordered the carriage to go across to see Lady Melville".

Westside House, like its neighbour, Warren House (already the home of the future Duke of Cannizaro), had been built over a century earlier during the reign of Queen Anne. In 1705 William Browne, a successful London merchant, bought a large estate alongside the Common, once known as The Old Park, but by then called The Warren (named after a large farm, "where the Warrener lived"). He built the two houses, lived in "the mansion house" (Westside House) and leased the other to wealthy friends.

Browne seems to have been very argumentative. He certainly had no time for the vicar, Edward Collins. In May 1722 he deliberately disrupted the morning service by leaving his box-pew as soon as the vicar mounted the steps to the pulpit, banging the door shut and walking out. Many in the congregation stood up to see what was going on. Some apparently roared with laughter; others simply remarked: "Old Browne had gone out of his pew". Not content with doing this once, he repeated the demonstration on at least eight successive Sundays!

The matter came to a head at a meeting of the Vestry held in the church that autumn. The "vexatious and wicked Browne" bitterly criticised Collins "in a brawling, noisy manner", calling him "rogue, robber of the church and cozener of the poor" (perhaps because he had recently increased the fees for baptisms, marriages and burials without consulting his Churchwardens). At this point the Churchwardens intervened on the Vicar's side and denounced Browne to the Archbishop of

Canterbury, both for disturbing the service and for "cohabiting" with Anne Needham and jointly abusing their neighbours "in most scandalous and defamatory language".

The case dragged on until June 1724. Browne was found guilty, ordered to pay Collins twenty pounds and excluded from the parish church. He refused to pay the money and so was declared excommunicate. Still, Collins was able once again to conduct his services in peace. Browne and his lady friend may ultimately have been reconciled to the church, as both were buried by Collins in St Mary's Churchyard, but against Browne's name in the Burial Register is the mysterious word "dung".

On Browne's death in 1738, his son sold the entire Warren estate to Thomas Walker M.P. Walker was a wealthy landowner, Surveyor-General of His Majesty's Land Revenue and, according to the inscription on his tomb in the Churchyard, "an intimate friend of Sir Robert Walpole", the Prime Minister. In 1746 he loaned the Vestry fifty pounds when it ran out of money and charged no interest. He died a bachelor in October 1748 and his estate passed to a nephew, whose daughter later married Thomas Grosvenor. She and her husband inherited the Warren estate in 1769 and from them it passed in the 1820s to the Drax family. Neither Grosvenors nor Draxes seem to have lived in their Wimbledon houses; their only concern was to lease

The garden front of Westside House in May 1913. The oldest part of the house is the central block.

69

Hanford Row — six labourers' cottages put up in the 1760s by William Hanford.

them to wealthy families who wanted to stay by the now fashionable Common.

Behind the two houses lay extensive grounds with views across the entire Grosvenor estate to Coombe Hill and its woods on the far side of Beverley Brook. A plan of the Warren about 1795 shows that the grounds covered nearly sixty acres. Behind Westside House there was then only a small "pleasure ground", surrounded by a "ha-ha" or sunken fence (in the next century the grounds were much bigger and included "a dense wood, the haunt of wood-pigeons and wild pheasants"). Next door the place we know today as Cannizaro Park was more extensive. Just over the wall from Hanford Row (six labourers' cottages put up in the 1760s by William Hanford), there was a small, enclosed garden. In front of the large rectangular Warren House a wide "pleasure ground" was surrounded by trees with paths leading down to a pond and a walled kitchen garden (and a gardener's cottage, pulled down in the 1960s). Beyond was a small copse and large open fields, full of cows.

CANNIZARO PARK

Several noteworthy people lived in the two houses during the reigns of George III and George IV. In the 1770s and early 1780s each was occupied by a banker: Westside House first by Hon. Henry Drummond, Director of a West End Bank, and then by Thomas Jackson, a Director of the Bank of England; Warren House by Lyde Browne, Governor of the Bank of England. Browne was a leading collector of Greek and Roman sculpture, and spent large sums on works of art from Italy. He displayed the collection in his Wimbledon house and many people called to see it, though some were critical of the cramped conditions in which the objects were shown. In 1787 he sold part of the collection to Empress Catherine the Great of Russia and it is now kept in the Hermitage, Leningrad.

From the late 1780s politicians succeeded the bankers. In 1785 Henry Dundas, later first Viscount Melville, a Scotsman and close ally of the young Prime Minister, William Pitt, moved into Warren House. A few years later he also took over the lease of Westside House and allowed first his eldest son Robert and then his daughter Anne use of it in their early years of married life. Dundas used his own home to entertain his many friends. He had an excellent wine cellar and his parties became so notorious that cartoonists alluded to "the dozing fountain of Dundas's port" and to his special emblem, "the bottle and the glass". Pitt was a frequent visitor (as he was to William Wilberforce's house on Southside and to Eagle House where lived another of his close allies, William Grenville). The two friends are said often to have settled political problems on their morning rides on the Common or evening walks in Dundas's Park. In 1792 they shut themselves up in the house for ten days to discuss a final settlement of the thorny problem of the revenue of the rich Indian province, Bengal. With only two experts from the East India Company to help them, they came to an agreement with far-reaching consequences for the future of India.

Another visitor to Dundas's home was the King. George III loved military reviews and Wimbledon Common was the scene of many during his reign. At the height of the French invasion scare in the summer of 1797, the King, accompanied by the Queen and several of their children, reviewed the Surrey Volunteers, including men from Wimbledon. *The Times* reported that "after the usual inspection and marching salutes, the firings were conducted with great precision, which was particularly commended by His Majesty". At the end, "the whole royal party went to breakfast with Mr Dundas, where they remained until three o'clock". The King came again for breakfast after further reviews in 1798, 1799 and 1801.

The visitor whom Dundas most wanted to please, however, was a young woman of quite extraordinary charm, Lady Anne Lindsay, daughter of the Earl of Balcarres. He had already been married once, but the marriage had ended in divorce. He was very fond of Anne and she liked and admired him, but was in love with another politician, William Windham. Dundas waited vainly for two years. Then in 1793 he married Lady Jane Hope and celebrated the event by planting in her honour a wood in his park. Lady Jane Wood still graces the modern Cannizaro Park, around the azalea glen.

Twelve years later, in 1805, Dundas, now Viscount Melville and First Lord of the Admiralty, was in serious political trouble. Accused by the opposition of corruption

Henry Dundas, first
Viscount Melville.

and with even Pitt convinced of his guilt, he was forced to resign from the government and was put on trial, the last impeachment of a minister in English history. In the end he was found innocent, but never held office again. His legal expenses were heavy and he leased Warren House to the young Lord Aberdeen (later Prime Minister during the Crimean War). Instead, he moved into a small cottage on the edge of the estate and then retired to Scotland, where he died in 1811.

His son Robert, now the second Viscount Melville and First Lord of the Admiralty, returned to live in Westside House shortly afterwards. In November 1820 his windows were smashed by a mob, probably because he was a member of the government which was trying to secure George IV's divorce from Queen Caroline. Two years later he left Wimbledon for good and was replaced at Westside House by another leading member of the Tory government, the handsome Attorney-General, Sir John Copley, son of a famous American portrait painter. In 1827 he became Lord Chancellor and took the title Lord Lyndhurst.

Meanwhile, next door at Warren House music rather than politics was the chief interest. In 1811 "a good-looking, intelligent, but penniless Sicilian of high birth", Francis Platamone, Count St Antonio, married a rich and beautiful Scottish heiress, Miss Johnstone, at St George's, Hanover Square. Six years later they moved to Wimbledon and took over the lease of Warren House. The Countess was said, by Charles Greville, to be "totally uneducated, but full of humour and vivacity", and to have an "all-absorbing interest" in music. She was a generous patron to all musicians, built up a valuable library of manuscript and printed music, "one of the most complete collections in the country" and held frequent concerts at her house, especially on Sundays.

About 1832 her husband succeeded to the Dukedom of Cannizaro (a tiny village, just north of Catania in Eastern Sicily). According to Greville, he had already "become disgusted with her" and went off to Milan to live with the "eminently pleasing and attractive" Madame Visconti. The enraged Duchess followed him to Italy, but found he was "irrecoverable". So she returned home and "consoled herself with her music and a strapping young Italian singer, who plundered her without shame".

In June 1841, aged only fifty-five, the Duchess suddenly died, after refusing a

Woodcutters in Cannizaro Park in the 1880s. Behind is the first Cannizaro House, the only known photograph of the building.

73

necessary operation until too late. Only nine months later her husband followed equally suddenly, "in consequence", reported *The Times*, "of taking three pills at a time, which his physicians had ordered him to take only at intervals of eight hours". The Duchess's "valuable library and collection of music", was sold at Christie's and when the census was taken later in 1841 the house was looked after only by servants.

It is in this census that the name "Cannizaro House" seems first to have been used. Perhaps because it sounded so exotic, the name stuck, even after the house had to be totally rebuilt on a different plan when a disatrous fire burnt it to the ground in October 1900. The only link with the past was the fine park that has survived almost complete, with the addition in 1932 of the grounds of an adjoining property, the Keir. It was sold to Wimbledon Corporation in 1948 and opened as a public park. Its beautiful grounds now provide an oasis of peace on the edge of a very busy Common.

WARREN FARM

The Farm, recently transformed into a fine modern house, has claims to be one of the earliest surviving buildings in Wimbledon. It is first mentioned in the 1617 survey as "the house where the warrener lives" — the man responsible for "two warrens of coneys" or rabbits, bred for their meat, as well as for fish ponds near Beverley Brook.

By the 1740s the farm was a large one of over 130 acres. Rocque's map of Wimbledon marks it clearly between the extensive Wimbledon Wood off Copse Hill and "the Rounds" by the Common. Estate maps of the same period show that it had twenty fields, with names like the Bog, Hilly Field, Fox Fields and Calve's Close.

Until the late eighteenth century the names of its farmers are not known. Then between 1785 and 1812 it was run by two Watneys: Thomas (son of Daniel, founder of the family fortunes) and his son, Matthew. Thomas started with a farm near the Crooked Billet, but moved to Warren Farm in 1785 and died there sixteen years later. After Matthew gave up the farm, no family seems to have stayed there long. Most farmers seem to have been in their fifties or sixties, helped only by their wives and children, and a single "agricultural labourer". Nothing else is known about them or the fortunes of their farm.

THE KEIR

The Keir was built in 1789 on an unused plot of land at the northern end of Westside. Its first owners, the Aguilars, were Portuguese Jews who owned extensive property in Jamaica. In 1812 it was bought by another family who had made their fortune in the West Indies, the McEvoys.

The brothers, Christopher and Peter McEvoy, and their widowed mother were Roman Catholics. For the previous twelve years they had been living in a large house on Southside which they had taken over from another Catholic family, the Brays. While there, they had continued a tradition, started by the Brays in the 1780s, of inviting a priest from London to say Mass for the family. They then got their chapel "licensed under Act of Parliament" and encouraged other Catholics to come. By 1808, according to the vicar, "there is considerable resort of that persuasion [i.e.

"Papists"] to attend service there on Sundays". So, as soon as they moved into the Keir, the McEvoys set up another chapel in the house.

The garden front of the Keir about 1900.

In the 1830s, to enlarge their garden, they pulled down a row of cottages lining Workhouse Lane. Two, however, they saved. One they transformed into a Victorian Gothic house for the use of their private chaplain, a Spanish priest, Fr. Lopez. (It still survives in the grounds of modern Cannizaro, by the wall on the northside of the park.) The other they converted into a small Catholic chapel where a public Mass was said every Sunday.

After Peter McEvoy's death, his sons sold the Keir in 1850, and the chapel was closed and demolished. The house was transformed by its new Scottish owners into a preparatory school — and given its present name, meaning fort.

South of the Keir are Stamford House and the White House. Stamford House was probably built in the 1730s, but had no noteworthy occupants in the Georgian period, except perhaps the vicar, Herbert Randolph, in the early years of the nineteenth century. Before 1798 the White House was an Inn, known as The Rising Sun. It was very popular with the labourers who lived round Workhouse Lane, but not with the wealthy families living in the big houses round the Common. So in that year it was closed by the local magistrates on the grounds that it was "injurious to the good order of society".

75

11

Chester House

Another oasis of peace like Cannizaro Park, though not open to the public, is the much smaller garden of Chester House. Despite being overlooked by some of the old cottages around the Crooked Billet, it breathes the atmosphere of a past age, with its long beech hedge, its fine modern cloisters and the beautiful garden in front of the old house.

Chester House is one of the oldest buildings in Wimbledon. Only the Tudor

The front of Chester House, drawn in 1827 by Edward Hassell.

The front of the house today, showing the changes made since Horne-Tooke lived there.

Rectory and Jacobean Eagle House are definitely known to be older. It dates back at least to the reign of William and Mary, as its first known owner, Benjamin Lordell a wealthy merchant who traded with Oporto in Portugal, was living there in 1692. But it is also said to have been built by James, Duke of York (the future James II), for one of his mistresses and the legend is reinforced by the burial in St Mary's Churchyard in 1724 of a possible royal bastard, a mysterious John Fitzjames of St Paul's, Covent Garden.

For most of the eighteenth century its occupants are little known. However, between 1792 and 1812 it was the home of one of the most interesting characters in Georgian England, John Horne-Tooke. Born John Horne in 1736, he added the name Tooke in gratitude to a friend and benefactor. He had wanted to be a lawyer, but was persuaded by his father to become a parson. He soon found he was quite unsuited to the work, resigned his parish and entered politics. Defeated in several elections, he finally got a seat in Parliament in 1801 for a "rotten borough", Old Sarum, and was then barred from standing again as an M.P. since technically he was still a clergyman. His real importance, however, was outside Parliament as a champion of the rights of the people (though not of democracy) and of the radical reform of the political system.

His connection with Wimbledon began in 1782 when he bought Chester House. He only came to live at the house ten years later when he was in his middle fifties, but for the rest of his life it became his "constant residence". He liked the country air and delighted in his large garden where he grew quantities of fruit, including grapes, and grazed two cows. He shared the house with his two illegitimate daughters, Mary

John Horne-Tooke, owner of Chester House from 1782 until his death in 1812.

and Charlotte Hart, and a large tom-cat which he fed himself.

Tooke still maintained a close interest in politics and in the early 1790s travelled up to London by coach for meetings of the Constitutional Society, a group agitating for the peaceful reform of Parliament. In 1793, however, war broke out with Revolutionary France and Tooke was suspected by Pitt and Dundas of aiming to start a similar revolution in England. So his activities were closely watched by a clever government spy, John Moody, who became a trusted member of Tooke's circle of friends at Wimbledon. He described Chester House as "the Headquarters" of sedition and Tooke as its "High Priest". As a result, in 1794 Tooke was arrested on a charge of high treason and sent to the Tower. At his trial he defended himself brilliantly and was acquitted by the jury. His return home was welcomed above all by his cat which had refused to appear in the house while his master was in prison. The cat jumped onto Tooke's shoulder during dinner and stayed there, purring contentedly, for the rest of the meal!

Tooke has been described as "friendly, kind and beneficent". He had a circle of friends whom he entertained at his house every Sunday afternoon. They included peers like Lord Erskine, a leading barrister and Lord Chancellor in 1806; rising young radical politicians, above all Sir Francis Burdett, who lived just across the Common at Wimbledon Villa (later the Grange) on Southside; university professors, notably Richard Porson, a famous Greek scholar at Cambridge; clergymen, including a learned Roman Catholic priest, Dr Geddes; the famous philosopher, Tom Paine, who wrote *The Rights of Man* and whom Tooke did not really like; his banker, Timothy Brown; a poet, Samuel Rogers; a chemist who was just making major discoveries, Humphrey Davy; and an ordinary shoemaker, Samuel Miller, accompanied by his young son.

The "motley assemblage" used to arrive about three o'clock in the afternoon. A few like Burdett came on foot; most travelled to Wimbledon by horse or carriage. They were taken first on a tour of the garden and did not sit down to dinner in the parlour overlooking the Common until about four. The meal was said to be "always excellent": meat, fish, veal, soup, pies, puddings, wine and fruit. The conversation was "very lively", particularly as Tooke placed people with radically different views or occupations next to one another. He himself kept everyone in good humour with his jokes.

His most frequent guest, the one who normally sat on his right at dinner, was his "disciple", Sir Francis Burdett M.P. Like Tooke, Burdett detested the "corruption" of both political parties and wanted to restore the "ancient principles of the constitution". Unfortunately, in May 1807 he infuriated a fellow Radical, John Paull, who claimed that comments Burdett had made in a letter to his constituents at Westminster were insulting. So in the early hours of Saturday, 2 May, Burdett was

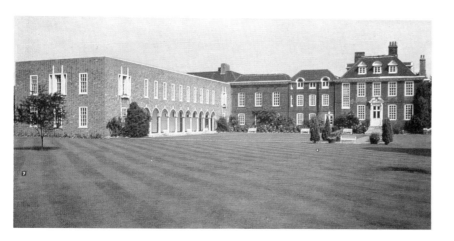

The garden front with the new wing built by Barclays Bank.

Sir Francis Burdett, who lived at Wimbledon Villa on Southside.

awakened by the arrival of Paull at his Wimbledon villa with a demand that he should withdraw the remarks. Burdett refused, so Paull challenged him to a duel and one was arranged for about half past ten that morning.

According to Burdett's second, Coombe Wood just off the Portsmouth Road was chosen as "it seemed to be a proper place for the meeting". The two contestants and their friends went into the wood "for a considerable distance". Pistols were produced

80

CHESTER HOUSE

and the duellists "fired together without effect". But their second shots were more accurate. Both men fell wounded, Sir Francis in the thigh, Paull far more seriously in the leg. While they were being carried slowly to one of the waiting carriages, Burdett's second rode to Wimbledon and returned with the apothecary, John Sanford. He helped the two victims as well as he could while the carriage rode up to London. There Burdett soon recovered. Paull nearly lost his leg and later committed suicide.

Tooke was very upset at the quarrel. By this time his health was failing. He had long suffered from gout and often needed help in moving about the garden or house. Now his legs had daily to be "dressed with great care and assiduity" by Dr Sanford. When his home-grown supply of grapes ran out he was supplied with foreign grapes by another member of Wimbledon's gentry, Lady Rush, whose husband kept a painting of Tooke in their drawing-room at Belvedere House. He still retained his interest in politics, waiting eagerly for the arrival of *The Times* and *Morning Chronicle*, brought daily from London on the stage coach. Finally, however, he had to accept that his end was near, so he had his tomb prepared — in his beloved garden. It was a large classical mausoleum, with pillars in front, and on the door an inscription: "John Horne-Tooke. Late Proprietor and now Occupier of this Spot. Died Content and Grateful."

Tooke died, aged seventy-six, on 18 March 1812. His friends thought that the presence of his body in the back garden would devalue the property for his two daughters so they ignored his wishes and buried him instead in the churchyard at Ealing, his birthplace. After his death the "Wimbledon Circle" of Radicals broke up. Burdett rarely gave dinner parties, preferring to hunt, and in any case gave up his villa on Southside soon after 1812.

Tooke's daughter, Mary, lived in the house for a short time, but first leased and then sold it. Later owners were always wealthy, but rarely well known. Then late in 1938 the house was threatened with demolition and replacement by a block of flats — or conversion into a trade union headquarters or home for the terminally ill. Instead, as soon as the Second World War broke out, the house was taken over by Barclays Bank as their new head office. Since the War it has become their training centre. Unsightly Victorian additions have been pulled down and a new wing in perfect keeping with the original five bay house has been built. Chester House is now one of the finest looking buildings in Wimbledon.

CROOKED BILLET

The legend that this small collection of pubs and cottages was once "Cromwell's half acre" finds no support in the records. Thomas Cromwell's father, Walter, is said to have moved from Putney to Wimbledon in 1513 and taken over "a brewery and inn called the Crooked Billet" at the south-western edge of the Common. Unfortunately, the first mention even of an ale house of that name does not occur until 1759 and a brewery only appears in the 1770s.

In fact, the earliest group of cottages (next to the present Crooked Billet inn) probably dates from the late seventeenth century, just about the time Chester House was being built. Twenty-five cottages are marked on a map of 1776, along with an

The Crooked Billet today. The oldest cottages are those behind the Inn sign; they probably date from the late seventeenth century.

The Hand-in-Hand just to the east of the Crooked Billet, in the early 1880s.

ale house (called the "Crookett Billett" in one document) at the corner of Westside. They were mostly occupied by labourers, often too poor to pay the rates. But several were rented by craftsmen — a wheelwright, carpenter, chandler and tailor — and two were owned by "gentlemen": William Walker, calico-printer, who managed a works on the Wandle, and Daniel Watney, farmer, who lived on the site of the present Hand-in-Hand.

So the Crooked Billet has a genuine claim to fame: it saw the rise to prosperity of the Watney family. Daniel settled there in 1730 as a young man of twenty-five, on his marriage to a local girl. He became a successful farmer, leasing fields on either side of Worple Lane and there grazing cattle and growing corn. He used his profits to buy half the cottages in the Crooked Billet and was able to give his children a good start in life. All prospered: his eldest son, William, set up the Wheatsheaf Brewery to the west of the cottages; Thomas started a farm nearby and later moved to Warren Farm; John, the youngest, took over his father's lands and in 1788 built a fine house on Southside (Rushmere, next to King's College Junior School); his daughter Mary married Samuel Mason, carpenter and innkeeper at the Rose and Crown.

Opposite the Crooked Billet stands Southside House, round which legends have also collected. It is said to have been built in 1687, around an old farm house. Neither house nor farm is mentioned in any known document before 1751. In that year John Lawson, a wealthy lawyer, took out an insurance policy on "two houses, adjoining, not quite finished" (though he may have been adding to an existing building). He gave the two a common Georgian brick facade with finely carved stone doorways and inside built some beautiful panelled rooms. The building, regarded as two houses until relatively recently, does not seem to have been occupied by anyone of real note, except Robert Wright after whom Wright's Alley has been named.

Southside House and Holme Lodge, then two separate houses, in 1913. The entrance to Wright's Alley lies behind the street lamp on the left.

83

12

The Windmill

John Watney, described as "a farmer of the old school, who brewed his own beer, dressed plain and wore an old top hat", seems to have been the first to think of putting up a windmill on the Common. In 1799 he applied to the manor court for permission "to enclose a piece of land of Wimbledon Common for the purpose of erecting a windmill thereon", and was told to provide a plan for the court to consider. For some unknown reason he never did so and the matter was dropped.

In 1816 a new application was made by Charles March, a carpenter from Roehampton, "praying for a grant of a small plot of ground for the erection of a mill". He was supported by several of the inhabitants of Wimbledon and his request was granted so long as he put up "a public corn mill for the advantage and convenience of the neighbourhood". Within a year the building was ready, an unusual hollow post mill, and to it March added a cottage for the miller and his family.

For the next ten years the miller was first Benjamin, then Anthony, Hallowell. Some time in the 1830s Thomas Dann, a married man with a family of eight, took over. He combined the duties of miller with those of special constable, sworn in to arrest robbers and especially to stop duels which had recently taken place nearby.

Before 1830 all the famous duels, such as those involving the Dukes of York and Wellington, William Pitt, Castlereagh and Canning had been fought on Putney Heath. In the 1830s, however, the fashionable spot had become a "lawn-like land" with a small stream flowing through it and dense woods all around (it lay just to the west of the Windmill and has since been turned into a pond known as Queensmere to commemorate Victoria's Diamond Jubilee). It was an ideal site for a duel. Most of the contests there ended harmlessly, with honour satisfied after one or both of the duellists had deliberately shot wide. In 1838, however, a Mr Mirfin was killed and the authorities decided to give the man living nearest the spot, the miller, full power to stop further duels and arrest the assailants.

Constable Dann, however, proved unable to stop the last and most infamous of the duels. In the late afternoon of Saturday, 12 September, 1840, as he was standing with his wife and one of his sons on the gallery outside the mill tower, two carriages drove along Parkside from opposite directions. They stopped near the mill and from each two men merged. One pair were carrying cases of pistols, while the other two went to take up position, not at the usual spot in the meadow, but about two hundred yards east of the mill, near "the road that leads by Earl Spencer's park".

One of the duellists was James Brudenell, Earl of Cardigan, later to lead the famous charge of the Light Brigade at Balaclava. In 1840 he was Colonel of the Fourteenth Hussars, the smartest regiment in the British Army, but was on very bad terms with his fellow officers. The feud was revealed in the *Morning Chronicle*. Cardigan was furious, discovered that the officer responsible was Captain Harvey Tuckett and challenged him to a duel.

According to a contemporary account: "The word to fire was uttered and immediately was followed by an ineffectual discharge of both pistols. The principals remained at their posts; a second brace of pistols was given them; again both fired and Captain Tuckett fell, wounded in the small of the back, bleeding profusely, but as it proved, not from a mortal wound."

At this moment the miller "ran up to the scene of the action and intimated to all parties that they must consider themselves in his custody". Poor Tuckett could hardly resist, but even Cardigan went quietly — to Wandsworth police station, where he was bound over to appear before the local magistrates.

The duel caused a sensation. The Earl, realising public opinion was against him, elected to be tried by his fellow peers. He employed a clever counsel who fastened

The earliest picture of the Windmill, engraved by George Cooke about 1825. Only the ground floor was then of brickwork.

on the failure of the prosecution to prove that the wounded man was in fact Captain Tuckett. So on this technicality he was declared not guilty and kept command of his regiment. But he had helped to bring duelling into disrepute and no further "matters of honour" seem to have been settled with pistols near the Windmill.

Nine months after the duel, in May 1841, the Danns witnessed a very different ceremony, a "perambulation of the parish" or "beating the bounds". On the surface, this was a day out for some of the inhabitants, including schoolboys, accompanied by a ten piece band. They inspected the boundary posts near the Windmill and then moved on to Earl Spencer's Park where at one of the posts several of the boys were ceremonially bumped — so that in future years they would remember the position of the boundary. On the way they had an "excellent dinner", complete with four bottles of wine and fifty-four of porter.

In fact, the practice of "men going the parish bounds" was directed particularly at their neighbours in Putney. For over fifty years there had been a dispute over the ownership of a large area south of the modern Tibbet's Corner. In 1787 the boundary had been settled by dividing the disputed land almost in half. The Wimbledon Vestry, however, was not satisfied and in 1813 went to "ascertain and claim the boundaries". Shortly afterwards there was a strong protest from the Putney Vestry which claimed that the Wimbledonians had taken down the posts marking the agreed line of 1787 and substituted new ones which increased their share of the Common by nearly two hundred acres. So they employed an impartial surveyor from Merton to work out the correct boundary, helped by old maps and surveys. Then, accompanied by a hundred inhabitants, they walked their bounds, threw down the new Wimbledon posts or simply sawed them off, and restored the old ones. Next year Wimbledon retorted by holding another "Grand Perambulation", putting up fresh posts and finishing with a grand dinner at the Dog and Fox.

There the matter seems to have rested until the perambulation Dann saw in 1841. Putney's reply did not come for five years, but then they called in another impartial adjudicator, Francis Martin, a Tithe Commissioner. He again looked at old records and also questioned old inhabitants who all claimed that time and again Wimbledonians had encroached on their part of the Common, especially near the Windmill. So he too found in Putney's favour and a line of new posts was put up west of Parkside from Heathfield House to just north of the Windmill and then south-west to Beverley Brook. This decision seems at last to have been accepted by both sides.

Meanwhile, the mill (along with the job of special constable) had been taken over by Anthony Holloway. He is said to have had a hand in the building of the mill thirty years before and was certainly involved with other mills in the area. At the time of the 1851 census, he was sixty years old and had his wife and six children living with him in the cottage. Ten years later the mill was being worked by John Marsh of Kingston, the owner of both watermills and windmills in the neighbourhood. In 1864, however, he was persuaded to sell his lease of the Wimbledon mill to Earl Spencer, who was aiming to enclose the Common, but insisted on removing the mill-stones and machinery to Kingston.

So after less than fifty years, the mill suddenly stopped working. It was converted by Earl Spencer into cottages used by officials of the National Rifle Association. Battered by wind and rain in its exposed position, it gradually fell into decay. In 1893

THE WINDMILL

a public appeal was made to preserve it as a landmark and enough money was raised to have it almost entirely rebuilt. After both World Wars, however, it needed further extensive repairs. Not until 1974, when the cottages were empty, could the full extent of the decay be discovered, and massive repair work started. Within two years the building was transformed and in 1976 it opened as the Windmill Museum.

Manor Cottage and the Windmill about 1860. The Mill is clearly still working.

PARKSIDE

Since before the Norman Conquest "the Road to Putney" has been travelled by generations of Wimbledonians. In 1729 with the building of the first Putney Bridge, it became their easiest route to London. Sarah, Duchess of Marlborough, found that it took her only an hour to get to London, while the second Earl Spencer used later to ride up to St James's and back home in a morning.

The road, however, was very lonely. Until the building of the White House (on the site now occupied by the Victorian Heathfield), probably in the 1760s, travellers from Wimbledon village would not have seen another building until they reached the top of Putney Hill. As a result there was always the danger of encountering a footpad or even one of the highwaymen who infested the Portsmouth Road.

87

The worst period for such attacks was between the years 1784 and 1795. In October 1784 Lady Spencer told her husband about "a robbery committed at ten o'clock this morning on the Common by a single highwayman on a coach and four". When he held the coach up, one gentleman refused to hand over his money and tried to seize the highwayman through the broken window. Instead he cut his wrist badly and nearly got pulled out of the coach by the robber. His experience so frightened Lady Spencer that she ordered her servants to carry loaded pistols when she went for an airing, and her guests at Wimbledon Park House started leaving early on their return journeys to London.

In the early 1790s a small band of highwaymen, led by a young man from Kingston, Jerry Abershawe, began operating on Putney Heath and Wimbledon Common. Their headquarters was the Bald Faced Stag, an inn on the Portsmouth Road near Beverley Brook. Their more important robberies were regularly reported in *The Times* and were sufficiently serious to alarm both local and central authorities. In Wimbledon a Patrol Guard, paid for out of local subscriptions, was raised to convoy travellers to Putney. In London the Bow Street Runners were set on their trail.

Abershawe evaded arrest for five years. Then in July 1795 he was cornered in a Southwark pub, tried to shoot his way out, killing one Bow Street Runner and severely wounding another, and was finally overpowered and arrested. Put on trial at Croydon Assizes, he was sentenced to death and hanged on Kennington Common. His body was then hung in chains from a second gallows, specially erected on "Jerry's Hill" by the Portsmouth Road. Thousands of people came to see "the spectacle", which was long remembered. Forty years later Captain Marryat described the scene in his novel *Jacob Faithful*.

The road to Putney was now much safer and the Wimbledon Patrol disappears from the records. But robberies "on the Common" still continued, though on a lesser scale.

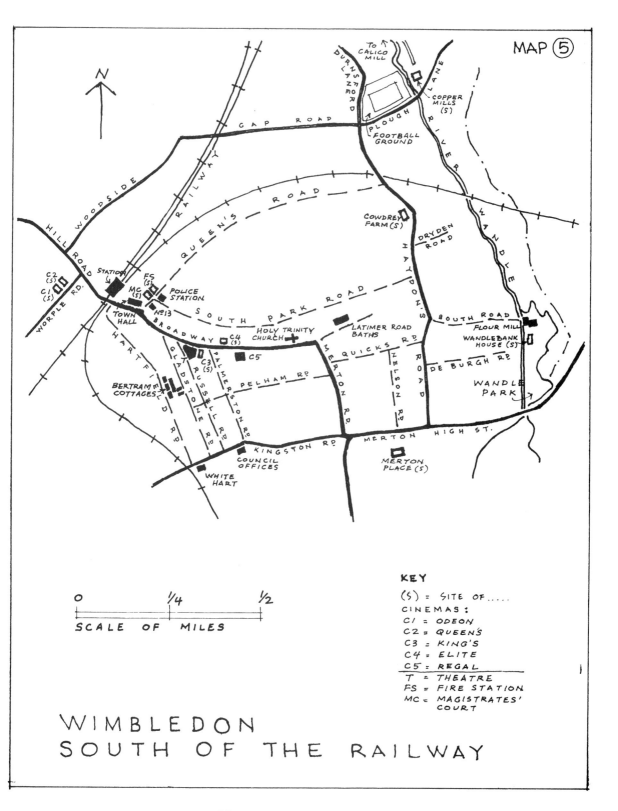

MAP ⑤

N

To CALICO MILL

DURNSFORD LANE

PLOUGH LANE

COPPER MILLS (S)

FOOTBALL GROUND

RIVER

GAP ROAD

RAILWAY

WOODSIDE

WANDLE

QUEEN'S ROAD

HILL ROAD

COWDREY FARM (S)

DRYDEN ROAD

HAYDON'S ROAD

C2 (S)

STATION

FS (S)

POLICE STATION

SOUTH PARK ROAD

SOUTH ROAD

C1 (S)

MC (S)

No 13

BROADWAY

HOLY TRINITY CHURCH

LATIMER ROAD BATHS

FLOUR MILL

WORPLE RD.

TOWN HALL

C4 (S)

QUICKS RD.

WANDLEBANK HOUSE (S)

HARTFIELD RD.

GLADSTONE RD.

RUSSELL RD.

C3 (S)

C5

PALMERSTON RD.

MERTON RD.

NELSON RD.

DE BURGH RD.

WANDLE PARK

BERTRAM COTTAGES

PELHAM RD.

MERTON ROAD

KINGSTON RD.

MERTON HIGH ST.

COUNCIL OFFICES

MERTON PLACE (S)

WHITE HART

KEY

(S) = SITE OF.....

CINEMAS:
C1 = ODEON
C2 = QUEEN'S
C3 = KING'S
C4 = ELITE
C5 = REGAL
T = THEATRE
FS = FIRE STATION
MC = MAGISTRATES' COURT

0   ¼   ½
SCALE   OF   MILES

WIMBLEDON
SOUTH OF THE RAILWAY

13

The Wandle

The Windmill on the Common ceased working in 1864, but other Wimbledon mills continued to operate, one for nearly another 100 years. These were watermills, situated along the banks of the Wandle. By the early nineteenth century, according to one authority, the Wandle had become "the hardest worked river of its size in the world", with forty mills drawing power from its waters between the source near Croydon and the mouth at Wandsworth. Three of them were just inside the parish of Wimbledon.

The oldest, often alluded to as "Martyn" or Merton Mill because it was only a little north of Merton High Street, may be one of the two mills mentioned in the

Wimbledon Flour Mill in April 1914. The River Wandle flows by the side of the road.

Domesday Book as part of the Archbishop of Canterbury's manor of Mortlake (which included Wimbledon). It was certainly in constant use in the thirteenth century, grinding the manor corn both from the Archbishop's lands and from the plots tilled by the ordinary farmers, who were banned from using small hand-querns at home. Manor documents list repairs to the waterwheels and the cogs, as well as costly new mill-stones, brought especially from Croydon.

The millers were important people in the community. In the late thirteenth century the De La Mares ran the mill, in the early fifteenth century, the Melewards, and in Queen Elizabeth's reign the Lingards. Hugh Lingard, a wealthy farmer as well as a miller, worked two other mills for fulling or cleaning cloth. The three mills seem to have been situated near each other, at the top of a special head of water made by diverting the Wandle from its normal course (this large mill-pond was partly filled in about 1906 and laid out as Wandle Park).

The Lingard family was notable for two unusual tragedies. In 1569 Hugh's wife died in mysterious circumstances, shortly after the birth of their thirteenth child. She was said to have been "wickedly and devilishly" killed by the "incantations and enchantments" of Jane Baldwyn, the wife of a leading Wimbledon farmer. Jane was arrested, put on trial, pleaded guilty to "murder by witchcraft" and sentenced to be hanged, but was then reprieved. Instead, she had to go to prison for a year and stand in the pillory for six hours on four separate days. What became of her is not known. Hugh Lingard long survived his wife and when he died in 1596 had outlived most of his contemporaries and several of his own children. He passed on his mills and his land to his eldest son, William, who was already in his forties but only recently in a position to marry. Nonetheless he and his young wife, Elizabeth, also had a large family. By 1603 there were ten children. Then, as in 1569, tragedy struck, but in an even more terrible way. The year of James I's arrival in England was marked by a serious outbreak of plague and during the summer the dreaded disease seems to have reached Wimbledon. In the short space of two months, 17 July to 15 September 1603, William Lingard and seven of his children caught the infection and were soon buried in St Mary's Churchyard. As two other boys had died earlier, only their mother, Elizabeth, and her youngest son survived the disaster — and they soon followed. By 1617 the mills were said to belong to "the heirs of Lingard" and no one seemed to know who they were. With this sad epitaph the family name disappeared from Wimbledon's records.

The next notable owner, James Perry, took over the mill nearly 175 years later, in 1791, shortly after buying a leading radical newspaper, the *Morning Chronicle*. Under his editorship it became, according to a plaque in the parish church, "a great moral instrument, devoted to the support of the oppressed and the promotion of public and private virtue". Perry was a great friend of Horne-Tooke, and of Horatio Nelson who bought Merton Place on the opposite side of Merton High Street in 1801. The Admiral and the Editor often went fishing near Perry's Wandlebank House. Perry rebuilt the mill in brick and installed seven pairs of mill-stones. He thus became a major producer of corn for the London market. To transport the corn more cheaply to that market, he enthusiastically supported a plan for an "Iron Railway", a track of iron rails linking the mills between Croydon and Wandsworth, on which would run a series of freight waggons drawn by horses. The Railway was opened in 1803. The

James Perry, who owned the Mill and lived at Wandlebank House between 1791 and 1811.

maintrack kept just east of Wimbledon's boundary and only Perry's mill had a branch line connecting with it. How much he used the line is impossible to say, but within eight years he seems to have left the area and let both the mill and the house. A little over a century later the mill was converted into the Connolly Brothers leather works.

At the opposite end of the Wimbledon section of the Wandle, near the boundary with Wandsworth, another mill had been constructed. It first appears in a deed of 1666 as a gunpowder mill, perhaps started during the Civil Wars to supply the New

Model Army. A hundred years later it had become a calico print works, managed by William Walker, the neighbour of Daniel Watney in the Crooked Billet. The owner between 1777 and 1820 was John Coleman, a Quaker who flatly refused to pay the church rate and every so often had some of his goods seized by the Churchwardens. But, as the vicar reported: "he soon redeems any articles so seized".

Between the corn and silk mills was a large copper mill. It stood on the Tooting side of a bridge over the Wandle (where Copper Mill Lane ends abruptly today with some of the old mill houses nearby). In the early seventeenth century an iron plate mill had been started here, probably by French Huguenot refugees. In 1636 the funeral of one of the workers, "Tussen, a Frenchman from the Irone Myles", was recorded in the Parish Register. By 1762 the mill had been taken over by "The Governor and Company of the Copper Miners". The works were large with a "copper hammer mill, tumbling bay, hoop or rolling mill", and furnace. But its chief claim to fame was a gigantic waterwheel, twenty feet in diameter and said as late as 1929 to be the second largest in Europe. Apparently it still existed fifty years ago and the factory, after becoming a leather works, only ceased production in 1960.

The manager of the copper mill between 1804 and 1813 was one of the most enterprising Wimbledonians of all time, Benjamin Paterson. His father, John, had been bailiff to Earl Spencer and a "yeoman farmer" who lived in the High Street. Benjamin moved down to the more fertile land in the Wandle Valley and in 1787 leased the best and oldest farm in the district, Cowdrey Farm. Known by many different names: Butler's in the late Middle Ages, Cowdrey's in the early eighteenth century and Heydon's later in the century, it was never better looked after than under Paterson, described as "a large scientific farmer". In the 1790s he introduced a newly-invented mill for threshing corn. It was worked by two or three horses, and separated the corn from the straw far more efficiently than normal threshing with flails. He clearly impressed Earl Spencer who had become very dissatisfied with the farmer who managed the eastern side of his park from Ashen Grove Farm. So in 1815 he leased over 400 acres of the park to Paterson, who therefore moved from Cowdrey Farm to Ashen Grove. That September Lady Spencer wrote to the Earl: "I had a visit from Mr Paterson after service and had a great deal of farming conversation with him. He appears to me to be in high feather, notwithstanding the pressure of the times on farmers." Two months later she had given him a nickname, "Splutter Paterson", but was still prepared to "talk [about farming matters] and walk with him" just before leaving for Spencer House, London. In the late 1820s Paterson, now in his seventies, moved yet again to Durnsford Farm. There he died in 1831 and was buried in a large family vault behind the parish church.

Meanwhile, in 1818, Cowdrey Farm had been put on the market. In the sale brochure it was described as "a most valuable farm, with a respectable brick-built residence and warm farmyard, surrounded by barns, cart- and nag-horse stables, cowhouse, cart and waggon sheds and granaries... highly distinguished for the superior quality of the soil, the excellence of the roads and the facility of carriage to the London markets". In the next fifty years its land was almost doubled in size so that when the "Cowdrey Estate" along with "two gentlemanly residences", Cowdrey House and Durnsford Lodge, were sold for development in 1872, it covered 332 acres north of the Broadway. The farm buildings were pulled down, streets laid out where

THE COPPER MILLS.

cows, sheep and horses had grazed for centuries and only one link was left with the past; the name of a short cul-de-sac, Cowdrey Road, over the site of the old farmhouse.

ASHEN GROVE

Until the early seventeenth century Ashen Grove was a "great" forty acre wood to the west of "Dunsford Lane" and part of the manor park. In 1633 Viscount Wimbledon leased it to a yeoman from Hertfordshire, John Halfhead. He cleared most of the wood and developed a farm with "yards, barns, stables, outhouses, orchards and gardens". During the Civil War he was chosen Village Constable with the job of collecting taxes for Parliament. He managed to raise most of the unprecedentedly large sums demanded, but seems to have kept his records slackly and got into arrears. In the end he was summoned to appear before the Parliamentary Accounts Committee, but never turned up. How he evaded the summons when every other constable in Surrey complied will never be known. But Wimbledon's accounts for the years 1642 to 1646 are still missing from the official Exchequer Papers.

Halfhead died in June 1648 and his farm passed through many hands before Benjamin Paterson took over in 1815. By then it was known as the Wimbledon Park Farm. Its buildings, along with a small pond, were situated just to the west of Durnsford Road and its fields extended nearly to the lake on one side of the road and to the Wandle on the other. In some of the fields large flocks of sheep and herds of cows belonging to Earl Spencer grazed, while in others wheat, barley, oats, cabbages and turnips were grown, as well as large quantities of grass for producing hay.

The first sign of change came in 1838, while Paterson's son, William, was in charge. The new London and Southampton railway embankment was built across some of the fields near the Wandle (just to the south-west of the modern Earlsfield Station). Then in the early 1880s the District Line was laid out in the fields near the lake. So in 1882 the farm was put up for sale as "freehold building land". For twenty years no building took place and the farmhouse was still being lived in as late as 1900. In the next few years, however, lines of houses were built including those in a road called Ashen Grove laid out over the site of the farmhouse. The last relic of the old farm was the small pond, which survived by the side of Durnsford Road for a few more years before the First World War.

Victorian Wimbledon

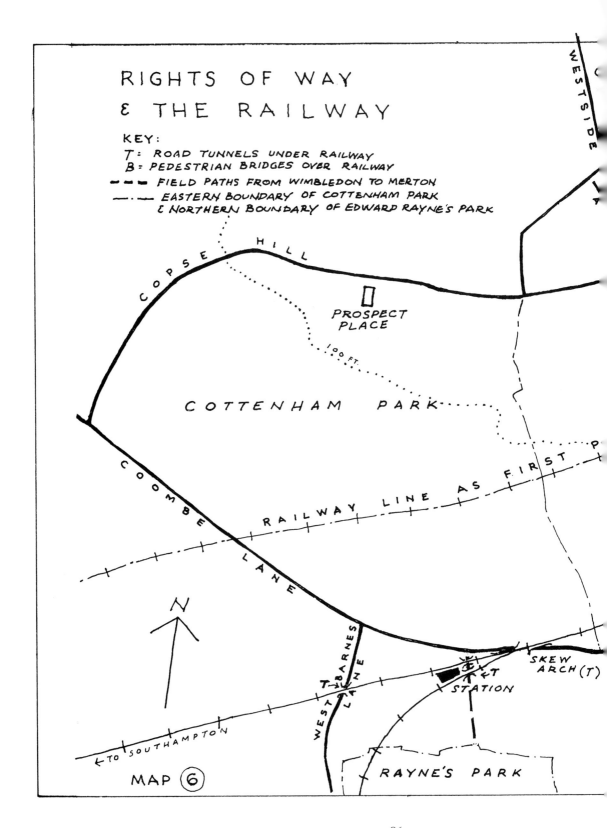

RIGHTS OF WAY
& THE RAILWAY

KEY:
T: ROAD TUNNELS UNDER RAILWAY
B: PEDESTRIAN BRIDGES OVER RAILWAY
▬ ▬ ▬ FIELD PATHS FROM WIMBLEDON TO MERTON
—·— EASTERN BOUNDARY OF COTTENHAM PARK
& NORTHERN BOUNDARY OF EDWARD RAYNE'S PARK

WESTSIDE

COPSE HILL

PROSPECT PLACE

100 FT.

COTTENHAM PARK

COOMBE LANE

RAILWAY LINE AS FIRST P

N

WEST BARNES LANE

T

SKEW ARCH (T)

STATION

← TO SOUTHAMPTON

RAYNE'S PARK

MAP ⑥

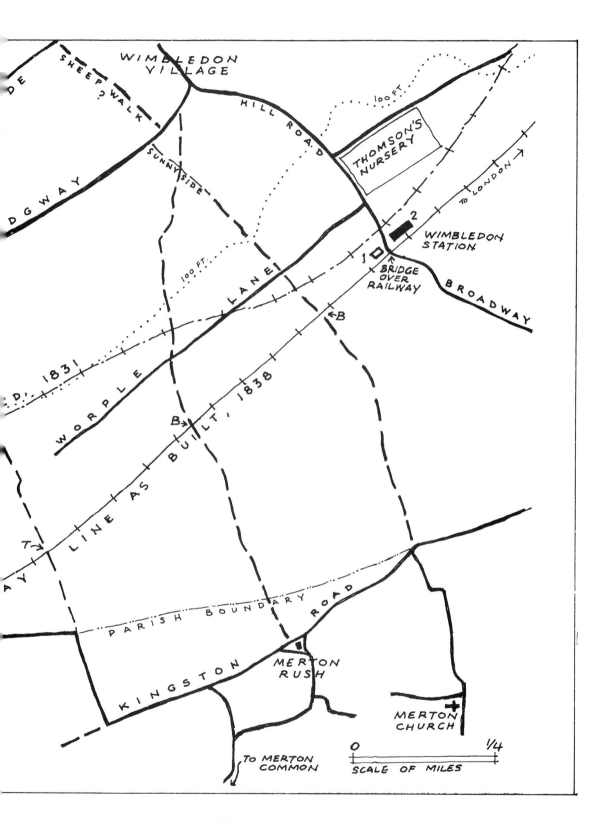

14

South Wimbledon

The railway that cut across the fields of Ashen Grove Farm in 1838 went on to cut the parish of Wimbledon in two. "Wimbledon South of the Railway" became an ever-growing section in local street directories and from about 1870 maps began to label the district "South", instead of "New", Wimbledon. They also changed the names of old roads there: "the Lane to Merton" became the Broadway (initially for the open area just below the railway, slowly extending to Holy Trinity church); "the Way to the White Hart, Merton" became Hartfield Road; "Heydon Lane", Haydons Road; and "Lower Worple Lane", Dundonald Road. "Upper Worple Lane", now Worple Road, was also nearly included in South Wimbledon.

In 1831 the newly-formed London and Southampton Railway Company engaged a leading canal engineer, Francis Giles, to survey a possible route for their line. He had a thorough look at the country to the south-west of London and finally drew a detailed map of his recommended route. He proposed that the railway should start by the Thames at Nine Elms, near Vauxhall, and go through the outskirts of Battersea and Wandsworth. After crossing the Wandle by Ashen Grove Farm, it would skirt Earl Spencer's Park and Kitchen Garden, cross Wimbledon Hill (about where Boots the Chemist is now located), go through a few fields below Worple Lane, then cross the road (where Spencer Hill was later built) to the higher ground, and in a small cutting travel over further fields (soon to be covered by houses on the bottom slopes of Denmark, Thornton and Edge Hills, the Downs, Arterberry, Pepys and Durham Roads), crossing Coombe Lane (near the bottom of the present Cambridge Road) and so on to Kingston.

Giles's plan immediately ran into fierce opposition. The Earl of Cottenham, who owned the fields between the modern Pepys Road and Coombe Lane, did not want dirty, noisy trains near his house up on Copse Hill and refused to sell his land. Kingston Corporation, with a vested interest in stagecoaches, did not want the railway either. So the company was forced to alter the route — first to a line just south of Worple Lane and then in 1834 further south still, "through the low lands", which the owners, Caroline Phillips in particular, were willing to sell.

As a result the company had to build a long earth embankment to keep the gradient for the primitive engines more or less level. Work started in October 1834. Labourers from Wimbledon were "obtainable", according to Giles, "at cheaper prices [three to four shillings a day] than at Battersea", and local farmers, like Edward Rayne at West Barnes, were willing to send "a horse on work for the Southampton Railway and to pull waggons for a whole week". But progress was slow. Heavy rain damaged the

new embankments, while severe frost held up the laying of rails. Above all the small, local contractors were inefficient. So after nearly three years of frustration, the directors sacked Giles and appointed a pupil of George Stephenson, Joseph Locke, as engineer. He was energetic and efficient, dismissed all the old contractors and entrusted the work to Thomas Brassey, who was later to build railways all over the world. He transformed the work. Edward Rayne noticed the difference: "They are now pushing on with the railway," he wrote in his diary on 7 April 1837, "gangs working night and day, and others over hours." He himself brought cartloads of gravel for the track and also some of the rails.

At last in May 1838 the line was ready to be opened as far as Woking. The first trains to use the new railway only carried the directors, the engineer and "persons of distinction". They covered the twenty-three miles "with perfect ease in forty-five minutes", while "on every eminence along the line admiring rustics gathered in thousands to cheer the trains". On Monday 21 May the line was opened to the public and people from London flocked to use the novel form of transport, above all on Derby Day when the terminus was invaded by a huge crowd wanting to get to "Kingston-on-Railway" (soon to become Surbiton), from where coaches would take them to Epsom.

One station that does not appear to have been well patronised was "Wimbledon and Merton" (so named because it was out in the fields halfway between the two villages). The platforms were to the west of the new bridge and passengers could have a very long wait there as trains only ran every two to three hours. But with only one stop (at Wandsworth Town, to the west of the later Clapham Junction), they reached Nine Elms in eighteen minutes and there could board a river steamer for the city or a horse bus over Westminster Bridge for the West End. One local man who certainly did use the line shortly after it opened was Edward Rayne, who on 19 July

The bridge over the railway and Hill Road in 1880. The photograph was probably taken from the Prince of Wales public house. The station entrance was still to the left of the bridge, while the platforms had now extended to the other side. The site of the present Booking Hall was then a goods yard. The south end of Hill Road is lined with large private houses: one at the corner of Worple Road has a garden. Beyond is a large field and, on the opposite side of Hill Road, are the grounds of Belvedere House. Above the railway lines there is a path soon to become Alexandra Road and behind that are the walls and shrubs of Thomson's Nursery with Ricard's Lodge in the hazy background.

A view from the same point, taken nearly 100 years later in the early 1970s. The only buildings that survive are the large houses at the bottom of Hill Road, by the banks.

A view of the bridge from the other direction, taken about 1910. The cab on the right is probably a private one, the one on the left was for hire in the station forecourt.

noted, "I went and returned from town by the railway and was home again by noon."

For about twenty years, life in Wimbledon seems to have been largely unaffected by the railway. An interesting water-colour painted in the 1850s from a viewpoint on the Ridgway shows the valley still covered with trees and green fields; in the middle, puffing its way along the embankment, runs a solitary train. The embankment in fact was the immediate legacy of the railway. Old rights of way had to be safeguarded by the building of Elm Grove bridge and tunnels at Lower Downs and Coombe Lane. Drainage was upset, especially in the future Raynes Park area, and floods were increasingly reported there. Above all a new barrier was created right across the centre of the parish.

This barrier became important from the middle 1850s when important changes began around the railway. More lines were opened — to Croydon, Epsom and Kingston — and Wimbledon became a junction. With better communications and more work available, people began pouring in. Street after street of semi-detached or terraced houses went up in "New Wimbledon". Many of these Victorian houses are still standing. Some, for instance in Pelham Road (dating from the 1850s) and Queens Road (from the 1880s) were clearly designed for "respectable" middle-class families. But most of the houses on both sides of the Broadway (such as in Gladstone Road, 1870s; Derby and Nelson roads, 1890s) and off Haydons Road (like De Burgh Road, 1870s; Dryden Road, 1890s) were put up as blocks of separate homes, each for one working-class family, since flats were felt to be out of place in a Victorian suburb. In addition a few specially designed model cottages (such as Bertram Cottages between Hartfield and Gladstone Roads) were built in the 1870s by charitable people to help "the deserving poor".

By the 1880s a railway suburb had been born. The census returns every ten years show the dramatic increase in population, above all in South Wimbledon:

1861   Population 4,644 including about 1,000 south of the railway.
1871   Population 9,087 including about 4,000 south of the railway.
1881   Population 15,949 including about 8,000 south of the railway.

Many of these people worked on the railway. Others were bricklayers, carpenters and plasterers, employed in putting up the new houses. Still more served the big mansions up the hill as domestic servants, gardeners, coachmen, laundresses, or as tradesmen — blacksmiths, whitesmiths, bootmakers and stonemasons. They were rarely local in origin. Many came from London and the Home Counties, from East Anglia or from Somerset and Wiltshire. They were escaping from a city whose inner ring of suburbs had by 1860 become congested or from rural areas which in the late 1870s were suffering a serious slump. They were in the main manual workers, like Mr Clark who in the 1890s was a railway blacksmith's assistant. He received just over a pound for working at the Wimbledon sidings from 6 a.m. to 5.30 p.m. six days a week. On the way to work he often called at a public house (which opened at 5 a.m.) for a halfpenny cup of coffee laced with a pennyworth of rum. At work he was allowed no teabreaks and risked the sack if he smoked. On such a wage men like Mr Clark could not afford to travel to work and would be hard hit by even a short spell of unemployment caused by bad weather.

In such circumstances families had to rely largely on charity. For the really destitute, there was the Wimbledon Charity Organisation (now the Guild of Social Welfare), founded in 1869 to "prevent mendicancy" by giving tickets with which the "deserving poor" could obtain bread, and by discouraging "indiscriminate alms-giving" which "fosters dishonesty and demoralisation". During the hard winter of 1882, for instance, when there was "great scarcity of work for many weeks" in South Wimbledon, a local painter with a wife and eight children was left unemployed and then got rheumatic fever. He and his family were "literally starving" when the Charity Organisation was informed of his plight — and that he was "sober and industrious". He was therefore given "relief" for three weeks until he found a new job.

To meet the ordinary hazards of life, however, the people of South Wimbledon seem to have looked to the Churches for help. The Church of England established a mission below the hill in 1859 when Revd J. Halcombe held the first service in a small room off Haydon Lane. The next year he was succeeded by a much more important clergyman, Revd William Bartlett, who came to Wimbledon a young man of twenty-eight, fresh from his first parish in the very different environment of Winchester. Bartlett lodged with his sister at 1 Waterloo Villas, near "the Quicks" (the edge of Nelson's old garden). His first job was to buy a plot for a new church and vicarage on the Broadway, and there to build Holy Trinity which at first served the whole of South Wimbledon and where he soon reported, "the seats are being filled extremely well". At the same time he did all he could to help the poor. He sponsored the New Wimbledon and Merton Soup Kitchen "to supply the poor with good soup during the winter months at a cost of a halfpenny a pint". He encouraged a Clothing, Bedding and Fuel Club "for the benefit of respectable labourers and their families", the Provident Medical Dispensary "to supply gratuitous medical assistance and medicines" and the Maternal Society "to help with medical aid and linen at the confinement of poor women of good character who had been resident in Wimbledon for at least a year". He was also concerned about the children and supported an Infants' School, Sunday School and Night School for Youths, as well as opening a new school (later known as All Saints Primary) for ninety boys and girls in South Road, and a local library with a penny a month subscription.

Yet amid all this work to make life in his district a little more bearable, Bartlett still found time to write Wimbledon's first genuine local history. His *History and Antiquities of the Parish of Wimbledon* was published in 1865, partly to combat the lack of reverence for the past shown by "this utilitarian, money-making, railway-projecting age", partly to encourage local pride in "those families who lived in our homes through years gone by". He went to a great deal of trouble over the research and used original documents, as well as information from "older inhabitants". Three hundred subscribers, including peers and the chief local landowners, helped to pay the cost of the book which was an immediate success and still remains the standard history of Wimbledon. (It was reprinted in 1971 and all copies of this edition have now been sold.)

In late 1868 Bartlett was made Vicar of Wisborough Green, near Horsham in Sussex, and there he remained until his death twenty-seven years later. Little is known of his personality, but photographs show him as strongly built with a full black

Left: An aerial view of the town centre, taken from an aeroplane in 1920. The church in the foreground was the Congregational in Worple Road. Behind in St George's Road, is the Drill Hall. In the top right corner is the Theatre, facing down the Broadway.

Far left: The top of the Broadway with a solitary car, about 1914. The side of the first Town Hall is on the left. The shop buildings in the centre mostly still survive.

Bottom left: A tram near the top of the Broadway in 1910. The tradesman's cart has a bag of oats for the horse slung underneath.

Left: Trolley-buses from Hampton Court near the Town Hall in the 1930s. A tram waits at its terminal to take passengers to London.

Revd William Bartlett who built Holy Trinity Church in the early 1860s and wrote Wimbledon's first history.

beard and a kindly expression. He was a great benefactor to South Wimbledon, yet his name was not even mentioned in the Holy Trinity church history.

The Church of England, however, did not monopolise the good works or the religious observance in the area. Before 1838 Nonconformists only had a small chapel up a narrow court off the High Street. But the railway brought not merely people in large numbers from all over the country, but many families with no links to the Established Church. So for the first time Presbyterians, Baptist and Methodists were able to stage a "religious revolution" and challenge Anglican supremacy in Wimbledon. Their success was shown by a survey made in 1903 which revealed that on the chosen Sunday in September there were more Nonconformists than Anglicans at morning and afternoon services there.

Among the men who made this possible, the greatest was undoubtedly the virtual founder of the Baptist church in South Wimbledon, Revd Charles Ingrem. He arrived in 1880 as a young minister of great promise, a protégé of one of the most famous of all Baptist preachers, Charles Spurgeon. He was faced by a tiny congregation of twenty, meeting in a small hall (which still exists) at the top of Palmerston Road. He looked frail, but had a strong voice, "a gracious manner and an outgoing personality". His eloquent sermons often lasted forty minutes or more, but they soon began to draw crowds. The hall was too small to hold them all, so he moved, first to a larger hall in Merton Road, then to a small church in Queens Road and finally in 1897 to the big church in the same road (which was in its turn replaced in 1988 by a new building). The 1897 building could seat a thousand, and he filled it Sunday after Sunday, drawing the largest attendance at any church in Wimbledon.

Yet, despite the unsparing work of clergymen like Bartlett and Ingrem, only a minority of Wimbledonians went to church on Sundays. Both the official religious census of 1851 and the unofficial census of 1903 showed the same result: about a third of all Wimbledonians attended a service, and the great majority came from the wealthier homes.

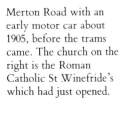

Merton Road with an early motor car about 1905, before the trams came. The church on the right is the Roman Catholic St Winefride's which had just opened.

Haydons Road at the junction with Gap Road and Plough Lane, about 1910.

RIGHTS OF WAY

The fields south of the Ridgway had been crossed "from time immemorial" by footpaths to Merton. The first, starting near the top of Wimbledon Hill (about where Grosvenor Hill was later laid out), ran diagonally across the slope to Upper Worple Lane (near the bottom of the modern Thornton Hill) and then straight to Merton Rush. The second, marked as "Footpath to Merton Church" on the Tithe Map of 1838, began a little to the west (where Sunnyside was later built and where the two paths crossed) and ran more or less straight down the hill and across the valley to the Kingston Road. Originally there was also a path (perhaps known as "The Sheep Walk") leading from the Common to the start of this footpath, but in 1794 it was made "very narrow, incommodious and dangerous for foot-passengers" by Gerard de Visme, the owner of Wimbledon Lodge on Southside, and seems to have fallen into disuse. The third path did start on the Common with Wright's Alley and continued as the Downs; it went to Merton Common.

When the railway was being built in the years after 1834, these rights of way had to be respected. The first two footpaths, to Mertonn Church and the Rush, were therefore provided with crossings at Alt and Elm Groves. But the Downs was clearly a more important route, probably used by animals, and so a tunnel was built under the railway. Other tunnels were provided for the Kingston Road at the Skew Arch, for the drive from Coombe Lane up to Edward Rayne's farm (by the side of the later Raynes Park Station) and for West Barnes Lane. All these rights of way still exist.

BERTRAM COTTAGES

These "model cottages" were one of the many works of charity carried out by Keziah Peache. She was the only daughter of James Courthope Peache, owner of Belvedere House, and a sincere Anglican. When her father died in 1858, she and her

BERTRAM COTTAGES

Bertram Cottages with
the date of their building,
1872, clearly outlined in
coloured brick.

brother, Alfred, a parson, inherited a large fortune. They used it jointly to found the London College of Divinity at Highbury. Then Keziah began to use her share for local good causes: a new organ for St Mary's Church, loans to help the Village Club enlarge their Lecture Hall, large donations to the Cottage Improvement Society for building homes in South (now Denmark) Road, careful supervision of the Belvedere Cottages built by her brother in Church Road.

In 1867 she decided to build some cottages of her own on a large plot of ground she had bought between Hartfield and Gladstone Roads. She asked a local engineer, H. C. Forde, to design them and he supervised "Mr Simpson, the builder" in putting up the first six for one hundred and forty-five pounds each. He was not very satisfied over "the quality of the bricks as far as the outside work is concerned" and advised Miss Peache to pay thirty pounds more for the next two cottages. The remaining eight cottages must have been built over the next few years, as the date "A.D. 1872" and the initials "K.P." are outlined in red brick on the fronts of two of them.

The cottages were let to poorer families "of good character and cleanly habits" at rents of about five shillings a week. They were soon occupied by a plate-layer from Norfolk, a dressmaker from Middlesex, a whitesmith from Brixton, a smith and bell-hanger from Gloucestershire, a turncock from Ireland and a bricklayer from Essex,

Keziah Peache who had
Bertram Cottages built.

as well as an accountant and, surprisingly, a lawyer, who had two lodgers, both
railway porters. Ever since, the cottages have been much in demand.

H.C. Forde, an engineer
who designed the cottages.

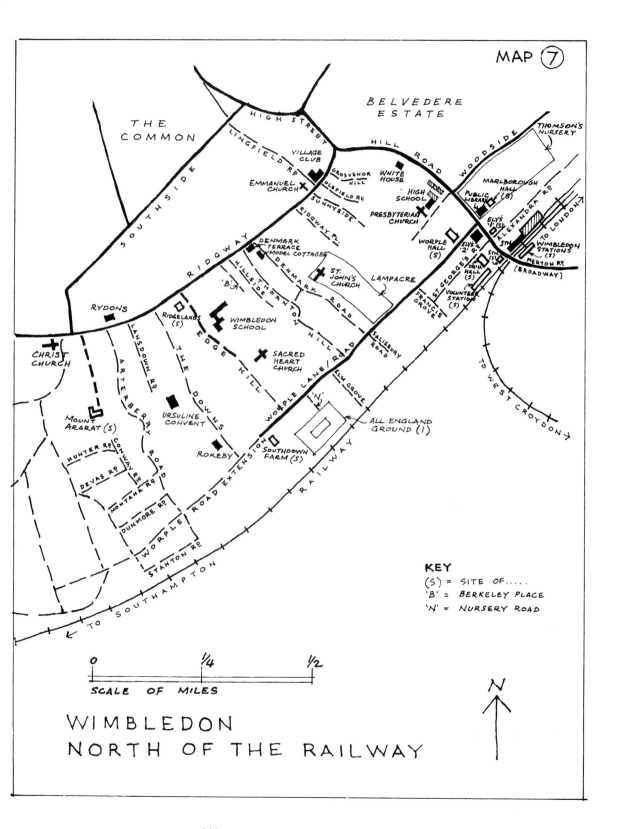

BELVEDERE ESTATE

THE COMMON

THOMSON'S NURSERY

HIGH STREET

HILL ROAD

WOODSIDE

LINGFIELD RD.

SOUTHSIDE

Village Club

GROSVENOR HILL

WHITE HOUSE

MARLBOROUGH HALL (8)

EMMANUEL CHURCH

OLDFIELD RD.

HIGH SCHOOL

PUBLIC LIBRARY

ALEXANDRA RD.

TO LONDON

SUNNYSIDE

PRESBYTERIAN CHURCH

ELY'S '1' (S)

STN

RIDGWAY PL.

RIDGWAY

WORPLE HALL (S)

ELY'S '2' (S)

WIMBLEDON STATIONS (S)

MERTON RD.

(BROADWAY)

DENMARK TERRACE MODEL COTTAGES

ST. JOHN'S CHURCH

LAMPACRE

GT. GEORGE'S DRILL HALL (S)

STN (S)

HILLSIDE

DENMARK ROAD

'B'

RYDONS

RIDGELANDS (S)

WIMBLEDON SCHOOL

THORNTON HILL

FRANCIS GROVE

VOLUNTEER STATION (S)

CHRIST CHURCH

EDGE HILL

SACRED HEART CHURCH

SALISBURY ROAD

TO WEST CROYDON

LANSDOWN RD.

THE DOWNS

WORPLE LANE / ROAD

ELM GROVE

'N'

MOUNT ARARAT (S)

ARTERBERRY ROAD

URSULINE CONVENT

ALL ENGLAND GROUND (1)

HUNTER RD.

CONWAY RD.

DEVAS RD.

ROKEBY

SOUTHDOWN FARM (S)

MONTANA RD.

WORPLE ROAD EXTENSION

RAILWAY

DUNMORE RD.

STANTON RD.

TO SOUTHAMPTON

KEY
(S) = SITE OF.....
'B' = BERKELEY PLACE
'N' = NURSERY ROAD

0   ¼   ½

SCALE OF MILES

N

WIMBLEDON
NORTH OF THE RAILWAY

15

Wimbledon Hill

Like the Broadway, Hill Road used to be known as "The Lane to Merton". During its long history it has had several other names. In Henry VIII's reign it was referred to as "Bishop's Hill", probably because the Archbishops of Canterbury were lords of the manor. For most of Queen Victoria's reign it was marked on maps as "Wimbledon Lane". The present name, Hill Road, only seems to have been used from the 1890s, although it was in danger during the Second World War when in 1943 after the victory of Stalingrad, left-wing Councillors proposed changing it to Stalin Avenue in recognition of "our brave Soviet ally". The proposal was rejected.

Hill Road after it had been widened in 1892.

The change of name to Hill Road came at the same time as the street was widened. For a long time it had been more like a country lane, overhung with trees and in places barely thirty feet wide. There was a pavement only on the western side; opposite was a high brick wall which extended from Church Road to Woodside and enclosed the grounds of the Belvedere estate. In 1892 the Local Board bought a strip of the estate, took down the wall, laid out a wide path inside the line of trees and added shrubs and seats. By the time Charles Cooper, its surveyor, had finished the work, he had created what a loyal Wimbledonian described shortly afterwards as "one of the prettiest roads in Surrey".

He had, however, also created a new main road. The Hill was increasingly used for horse-drawn carts, often with heavy loads of coal, or horse-buses from Putney carrying many passengers. Ethel Crickmay of the Dumb Friends League noticed the suffering of the animals as they struggled up the steep hill and appealed to the Council to provide money for a trace-horse (like "Kitty" at Putney Hill) to help pull the carts. The Councillors, however, maintained that legally they were unable to pay for it out of the rates, but gave ten guineas to start a public subscription. This in fact raised enough money to enable a horse to start work in May 1908 from a box at the bottom of the Hill, just above the junction with Woodside.

For the next thirty years, Jack, as each new horse was called, stayed at his post and became a real institution. He used to make about twenty journeys a day up the hill,

Jack, the trace-horse, waiting for customers at the bottom of the hill.

113

One of Jack's customers, the horse bus to Putney, waiting near the Town Hall about 1910. Soon afterwards, motor buses took over.

Ely's Corner in September 1905, before the coming of trams led to a widening of Worple Road. Hill Road was then more notable for its trees than its traffic.

helping to pull loads of two tons of more. He also won prizes at cart-horse parades in Regents Park — and in 1914 was saved from being "called up" by the Army Remount Department because of his "usefulness". The increasing use of lorries in the 1930s, however, meant that he no longer earned his keep. So the Dumb Friends League threatened to remove him, until local residents petitioned for him to stay and promised to pay for his support. He finally disappeared about the start of the Second World War.

The origin of all these changes on the Hill lay at the bottom — the station and its large goods yard. Near the station shops were soon erected on both sides of Hill Road. Among the first was "Joseph Ely, tailor, outfitter and draper". Ely, a young man in his early thirties, whose family came from Suffolk, opened a small shop on the corner of Alexandra Road in 1876. He is said to have first tested the possibilities of trade by counting the number of people who passed the corner in the course of an hour. Only twenty went by, yet he took the shop, sure that its position just above the station would bring business. He was proved right. Starting with the help of his wife and only one assistant, he soon found he needed more and more staff. After ten years he decided to move to a large shop across the way at the corner with Worple Road. But

A more lively photo of Ely's Corner, taken at about the same time by Russell's who were forced to move when the road was widened. The three men on the balcony are Ernest and William Fielder and in the middle is James Russell. In 1928 Ernest and William founded Fielders Booksellers and Stationers on its present site in Hill Road.

real success only came in 1907 with the arrival of the trams, bringing people into Wimbledon from areas like New Malden and Raynes Park. With gifts such as pullovers, the conductors were persuaded by Ely to shout out "Ely's Corner" at the right moment. His business flourished and in 1926 celebrated its first half-century with a banquet on the ground floor of a rebuilt store.

At the same time as Ely's was settling in on its present site, a "Free Library" was being built on the opposite side of Hill Road. It had first been proposed in 1880 by James Van Sommer, a local solicitor, but after a stormy debate his proposal had been narrowly defeated in a poll of rate-payers. Six years later, however, a new scheme was approved and a site (part of Thomson's Nursery) was bought from the Church Commissioners (who owned much land both above and below Woodside). Early in 1887 the building was finished and on 9 March was formally declared open by the champion of free libraries, Sir John Lubbock M.P. (later Lord Avebury). "The ceremony was graced", wrote a local reporter, "by the presence of all the men and women of note in Wimbledon." They included two Members of Parliament — Sir Henry Peek, M.P. for Mid-Surrey, and Cosmo Bonsor, M.P. for Wimbledon — the Vicar of Wimbledon, Canon Henry Haygarth; London's chief engineer, Sir Joseph Bazalgette; the Chairman of the Local Board, John Townsend; and 620 other guests.

The Public Library about 1901, shortly after new reference and lending sections had been added to the original building, with its railings and shrubs in front.

In front of the platform in the Reading Room (now the Fiction Department) there was "a choice selection of foliage plants, kindly lent by Messrs Thomson and Son" from the Nurseries next door. A Guard of Honour was provided by the Volunteer Fire Brigade. The ceremony started with prayers, read by the vicar. Then Sir John Lubbock "gave a scholarly and masterly address", illustrated by frequent quotations from Greek and other authors. He was followed by both M.P.s, Sir Joseph Bazalgette and the Chairman of the Local Board. Finally the Library was declared open and the ceremony ended with the National Anthem.

Unfortunately, only the Reading Room for newspapers could be opened at once. The Reference and Lending Libraries started nine months later when they had a sufficient number of books — 6,000, helped by many gifts, including money for reference books from the Queen's Diamond Jubilee Commemoration Fund (used to buy the new *Dictionary of National Biography*). It certainly filled a real need. Only a year later the Librarian, Mr T. A. Rabbitt, could claim over 2,000 members or one in twelve of the adult population of Wimbledon. It is hardly surprising, therefore, that in 1901 it was necessary to build new lending and reference sections. By a strange coincidence, the architect was Robert Thomson, son of the nurseryman.

Another institution founded in the 1880s which still flourishes in Hill Road is the High School for Girls. In 1880 Miss Mary Gurney, a member of the Girls' Public Day School Trust, who lived on the Common, was asked by some of her friends if the Trust would found a school in Wimbledon. She liked the idea, bought one of the large houses recently built towards the bottom of the hill, engaged some mistresses (who wore "dresses to the ground with long trains") and started with twelve girls. Soon there were over a hundred pupils and a new building was needed. It was opened in Mansel Road by Princess Louise in 1887. By then there was a small sixth form. Of its nine members, three won university scholarships.

A major reason for the success of the school was the remarkable personality of the first headmistress, Edith Hastings. At a time when girls had far fewer opportunities for education than boys, she was a headmistress in Nottingham at the early age of twenty-five and was only twenty-nine when chosen to found the High School. She was a disciple of the gospel of work for its own sake. She refused to give prizes and regarded public exams as incidental to the real purpose of education. When she retired in 1908 to become a Schools' Inspector, one of her old pupils wrote: "For me, the intense interest of the work emerges, and a gallery of faces, interesting people, mistresses and girls, but behind this shifting panorama was one quiet, strong personality that did not change."

Just above the High School is the only survivor of the five original homes built halfway up the hill in the early 1860s. Popularly known as the White House, its original name was a strange one, Loubcroy. Rightly described by Prof. Pevsner as "an unusually handsome stuccoed villa", it is now famous as the only house in Wimbledon with a well-authenticated ghost. Since the building became the London headquarters of City Assurance Consultants Ltd., several people, including the Managing Director, claim to have seen an elderly gentleman, immaculately dressed, with grey hair and piercing blue eyes. He can only be a member of the Jones family who owned the house from the time it was built until the outbreak of the Second World War.

The original owner, Charles Jones, came from Montgomeryshire on the Welsh

George Edwards-Jones
K.C., who was born in the
White House.

border. His son John at some stage added Edwards to the original Jones. He was a great sportsman and filled the entrance hall with stuffed birds. He died about 1900 and his widow and then his daughter Fanny (who rode everywhere on a tricycle and lived to be ninety) managed the house until 1939. The outstanding personality in the family, however, was Fanny's brother, George Edwards-Jones K.C. A well-known barrister, he chose to live in North View on the Common and from there walked to Wimbledon station in a black top hat, swallow-tail coat, striped trousers and boots, carrying his documents in a brown Gladstone bag. He never wore an overcoat, even in the coldest weather. He loved the Common and as a Conservator did all he could to have Caesar's Camp declared an ancient monument. He was also very interested in education and was Vice-Chairman of the Wimbledon Education Committee from 1911 until his death in 1936.

In that same year his son, Humphrey, became the first RAF officer to fly the Spitfire. His favourable report played a vital part in ensuring that a contract for over three hundred of the new aircraft was signed for its immediate production. "Perhaps the Spitfire would eventually have been ordered anyway," a fellow airman wrote, "but it certainly would have been delayed, with probably disastrous results in 1940." The young flying officer went on to become Air Marshal Sir Humphrey Edwards-Jones and only died in 1986.

THOMSON'S NURSERY

David Thomson, a quiet unassuming Scotsman with a great spade beard and piercing eyes, settled in Wimbledon as a gardener in 1838. After the Spencer estate was sold

Thomson's Nursery in 1926, just before building started at the corner of Woodside and Hill Road.

in 1846, he leased the fourteen acre kitchen garden which the first Earl Spencer had established just below Woodside at the bottom of Wimbledon Hill. His predecessor had been James Paxton, elder brother of the famous designer of the Crystal Palace who had himself worked in the garden for a time about 1825.

Thomson developed the garden into a nursery for fruit trees, and for flowers and vegetables which he grew in lines of greenhouses. He sold his produce from a shop on Hill Road, "with a spacious conservatory, containing a large assortment of beautiful palms, ferns and flowering plants", and lived with his wife and six children in a house opposite the end of Hothouse Lane (later renamed St Mary's Road). His services as landscape gardener were in great demand from the wealthy business and

David Thomson who ran the Nursery between 1846 and his death in 1905.

professional men settling on the hill and around the Common. By 1871 he was employing ten men and two boys.

In 1884, however, his original lease ran out and his landlords, the Church Commissioners, decided to sell part of the land for a Public Library. Thomson only kept his shop and the land immediately below Woodside for his greenhouses. He moved his main nursery south of the railway to the west of Merton Hall Road (where Toynbee Road and Abbott Avenue were to be built soon after the First World War). He died in 1905 at the age of eighty-eight, a man said to have been "upright in all his dealings".

The rest of the original nursery was sold for development in 1894. The new roads were named after the Dean of Worcester in the 1880s, Lord Alwyne Compton, who theoretically had owned the land. The only relic of the old nursery, apart from a few pieces of its old wall, is the flower shop which first became Luffs and later Dellers (located opposite Fielders Bookshop, which opened in 1928).

MANSEL ROAD

The road is named after the wealthy family that under different guises — Hopkins, Bond-Hopkins, Phillips and Mansel — owned the land on which it was laid out. Before it was covered with houses, the land had been part of one of the largest fields in Wimbledon. Known as Coppins Field, it extended from Hill Road to the site of Malcolm Road. In the first half of the nineteenth century it was farmed by the Watney family who used it as a meadow for grazing their cattle.

In 1878 Sir Richard Mansel sold the field for development. The Wimbledon Building Estate Company bought the land, set up an estate office on the corner of Hill Road opposite the new Elys and built a number of large houses in their own grounds along Worple Road.

In Mansel Road the High School bought a large plot on the north side for its new building which was opened in 1887. Two years earlier the Presbyterians had bought a neighbouring plot and there put up a church hall which they used for services. They then had plans made for a large church and a drawing appeared in the local paper in 1886 (probably the first picture to be printed in the paper). But the church was not built until 1891, a fine red-brick building with a spire. It is now the United Reformed Church.

16

Arthur Road

Between the top of Hill Road and the start of Arthur Road lies the Belvedere Estate. In Victorian times it was owned by the Peache family, but after the death of James Courthope Peache in 1858, the house was leased to a number of families, including the Wingfields who made it famous for their séances. These were held by Miss Wingfield, described by a lady who knew her as "a remarkable medium" with "a circle of admirers and believers who are constantly holding séances at Belvedere". "She is", the lady added, "no doubt a perfectly honest person, but the things that

An engraving of Belvedere House in the 1820s.

happen at the séances are extraordinary and often ludicrous." What these happenings were she did not reveal, but they were witnessed by many well-known people such as Lord and Lady Radnor.

Belvedere House was pulled down in 1900. Just beforehand, a little girl of six was taken by her nurse to see the empty building. Years later she remembered "going through massive wrought-iron gates". The house, "looking very large, square, and a grey musty colour, so gaunt and forsaken, made me very sad". They then walked round to the back. "There was one huge meadow or hay field, with a few big trees dotted about and in the distance a row of tall trees, edging Wimbledon Hill. Over this meadow in the next few years rose the houses that now line Belvedere Drive, Avenue and Grove.

Thirty years earlier, opposite the wrought-iron gates of Belevedere House, Arthur Road had just been laid out, linking one entrance of Wimbledon Park by Stag Lodge to another on Durnsford Road. It was part of a second stage in the development of the Park by its owner, John Augustus Beaumont. Beaumont was the Managing Director of the County Fire Insurance Company, which had been founded by his father in 1807, a year after John was born. Not content with managing a flourishing insurance business, he secured a large loan from his Company and bought two estates

John Augustus Beaumont, who bought Wimbledon Park from Earl Spencer in 1846 and developed it with large middle-class houses.

Arthur Road about 1900.

in south-west London in order to develop them for large middle-class houses. First, in 1845 he paid £43,000 for West Hill, Wandsworth, and then early the next year he paid the fourth Earl Spencer at least twice as much for the neighbouring estate, Wimbledon Park.

The deeds of this estate show that at Wimbledon he became the owner of three major properties: Wimbledon Park House, with its "waterhouse, brewhouse, lodge, gardens, stables, coach-house, paddocks and pleasure grounds", as well as Vineyard Hill Wood and Field; the Rectory, "formerly the Parsonage House", with its Tithe Barns, and the kitchen gardens and orchards "south of the road from Wimbledon to Wandsworth [now Woodside] in the occupation of James Paxton"; and Wimbledon Park, "with its lodges, barns, stables, cowhouse, orchard and paddocks", as well as the fish in the large lake.

Until 1860 Beaumont could not live in the Spencer House, as it was still under lease to the Duke of Somerset. Even then, he and his family seem to have spent only a few years there. He is said to have looked after the place well and kept peacocks "strutting about on the lawns", as well as hiring a nightwatchman to see that there were no intruders — and building Gap Lodge where intruders had regularly climbed through the park pale. His children invited friends for shooting, boating and fishing parties. His daughter married a Colonel Lane who, when serving in India, had saved the life of Queen Victoria's third son, Arthur, Duke of Connaught. By 1872, however, the family had definitely left Wimbledon. In that year Beaumont sold the house and its immediate grounds (now the playing fields of Park House and Ricard's Lodge Schools and the grounds of Bishop Gilpin School) to a Mrs Evans.

In the meantime he had patched up the Rectory and saved it from complete ruin. He used it for a time as a gardener's cottage, but in 1882 he also sold this house. Its new owner, Samuel Willson, then thoroughly restored it and lived there for over twenty-five years.

Beaumont's chief interest, however, lay in developing the park. He started with the northern half in 1850, laying out Inner Park Road, Princes Way, Augustus Road and, in the parish of Wimbledon, Somerset Road (named after the Duke, then living in Wimbledon Park House). Along these new roads, as well as on the older Parkside and Victoria Drive, sizeable plots of land were offered for sale and were quickly bought by wealthy business and professional men, who then employed architects to design large Victorian mansions and landscape gardeners like David Thomson to lay out their grounds. John Murray, a leading London publisher, established his family at Newstead, Somerset Road, and there entertained Gladstone and his many other friends. Joseph Toynbee, an eminent ear surgeon, settled in 1854 at Beech Holme, Parkside (a house which has recently been beautifully restored, but incongruously renamed Jenny Lind House). A third large house, Oakfield, was the home of Mr Schwann, a wealthy businessman and founder of the London Metal Exchange, whose house was "set among lawns, lovely trees, greenhouses and stables". As a result of the arrival of such distinguished men, *The Times* could report in 1865 that "Wimbledon Park which a few years ago could have been bought at £150 an acre is now worth £1,000 an acre and is covered with stately villas." It might even have been worth more had Beaumont accepted a proposal from the company that managed the Great Exhibition of 1851 to buy part of the park (where Vineyard Hill and Dora Roads were later built) as a new site for the Crystal Palace. His price, however, was felt to be too high and the Palace was put up on Sydenham Hill instead. "Mr Beaumont", it was reported, "was sorry afterwards he refused the offer".

Nonetheless, by 1872 he was ready to start the second stage in the development. After selling the manor house, he began laying out roads in the land immediately around it: Arthur (named after the Duke of Connaught whose life had been saved by his son-in-law), Leopold (after Arthur's younger brother), Home Park and Lake Roads. At the bottom of Lake Road he put up a house for his "Surveyor and Resident Agent", Alfred Osborne, where those interested could buy the building plots, and by it two large brick pillars to mark the entrance to the estate. Finally, he commissioned a Mr S. C. Hall F.S.A. to sing the praises of the district. Hall produced a small booklet, *Wimbledon: Illustrated Details Concerning the Parish*. Under the guise of local history (largely borrowed from Revd William Bartlett's recently published work)

Entrance pillars to the Wimbledon Park estate at the bottom of Lake Road, with Queen Alexandra Court in the background.

and with some fine illustrations, he wrote unblushing propaganda: "Wimbledon possesses peculiar attractions and natural advantages such as are rarely met with in a suburban district." Its rate of mortality "is proverbially low"; it has "magnificent trees and luxurious shrubberies"; its heights command views "such as no other spot in any other part of the world can supply"; it has a village which is "remarkably pretty" and "full of shops for the supply of all things that are needed by the surrounding mansions"; above all, "nightingales sing all the night long in springtime and early summer". No wonder Mr Hall could conclude that nowhere in the world was there "a site for villa-dwellings which presents so remarkable a combination of arguments", and that "Wimbledon Park when dotted with villas will have no rival in England".

Unfortunately for Beaumont, his second development came at a time of relative slump in the Victorian economy, when middle-class families were not so ready to move to a new estate, however pleasant it might sound. A map of 1882 shows that after ten years very few of the latest plots had been sold, but at least two of them had been bought by well-known individuals.

The first was Sir Joseph Bazalgette C.B., chief engineer to the Metropolitan Board of Works from 1856 to 1888. He had already had a dramatic effect on the health of Londoners by planning and building a major system of sewers under the capital (although the nearest he got to Wimbledon was Putney). Later he was also responsible for building the Thames Embankment, as well as new bridges at Putney and Battersea. In 1873 between these two major works, he decided to move his large family (six sons and four daughters) to the country air of Wimbledon Park, bought a large plot in Arthur Road opposite the parish church and appropriately called his new house St Mary's. There he was able to relax when he could tear himself away from his never-ending work. No details of his life in Wimbledon seem to have survived, except that he was very interested in the building of the Public Library. He died at St Mary's in 1891 and was buried in a large family mausoleum in the nearby churchyard. His home was replaced in the early 1930s by a smaller, modern house which has kept the name — and added a plaque of the Virgin by the gate.

The other important purchaser of one of Beaumont's plots was Percy Mortimer, who claimed to be descended from one of William the Conqueror's followers. He was an Old Etonian who trained to be a civil engineer, but instead became a wealthy stockbroker and director of several railway companies. In 1874 he bought three of the plots in Leopold Road, as well as a further one in Lake Road, and had a large house he called Ricard's Lodge built, where he could bring up his eight children. Next to the house he put up a dairy, served by cows which grazed in the field at the top of Lake Road. Behind the house he laid out a large garden with fine trees and shrubs, engaged five gardeners to look after it and every year held a big flower show.

He has been described as "stern and forbidding". His fellow J.P.s regarded him as "dour and difficult". But he played a leading part in local affairs as Councillor, Alderman (in the first Borough Council of 1905), and supporter of the Conservative Party. He was twice offered the office of Mayor, but each time declined it. He survived until 1939, dying not long before the start of the Second World War at the age of ninety-seven.

Beaumont had died long before, in 1886, just before the breakthrough for his second development scheme, the building of the District Railway. Throughout the 1880s projects had been discussed for lengthening the line from Putney Bridge. The first idea was to take it to Kingston across the northern part of the Common with stations at Tibbet's Corner and Coombe. But this scheme aroused too much opposition. So in the year Beaumont died a second plan was put forward: to build a much shorter line from Putney to Wimbledon, with stations at Southfields and Wimbledon Park. It was sponsored jointly by the District and the London and South-western Railway companies, and secured the necessary Act of Parliament.

On 3 June 1889 the first District train reached Wimbledon. It pulled in to a new station specially built north of the main line and launched a half-hourly service with about thirty trains a day. Its claim to provide a new, quick and cheap route to London did not convince everyone — until 1905 when the District introduced electric trains, ten years before the London and South-western Railway.

Already Wimbledon Park was being transformed. In the 1890s the growth was mainly near Wimbledon and roads like Woodside, Alexandra, Vineyard Hill and Kenilworth Avenue were built up, while the remaining plots in Arthur Road were at last sold. After 1900 houses spread to the land north of Wimbledon Park Station. George Ryan and Henry Penfold started their builders' and estate agent's office (now

The site of Kenilworth Avenue about 1890.

127

H. E. Rushbrook and Son) at the end of Arthur Road opposite the station in 1905. Before the First World war they put up rows of new villas all along the railway to Southfields.

The whole of the park might then have been lost but for Beaumont's daughter, Lady Lane. In 1889 she leased, then ten years later sold, land on the eastern side of the lake to cricket, tennis and golf clubs. In 1914 she sold the rest of this land, extending to the new houses by the railway, to the Council for use as a public park.

STAG LODGE

The Lodge at the western end of Arthur Road was put up by Beaumont in 1850. It was built to replace the old "Spencer Lodge" by the Portsmouth Road, after the development of the northern part of Wimbledon Park. For the next twenty years it was simply the entrance lodge to Wimbledon Park House and was the home of one of the gardeners who opened the large gate of which the hinges still survive.

In 1872, when Arthur Road was laid out and the manor house sold, the lodge lost its main function. It was then probably sold as a private house and the gate dismantled. By 1881 it was known as Stag Lodge, although whether the ornamental stag was put on its plinth by the first owner, Mr Cole, is uncertain, and no satisfactory reason has ever been found for placing it there.

The fine-looking animal survived until the start of the Second World War. Then in taking it down for safe-keeping, a builder accidentally dropped and smashed it. A new and even finer stag appeared on the lodge in the summer of 1988, put there by the owners, Mr and Mrs Hedges.

Stag Lodge about 1910.

St Mary's Church, from Arthur Road.

ST MARY'S PARISH CHURCH

The church with its two hundred foot spire is probably the fourth to stand on the site. Its Gothic Revival nave and tower, designed by Sir George Gilbert Scott and William Moffat, date from the early 1840s, the restored chancel from 1860.

    The two architects had to carry out the work under certain difficulties. They had

Canon Henry Haygarth, Vicar of St Mary's from 1859 until his death in 1902.

to lengthen the nave to allow for a growing congregation, yet had to carry out the major changes on a tight budget. They employed a local builder, William Parsons, used as much of the Georgian fabric as possible, yet made the whole building look of one period by covering it with flint. They added a fine hammer-beam roof, supported on iron girders, which were carefully covered with plaster to look like genuine stone pillars. The new nave and tower were then consecrated by Archbishop Howley of

Canterbury in November 1843. Seventeen years later the chancel, which still retained its medieval walls, had its Georgian additions removed and was redesigned to fit in with the rest of the church.

The vicar who presided at the second ceremony of consecration in 1860, Revd Henry Haygarth, had only been in the parish a year. He was then in his late thirties and was to stay at St Mary's (from 1878 as an honorary Canon of Rochester) until he died at the age of eighty-one in 1902. A man of deep principle who had to face personal tragedy when first his wife and then his only son died within a few years of each other, he won general respect and affection. "His face was the index of the man," wrote one of his curates, "it was kindly, open and sincere." He was a hard worker, very practical, with great common sense, a stabilising influence on the parish at a time of great change.

By nature, he was a conservative, Low Church Anglican. He strongly disapproved of the new *Hymns, Ancient and Modern* and of a surpliced choir. His services were very traditional, based on prayers with a long, learned sermon. But he realised the need to build churches in New Wimbledon and to create a variety of charities to meet the pressing needs of thousands of new and often poor parishioners. Out of his own pocket he provided the parish (still the whole of Wimbledon, except for Holy Trinity which was made a separate parish in 1872) and his growing band of curates (six by 1900) with a centre by building a Vicarage, now Steeple Court, at the corner of Church and St Mary's Roads. There he entertained friends and parishioners, helped by several servants; in the garden he lovingly tended his roses; in his study he organised fund-raising for new parochial schools and wrote pamphlets on temperance reform.

He lived for his parish and continued working almost to his death. He is commemorated by a large plaque in the chancel of his church.

17

The Common

In 1857, just as Beaumont's development of the northern part of Wimbledon Park was showing results, the man who had sold him the estate, the fourth Earl Spencer, died suddenly. His twenty-two year old son John had returned only a few days earlier from a visit to Canada and the United States, and was immediately plunged into the cares of the Spencer estates. In time he became a leading Liberal and close friend of Mr Gladstone. Twice he was made Viceroy of Ireland and in the early 1890s followed his grandfather in becoming First Lord of the Admiralty. Known as "the Red Earl" because of his great red beard, he was said to be a man of "commanding presence" and "transparent sincerity".

His father had virtually washed his hands of Wimbledon; he had even been willing to sell his rights as lord of the manor. The fifth Earl, on the other hand, became ever more involved in Wimbledon affairs, at least in the 1860s. Like many of his contemporaries, he was very worried at Emperor Napoleon III's powerful new iron-clad, "La Gloire" launched in 1859 and the possible threat of sudden French invasion. He therefore strongly supported the formation both of a Volunteer Corps to act as a home defence force and of a National Rifle Association to encourage the new soldiers to become good marksmen. So, despite some local opposition, he offered to let the Volunteers and the N.R.A. use Wimbledon Common as a training ground. A shooting range was set up south of the Windmill and members of London Volunteer units, including one from Wimbledon, were allowed to fire at the butts for several hours every weekday except Wednesday. Then in June and July the plateau around the Windmill was fenced in, a forest of tents and large marquees set up, and hundreds of riflemen arrived to compete for prizes put up by the N.R.A., including one given by Earl Spencer himself.

The inaugural N.R.A. meeting began on 2 July 1860. The Queen, accompanied by Prince Albert, drove through Wimbledon village and along Parkside to a gaily flagged arena near the Windmill. There she was welcomed by the Prime Minister – Lord Palmerston — Earl Spencer and a large crowd. She was then invited by Mr Whitworth to fire the first shot with his new rifle which had been placed in a special mechanical rest. She pulled the red silk cord and scored a near bull's-eye on the target four hundred yards away.

For the next twenty-nine years the N.R.A. summer meetings made Wimbledon one of the best-known places in Britain. "The shooting itself," according to Dickens's *Dictionary of London* of 1879, "except to experts and the friends of competitors, is not particularly interesting. But the camp itself is well worthy of a

John, fifth Earl Spencer, who tried to enclose the Common in the 1860s.

long visit. The remarkably successful sanitary arrangements should by no means be overlooked", and "the refreshment department" will supply "everything a visitor can reasonably require". Perhaps as a result, the number of spectators grew steadily. There were two entrances to the huge enclosure, one north of the Windmill for those coming from London, the other near Wimbledon Pound. Linking the two along Parkside was a horse-drawn tramway which took passengers behind the firing-points to a grandstand. At Wimbledon Station a special platform, known as "the

Queen Victoria listening to an address of welcome at the first N.R.A. meeting on the Common, 2 July 1860.

Volunteer", was built well to the west of the bridge, where trains bringing soldiers and their equipment could stop.

Earl Spencer himself was a keen marksman. At Althorp there is a painting of him at Wimbledon in 1864, resting on his elbow ready to fire. It is in fact a very significant picture because in that same year he introduced a bill in Parliament to enclose Wimbledon and Putney Commons. Almost certainly it was the sight of the Common at close quarters during the preceding four years that played an important part in his action.

The Common, he claimed, had got out of control. The land was undrained and in places had become a swamp. Rubbish of all kinds was frequently dumped there, especially near the Pound on Parkside. Outsiders were taking gravel and wood, and even pasturing their animals. Above all, gypsies were setting up camp near Caesar's Well and "besides being very often immoral characters, they bring contagious diseases and do not submit to sanitary and other regulations, commit depradations and in other respects are not desirable neighbours to the houses that are now found near here".

So at a meeting held in the Lecture Hall of the Village Club in November 1864, the

Earl put forward his plan to restore control. He would turn the largest part — Wimbledon Common or "the waste" south of the Portsmouth Road — into a public park "for the enjoyment and recreation of the inhabitants", and to pay for its upkeep (and for a new manor house which he intended to build on the site of the Windmill) would sell the rest — Putney Heath — to developers. To disarm opposition, he promised to drain the swamps, to construct new roads across the Common to make access easier, to get rid of the gypsies and to keep the fence around the new park as

Part of the elaborate N.R.A. camp, put up for the annual meetings. On the left the Refreshment Pavilion, first used in 1871. On the right the Umbrella Tent, the social centre from 1864.

The XI Surrey Regiment of Volunteers from Wimbledon.

The N.R.A. Camp, photographed from the Windmill, about 1885. In the centre is the Administrative Building which is still in use at Bisley. Beyond is the Umbrella Tent. On the right edge is the Clock Tower. Just to the left of this is an electric engine with the carriages for spectators beyond. To the left of the Umbrella Tent is the Refreshment Pavilion. In the foreground is the Windmill Garden and on its left tented shops, one selling accident insurance. In the distance are the trees lining Parkside, where the firing points were located.

small as possible with plenty of gates, "so that the Common would be practically as open as it is now".

He won considerable support for his plan. The few remaining copyholders agreed to accept compensation in return for giving up their rights. Representatives from Putney and Roehampton thought he was right to deal firmly with the gypsies. *The Times* and *Punch* also printed articles in favour of the plan, while the vicar of Holy Trinity, Revd William Bartlett, added a note to his History which was about to go to press praising the Earl for his "most liberal motives".

From the start, however, the chief landowners of Wimbledon (supported by *The Daily Telegraph* and *The Spectator*) were flatly opposed to the plan. At the meeting in the Lecture Hall, Sidney Smith, who lived in one of the new houses on Parkside and was soon to become the first Chairman of the Local Board, set the tone by rejecting the Earl's claims that the swamps were "prejudicial to health" and that the gypsies caused "inconvenience". He was supported by others who were horrified at the idea of any enclosure around the common or any sale of Putney Heath to pay for it. Led by Henry Peek, the owner of Wimbledon House, Parkside, and supported by leading Wimbledonians like John Murray and Joseph Toynbee, they formed a Wimbledon Commons Committee for "the preservation of the whole of Wimbledon Common and Putney Heath unenclosed, for the benefit of the neighbourhood and public".

Faced with such strong opposition, the Earl decided to compromise. He had

promised at the start: "If I meet with a general and considered opposition, I do not wish to proceed with the Bill." First, he modified the terms, but then seeing that this did not satisfy the Wimbledon Committee, he finally dropped the Bill. Instead, however, he claimed that as he had now bought out the remaining copyholders, he was legally the sole owner of the Commons and, apart from assuring public rights of way, could do with them as he liked. He therefore began to drain some of the worst swamps and to raise the necessary money by opening a large brickfield with a kiln near Caesar's Well, expanding gravel digging on a big scale near Parkside and leasing part of the Common to the Wimbledon Local Board for use as a sewage farm.

The Wimbledon Committee denounced these moves as making the Commons even more unsavoury. They were helped by a swing in national opinion, led by a recently formed general Commons Preservation Society. So in the end Earl Spencer decided to come to terms with the Committee.

In 1871, after long negotiations, the Wimbledon and Putney Commons Act was passed through Parliament. In return for an annual sum of £1,200 (finally paid off in 1958), the Earl gave "his estate and interest in the Commons" to a body of Conservators whose duty was "to keep the Commons open, unenclosed and unbuilt on, to protect the turf, gorse, timber and underwood", and to preserve it "for public and local use for the purpose of exercise and recreation".

The Commons had been saved, but the Conservators could do little to improve conditions until the N.R.A. and the Volunteers ceased to use the ranges. The shooting made large areas unsafe during the week, while a Volunteer Field Day on Easter Monday 1874 left several hundred acres burned or severely damaged. In 1889 the final N.R.A. meeting was held before the ranges were transferred to Bisley (perhaps because an unfortunate grave-digger in Putney Vale cemetery had been killed by a stray bullet). Then in 1891 the final Volunteer review was held on the Common, with Kaiser William II taking the salute.

One man who could watch this review in comfort from his mansion, Wimbledon House, Parkside, was Henry Peek, now a Baronet and Conservative M.P. for Mid-Surrey. Son of the founder of Peek Freans, the biscuit firm, he had played a crucial part in securing the Commons Act of 1871. "A generous supporter of good causes", he was prominent in public life, both national and local, for forty years. He bought Wimbledon House from the Marryat family in 1854, just before the large estate could be sold for redevelopment. He lived there with his wife and son Christopher who was a keen astronomer and built a small observatory in the grounds (its tower is still there, in the garden of Heatherhurst). They were looked after by a cook, lady's maid, three housemaids, a kitchenmaid and a footman. Their fine garden, supervised by Lady Peek, was tended by six gardeners. Once a year it was opened to "the private inhabitants" of Wimbledon, who had to sign their names at the gate under the watchful eye of an old soldier. Once inside the eight foot high wall, which "screened [the garden] from the vulgar gaze", they would see many fine trees and shrubs (some of which still survive), as well as cages containing rare birds and animals, and an extensive series of greenhouses, where a monster bunch of bananas was grown for exhibition. Beyond was a large lake, later known as Margin Lake, which has since been drained.

Peek retired to Devon in 1894 and died there four years later. His son then sold the

Sir Henry Peek M.P. who
lived at Wimbledon
House, Parkside from 1854
to 1894 and played a
leading part in saving the
Common.

Parkside in the 1890s
before any houses were
built. The Pound is in the
trees on the left. On the
right is the high wall of
the Wimbledon House
estate.

estate to a development company. Its surveyors split the area up into roads, several named after previous owners of the house: Calonne, Marryat and Peek himself. Hamptons, the estate agents, then set up an office near the site of the old house and over the next fourteen years sold the plots to wealthy professional men. They employed leading architects like Stanley May to design their homes (some with the new "motor houses") whose style and spacious gardens certainly added to the attractions of the Common which they overlooked.

An aerial view of Marryat Road in about 1920. Margin House and Lake are in the foreground. In the centre is St Mary's Church, with the Old Rectory, the Well House and Wimbledon Park House to its left. In the background are lines of houses near the railway.

MANOR COTTAGE

This small house near the Windmill is the headquarters of the Conservators. The date of its building is uncertain, but it is first mentioned in the census returns for 1851. There it is described as "the Keeper's house", the home of Richard Riseley, "agent to Earl Spencer".

From 1860 to 1889 it was the official residence of the Chairman of the National Rifle Association during the summer meetings. On the lawns "At Homes", important events in the London social calendar, were held every year. Otherwise it was occupied by the Head Common Keeper and at some stage became the headquarters of the Ranger and the Conservators.

WINDMILL ROAD

WIMBLEDON
COMMON

This straight, rough road which links the Windmill and Thatched Cottage was probably laid out in 1845. It was the track for William Prosser's "experimental railway", which used an engine whose wheels dispensed with flanges. Instead it was given stability by smaller guidewheels running against the inside of the track.

The train's large turning circle north of the Windmill is still outlined in one of the footpaths and can be seen on a good plan of the Common.

WIMBLEDON COMMON GOLF COURSE

Golf was first played on the Common in 1865. Earl Spencer then allowed the London Scottish Volunteers, who were using the ranges, to make a seven hole course near the Windmill. When the Conservators took control they insisted that "every person playing golf shall wear a red coat or other outer red garment", but they also permitted the club to extend the course to eighteen holes.

In 1882, after two years of debate, the military and civilian members of the original London Scottish Club split. The civilians formed the Royal Wimbledon Golf Club with their clubhouse at Camp Cottage (a house dating from the 1820s). Both clubs continued to use the Common until the Royal Wimbledon opened their present course in 1908. In that year the Wimbledon Town (later Wimbledon Common) Golf Club was founded. They too used the London Scottish course, but started at the opposite end by Camp Road.

18

Southside

The Common has long been noted for its springs, while wells are not difficult to sink in its shallow gravel soil. By the early nineteenth century five wells were in regular use; one on the Village Green (just below the site of the War Memorial); another by the Crooked Billet (on the Green, according to one account; by "Mr Dosset's", at the corner with Westside, according to a document of 1823); a third opposite "Croft's timber yard" at West View; the fourth, Caesar's Well; and the most popular one, "the well on the Common".

The site of this well, opposite the end of Murray Road, is now marked by a large circular stone, put there by the Wimbledon Society. The well is first mentioned in 1574 when Edward Atkins was told to fence it in "so that the cattle may receive no harm". This fence, as well as the brickwork of the well shaft and the paving around it, needed regular repair. In 1815, however, a major change was made: a pump was fixed by its side and the well hole itself covered over with a dome. It then became "the Village Pump", to which "in the early morning came a crowd of villagers from all around, each one bringing his tub or barrel, each having to wait his turn". The big attraction was apparently the fact that the water was beautifully soft. Unfortunately, in 1882 a member of the Local Board, Mr Twentyman who lived in Southside House, happened to test the water and to his horror discovered that it was quite unfit to drink. The well was promptly closed and filled in. The people living near Southside now had to wait for two years until piped water could be laid on from Battersea.

A century earlier, Southside had been described in a guidebook as "an assemblage of gentlemen's houses, most delightfully situated", with large gardens "from whence is a pleasant prospect over the luxuriant vale beneath". The road on the southern edge of the Common, "across the Green to the Crooked Billet", had not long been built. Until 1759 there had only been a "pathway". The road therefore was a sign of the growing social importance of the people who lived in the houses. In the 1780s William Wilberforce at Lauriston House was the only individual of national importance there, but ten years later two successive Dukes of Newcastle, followed by the Countess of Bristol, were living in the Grange (or Wimbledon Villa) and the Earl of Lucan, father of Countess Spencer, had rented Oakholm (by the side of the present Clifton Road). At the start of the nineteenth century Sir Francis Burdett M.P., the friend of Horne-Tooke, had taken over the Grange, while next door at Wimbledon Lodge (on the site of Murray Road) there was Earl Bathurst, a great friend of William Pitt and a minister in almost every government between 1789 and

The front of Wimbledon Lodge, the home of the Murrays, photographed in 1905, just before it was pulled down. The lions on either side of the porch have already been removed to a house in the High Street.

1830. In the early 1820s Lauriston House was leased to Lord Almeric Churchill, son of the third Duke of Marlborough and his political agent.

Only one of the houses had any architectural distinction. This was Wimbledon Lodge, whose semi-circular entrance drive has been retained at the top of Murray Road. It was built about 1792 for Gerard de Visme, the son of a Huguenot nobleman, in the latest Greek Revival style. The entrance gates were flanked by lodges, looking like small temples. The two-storeyed house had round-headed windows on the ground floor and an elaborate pillared porch, flanked by coad-stone lions (later moved to a house in the High Street). Above the porch were statues, with others on a large pedestal on the roof. The garden front was equally elaborate with a decorated balcony, supported by large Greek caryatids. Even in death de Visme clearly liked to show off to his neighbours. In 1797, the year Napoleon conquered Egypt, he was buried near the main door of St Mary's under a small pyramid and left money to ensure that it was kept in repair. The money must have disappeared as the tomb is now in a very sad condition.

The rest of the houses on Southside may have been plain, but the life in at least one of them caused some comment. At Lauriston House in the early 1780s the arrival of William Pitt as guest generally provoked horse-play. In his diary for 1783 Wilberforce recorded:

"3 April. To Wimbledon where Pitt dined and slept. Foyned [i.e. ragged] Mrs Hayes [his next-door neighbour]. Evening walk. Bed a little past two.

142

The front of Lauriston House in 1826, drawn by Edward Hassell.

The garden of Lauriston House before the First World War.

4 April. Delightful day. Lounged morning at Wimbledon with friends, and ran about the garden for an hour or two.
6 July. Morning fine. Persuaded Pitt to church. At night walked ladies on the Common."

To a friend he also wrote: "One morning we found the fruits of Pitt's earlier rising in the careful sowing of the garden beds with fragments of a dress hat with which Ryder [another friend] had come down from the opera." And later the two of them with a third friend went boating and fishing on Rushmere. No wonder the neighbours became alarmed as further stories of "some little excess" spread. In 1786, to their great relief, Wilberforce gave up his Wimbledon home to concentrate on his crusade against the slave trade. The house was then bought by a very sober wine merchant.

Most of the families living in these houses seem to have led temperate, ordinary lives. The only other extraordinary event recorded of this eastern half of Southside took place nearly a century later in 1878. Lingfield House, left empty after the development of its long garden for building houses, was the setting of a Batchelors' Fancy Dress Ball. The ballroom, lighted by large chandeliers, was decorated with flowers, large mirrors and statues placed against a blue background. The music was provided by Dan Godfrey's Band. The stewards were members of well-known Wimbledon familes, including Christopher Peek and two of Percy Mortimer's sons. There were over three hundred guests, among them the daughters of Dr Huntingford of Eagle House School who came as a grape-gatherer and a haymaker, and the engineer and amateur architect, H.C. Forde, who appeared as the Pasha of Baghdad. The ball seems to have been a great success.

None of the old houses between the village and Lauriston Road survive. Their estates were sold to developers between the late 1850s and the early years of the present century, and the mansions were pulled down. The last house to disappear (as recently as 1957) was Lauriston and the fine allegorical paintings by Angelica Kaufmann on the well of the staircase disappeared at the same time. Fortunately the seventeenth century cottages by its side, which had been converted into a stable block, still stand. Four roads were laid out on their site, three named after the houses: Lingfield, the Grange and Lauriston, while the fourth commemorates the Murrays, the family who lived at Wimbledon Lodge from 1812 to 1904.

In 1810 General Sir Henry Murray, one of the great characters of early Victorian Wimbledon, married Gerard de Visme's illegitimate daughter, Emily. He had just returned from serving "with distinction" in Egypt and in a disastrous attack on the island of Walcheren. Shortly after they married, they took over the Lodge from Earl Bathurst, but Murray then had to go abroad again to lead the Eighteenth Hussars in the later campaigns of the Peninsular War, where he finished in hospital with an abscess on his knee. In the final campaign, against Napoleon in 1815, however, he covered himself with glory, first in the retreat from Quatre Bras and then at Waterloo where he led his Hussars in "the brilliant charge" of Sir Hussay Vivian's brigade at the end of the battle. After the War he commanded the Western District for ten years.

Only then was he able to play a part in Wimbledon's affairs. In the late 1830s and early 1840s he earned the respect of his neighbours for the forthright way in which he spoke his mind at meetings of the Vestry. He strongly opposed "the demolition and rebuilding of our Parish church" in 1840, claiming it an unnecessary expense. He was equally critical of the suppression of the High Street Fair, which had, he said, "been held for many years by local custom" and was one of the few festivals "which the labouring classes have the opportunity of enjoying". He was heavily outvoted on both occasions. Yet when he had to leave Wimbledon two years later, "on appointment to the staff of the Army in Ireland", his fellow Vestrymen unanimously thanked him for "his advice and urbanity" and hoped he would soon return as "his politeness and kindness have rendered him highly respected".

When he did return, he was a sick man. His last years are recorded at the end of

John Townsend, a leading Wimbledon builder and Chairman of the Local Board, 1885–1894.

a large memorial tablet on the wall of St Mary's Church: "After a long and painful illness, borne with the most Christian resignation and fortitude, he died at Wimbledon on 29 July 1860, deeply lamented by his family and by all those who had known his excellent qualities." His widow stayed on in the house with their only daughter, Gertrude, "the loveliest girl I have ever seen", according to a contemporary. When her mother died "Miss Murray" ran the house on her own. She never married, survived into the present century and died at the age of ninety in 1904. The next year the large estate, which extended across the Ridgway, was sold to the British Land Company, and the land was divided into small plots. These were then bought by wealthy individuals who employed architects like James Ransome to design the fine houses that now line Murray Road.

Equally fine houses line the neighbouring road, the Grange. Here the land was sold in 1888 by Sir Richard Mansel not to a developer, but at an auction, and was advertised as "ripe for immediate building operations". Most of the forty-eight lots (which produced only twenty-three houses) were bought by three men: Sir Henry Peek and two local builders, John Townsend and Henry Harmer. Townsend was the most experienced master-builder in Wimbledon. He had married the daughter of William Parsons, the craftsman responsible for rebuilding St Mary's in 1840. As Parsons and Townsend, the firm worked not just in Wimbledon (building, for instance, the houses in Homefield Road) but in Bloomsbury and Brighton. In the Grange they erected a number of large, detached villas for business and professional men, some with grass courts for the latest sport, lawn tennis. A typical purchaser of one of their houses was Henry Horne, a leading barrister. Like Townsend, he was a member of the Local Board; he was also a Commons Conservator. The architect who designed the house was Robert Thomson, son of the nurseryman. It was clearly possible to rise in the world in Victorian Wimbledon.

The four roads off Southside nearest the village — Lingfield, the Grange, Murray and Lauriston — were only followed by one more, nearer the Crooked Billet — Clifton Road, laid out in the early 1880s. As a result, some of the older houses on the western half of Southside have managed to survive: South Lodge by the end of Lauriston Road (the third house on the site, put up in the 1840s); Rushmere House just beyond the end of Clifton Road (built in the 1780s for John Watney, the farmer); King's College Junior School and Southside House, by Wright's Alley.

South Lodge is notable for its late Victorian owners, the van Sommers. Like de Visme of Huguenot ancestry, they settled there in 1883 after living for the previous eight years in Wimbledon Park. They were fervent Evangelicals, full of "good works", above all in the cause of temperance. James van Sommer, a wealthy solicitor, and his mother played a leading part in the opening of "The Welcome Reading and Coffee Rooms" in the High Street, while other ladies in the family did "missionary work" persuading boys and girls to join the "Band of Hope" temperance league and talking to young workers at one of the laundries on the Common. James van Sommer was also very involved with the Y.M.C.A. in South Wimbledon and in the campaign for the establishment of a Public Library. His one blind spot, which he shared with some of the other Evangelicals, was "Popery". In 1887 he wrote a series of letters to the *Surrey Independent*, bitterly attacking the building of the church of the Sacred Heart in Edge Hill and above all the arrival of Jesuit priests in Wimbledon, "unwelcome

King's College School Hall, as designed by its architect Sir Banister Fletcher in 1899.

strangers who are trying to settle in our town to poison the fountain-head of knowledge". Despite his protests, the Jesuits stayed and by the time he died in 1901 they had helped to make Wimbledon one of the most Catholic areas in south London.

A very different series of individuals lived further up Southside at the house now known as King's College Junior School. The building is now probably the oldest in the road, about the same age as Gothic Lodge in Woodhayes Road. It was built about 1760 for a leading Doctor, Peter Shaw, "Physician in Ordinary" to both George II and George III. It was then occupied by a number of interesting characters: Baron Smythe, an Exchequer judge and "the ugliest man of his day"; James Meyrick, a Parliamentary agent, who later moved to Cottenham Park; Thomas Eden, brother of Lord Auckland and a "Virginia Merchant"; Revd Samuel Catlow, a dissenting minister who set up a "Literary and Commercial Seminary" here between 1811 and 1817; Joseph Marryat junior, elder brother of the novelist, Captain Frederick Marryat; and Mrs Phillips, the heiress of the Bond-Hopkins fortune and owner of the house.

It did not become part of King's College School until 1897. In the year of Queen Victoria's Diamond Jubilee the school moved to Wimbledon from the Strand as its numbers were declining and the Headmaster, Revd C.W. Bourne, feared that the school would disappear. He boldly bought the old house on Southside with eight acres of ground and employed the famous architect, Sir Banister Fletcher, to design new buildings by its side, including a great hall. These were opened by the Duke of Cambridge in 1899. By 1904 when the cricket field on the other side of Wright's Alley was added to the grounds, the school was again flourishing. There were about three hundred boys, the fees were twenty-four pounds a year, but already there was a premonition of the future: "the modern side shows a slight tendency to predominate over the classical side".

GOTHIC LODGE

This "genteel house with some pleasant shrubberies" is situated just off Southside, opposite the Crooked Billet. It was built about 1763 (the date on a lead pump head) and was known first as Gothic Cottage, then as Gothic House and now as Gothic Lodge. Its front is certainly in the "Gothic" style, popularised by Horace Walpole at Strawberry Hill in the middle of the eighteenth century, with "pretty ogee-arched and crocketed heads to the upper windows" (the words of an expert, Prof. Pevsner).

A blue plaque on the front proclaims: "Here lived Captain Frederick Marryat R.N., 1792–1848. Novelist." In fact he can have stayed there little more than a few months. He leased the house between 1820 and 1827 as a pleasant place for his wife and children to stay (and not far from his parents at Wimbledon House, Parkside), while he was at sea, guarding Napoleon on St Helena or fighting the Burmese.

A much more important occupant was Sir William Preece who lived there for nearly forty years from 1874 until his death in 1913. He was Chief Engineer at the Post Office and author of textbooks on the new telephone. He was very friendly with Marconi, who on one of his frequent visits to Gothic Lodge, set up in the garden a

Gothic Lodge in the mid-nineteenth century.

Gothic Lodge today.

transmitter for his newly-invented wireless telegraph and sent messages to the Post Office in London. Above all, he was keenly interested in electricity. His house was the first in the London area to have electric light (and an electric kettle and iron, as well as a telephone). In 1894 he put on a public demonstration of electricity — lighting the High Street — and then proposed that the Council should build a local power station and supply electricity to the people of Wimbledon. His suggestion was finally approved and Durnsford power station, designed by his son, was opened in 1899.

Besides his interest in electrical engineering, Preece was a member of the Wimbledon Literary and Scientific Society founded in 1891 and was its first President. He was also knowledgeable on Egyptology and Oriental Art, and turned Gothic Lodge into a miniature museum with his collection of old weapons, suits of armour, sculpture and Persian antiques.

19

The Ridgway

The Ridgway is a much older road than Southside. It was possibly a salt route in Neolithic times and it was certainly in use during the Middle Ages. By the reign of Elizabeth I anyone daring to plough within ten feet of "a highway called the Ridgewaye" was liable to a fine of "twelve pence". Yet although this highway was the main road to Kingston, it remained a narrow country lane until well into the reign of Queen Victoria. Indeed, in the 1841 census it is called "Ridgway Lane".

Year after year it was churned up by hundreds of Welsh cattle which used to be fattened on meadows near the village before being driven to market. One of the animals may be behind the story told by an old lady of her childhood in the 1840s:

> "Some children, coming home along the dark Ridgway, saw a white object above them on the bank and heard cries of distress. They fled onwards, thinking that it was a ghost. It was in truth a poor white cow, caught in some way on the fence and released later by the farmer on his rounds."

Careful study of the tithe map for 1848 shows that the Ridgway was indeed a country lane. While the garden fences of the great houses on the Common lined the north side, there was a continuous ditch, bank and hedge bordering long, narrow fields on the south. Most of these fields were meadows used for pasture, but two on either side of the Downs grew wheat. There were also "allotment gardens, leased by the Churchwardens" of St Mary's on the site of Hillside and Berkeley Place. But already the first signs of development were appearing. In the years immediately after Waterloo, William Eades, a grocer in the High Street, built "Brickfield Cottages" (now Oldfield Road) with their "glorious and uninterrupted view across the Epsom Downs". Then in the early 1820s William Croft, a timber merchant of West Place, bought a narrow piece of land from Richard Thornton of Cannon Hill and on it laid out South Place with twenty-nine small cottages, one a Beer Shop known as "The Jolly Gardeners" (South Place no longer exists, although some of the cottages survive up alleys off Thornton Road). By the 1830s Prospect Place, a line of six cottages, had been built along the Ridgway just to the west of Brickfield Cottages, followed in the 1840s by Ridgway Terrace, a line of much larger early Victorian houses a little further west. (Both survive, on the opposite side of the road to Emmanuel church.)

The real transformation of the Ridgway, however, started in the late 1850s. In 1857 a public appeal was made for funds to build a Chapel-of-ease to the parish church, St Mary's, at one end of the road and a Village Club at the other end near the High

Street. The appeal was launched by the Vicar, Revd Richard Adams, and leading parishioners, men such as Thomas Devas (a businessman who lived at Mount Ararat, just below the Ridgway), John Ludlow (a barrister of the Firs, Copse Hill) and John Reeves (a Fellow of the Royal Society, whose home was Woodhayes House). They felt that a second church was needed to cater for the growing number of "good class" people living south-west of the Common, especially in the new district of Cottenham Park. They also wanted a Club "to afford to the inhabitants, and more especially the working and middle-classes of Wimbledon and its vicinity, the opportunities of intellectual and moral improvement, and rational and social enjoyment".

For both projects they engaged the same architect, Samuel Teulon. Of Huguenot ancestry, he had already built up a large and successful practice, particularly in designing and restoring churches in the fashionable Victorian Gothic style. His work, according to one expert, "later acquired a reputation for extreme ugliness". It is hard to judge his Village Club, as it has suffered in the course of later enlargements. But the church has rightly been described as "one of his more successful designs, a

Christ Church, as designed by Samuel Teulon in 1858. He later added a stair turret.

The Village Club and Lecture Hall, as designed by Samuel Teulon in 1858. Later additions were made by Sir Thomas Jackson.

building of simplicity and charm, which gives the impression of compactness and strength."

Both buildings were opened in 1859. The chapel, consecrated by the Bishop of London and named Christ Church, could seat nearly six hundred people. Most were well-to-do as they had to pay for their sittings. Only a third of the benches were said to be "free", although, it was added, "any poor person wishing to secure a seat can do so by an annual payment of half a crown". The church was soon full and in just over twenty years the nave had to be extended.

The Club, too, quickly proved a success. Its chief originator seems to have been Joseph Toynbee, the ear specialist, who wanted to share his great advantages, particularly in education, with others less fortunate. The Club therefore provided a reading room for newspapers and magazines, a library and above all a special hall for fortnightly lectures and "penny readings" of poems and stories. In 1863 Toynbee put on what he called "a chat meeting". He described it in a letter to a friend:

"We had nearly two hundred and fifty working people (each paid two pence admission) who quietly and pleasantly walked from table to table looking through microscopes and stereoscopes, and watching a variety of useful instruments at work. I stood at my table showing with my microscope one object the whole evening, and letting everyone see and enjoy it. I assure you it was a great pleasure to be able to chat with and amuse the working people, and witness their real enjoyment."

Immediately he finished the Club and the church in 1859, Teulon was

152

Denmark Terrace just before the First World War. The shops next to the King of Denmark are a butcher, baker, grocer and post office. On the other side of Denmark Road, Jenkins is running a "Registry Office for Servants".

commissioned to build twelve model cottages half way between the two, on land just to the east of South Place. Such cottages were badly needed to deal with "the overcrowding of the poorer population" which had greatly aggravated "the evils of defective drainage and ventilation in most local cottages". To meet the problem the Wimbledon Cottage Improvement Society was therefore founded by some of the same men who had wanted the Club and church, such as Devas and Toynbee, as well as other leading gentlemen like John Murray, the publisher, and Sir Henry Peek. They offered a "profitable investment" to fellow Wimbledonians, raised a large sum of money and built some attractive cottages at a cost of about £125 each. These homes were then offered at very moderate rents to "applicants of good character and cleanly habits". In the next five years fifteen more cottages were built and the Society flourished, paying a dividend of five per cent. They had to evict some tenants for nonpayment of rent, but were known as good landlords and always found plenty of families ready to take their place. The Society was not wound up until 1952 and the cottages are still in demand, although now for sale at greatly inflated prices.

Around the cottages in the early 1860s there grew up a small settlement. A row of shops known as Denmark Terrace was built along the Ridgway with a grocery and post office run by Henry Jenkins (whose brother Edwin later opened a chandler's and confectioner's on the opposite corner of Denmark Road, where the shop survives today). There was also a coffee shop and a beer retailer at the sign of the King of Denmark. A little further on was the new Swan Inn, with Livery Stables at its side where horses and cabs could be hired for a journey to the station. Behind were the first two roads to link the Ridgway to Worple Lane: South Road, which half way along became Denmark Road, and Thornton Road. As far as the slope of the hill, both

153

were already lined with Victorian houses, small at the top, very large on the slope. A third road, Hillside, had also been built behind the Swan, although mostly with large middle-class houses only on its eastern side. Even larger houses had been put up about the same time along other new roads running south from the Ridgway: Grosvenor Hill, Sunnyside, Ridgway Place and, beyond the Downs, Lansdowne Road. For some reason three of these roads along with Hillside were never carried through to Worple Lane. However, by 1865 there were already more than enough people living in the area to justify the opening of a beer shop and inn as close together as the King and the Swan.

Their presence, however, can hardly have been welcome to a great Headmaster who had founded Wimbledon School nearby just before they were opened. Revd John Brackenbury was an Anglican clergyman who lived between 1816 and 1895, married three times and had seventeen children. At Cambridge he had only gained a third-class degree, but as a schoolmaster he proved first class. He helped to found Marlborough College, then in 1849 went into partnership with Mr Mayer, who was running a small Military Academy in the High Street, Wimbledon. This was Nelson House School, founded in Eagle House by Revd Thomas Lancaster in 1790 and named after the famous Admiral following a visit he and Lady Hamilton had made in 1803. Here Brackenbury proved so successful that numbers began to outgrow the existing buildings. So in 1860 he bought two large meadows below the Ridgway from Mrs Phillips for a new and much larger school. Inevitably the architect was Samuel Teulon. The buildings he designed, above all the school hall and family rooms overlooking the valley, were generally considered his finest work in Wimbledon.

For the next twenty years the school went from strength to strength. It mainly prepared older boys from fifteen to eighteen for entry into the Royal Military Academies at Woolwich and Sandhurst. By 1871 there were 91 "scholars" there, taught by Brackenbury and five assistant masters (among them ten years later was a future composer, then known as Edward German Jones). The school's results were excellent. A contemporary wrote of Brackenbury: "He was one of the most conspicuously successful teachers of his day. For many years his school held an

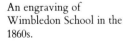

An engraving of Wimbledon School in the 1860s.

154

Revd John Brackenbury, founder and headmaster of Wimbledon School, and Chairman of the Local Board, 1871–76.

absolutely unique position as a successful training place for Army exams. As a teacher and organiser he could hardly be excelled. He loved his work in all its details and threw himself into it with never-ending energy. In private life he was one of the kindest and most delightful of men. He was generous and his house was the centre of hospitality".

Brackenbury also played a big part in local affairs. He was on the committee of the Village Club, strongly supported the Cottage Improvement Society and regularly sent his boys to Christ Church for services. Between 1871 and 1876 he was Chairman of the Local Board. His Sports Day at the school was a major social event. In 1882 it was graced by some of the leading officers in the British Army and music was provided by the Band of the Royal Horse Guards. Shortly afterwards Brackenbury, now in his late sixties and suffering from ill-health, decided to retire. He handed control over to his partner, Revd Charles Wynne, and went to live in Norwood where he died in 1895 after a stroke. By then his school was in very different hands. Under Wynne "Brackenbury's" went to pieces and had to be closed. For five years the buildings remained empty. Then in 1892 they were bought by the Jesuits who had recently come to Wimbledon to serve the new Roman Catholic church of the Sacred Heart. They opened a school which they called Wimbledon College. For nearly a century it has proved at least as successful as its predecessor, although the original buildings have been swamped by later additions and the hall was sadly burnt down in the 1970s.

In all this change and development south of the Ridgway, the hedges and fields inevitably disappeared. Winifred Whitehead, who came to live in one of the big houses in Ridgway Place in the 1880s, has recorded the sad effect of the disappearance in 1905 of the grounds belonging to Miss Murray to the west of her house: "Many splendid trees were lost and also the two meadows stretching to St John's Church, where a flock of sheep used to graze." Yet the country atmosphere remained. The famous illustrator, E. H. Shepard, spent a summer holiday in a house off the Ridgway in 1890. From the upstairs windows he could see miles of countryside below the hill and once a week a massive firework display from Crystal Palace.

Three years later Sir Richmond and Lady Ritchie, daughter of William Thackeray, the novelist, moved into a fine house, designed by James Ransome, at the end of Berkeley Place. Life for such people was leisurely. Their daughter, Mrs Fuller, later recalled that "nothing could be done quickly or on the spur of the moment". Great ladies, like Lady Cloncurry, "a most delightful old Irish lady", who lived in Hillside, held "Salons where extremely good talk was the order of the day". Famous visitors were constantly calling to see her mother: Henry James, W. H. Leckey the historian, Leslie Stephen, Gertrude Bell the explorer, Mrs. Oliphant a prolific novelist who lived at the Hermitage on the Common, and Sir Thomas and Lady Jackson from Eagle House.

Life on the Ridgway was radically changed, Mrs Fuller maintained, by the invention of the bicycle about 1894. "Wimbledon ceased to be country town and became a part of London — but before this happened, everyone had to learn to bicycle", including J. M. Barrie who went wobbling round and round their lawn. Winifred Whitehead recalled cycling in a group "along the empty, dusty roads to such places as Ewell, Ripley, Epsom or to the Star and Garter in Richmond for watercress teas".

Ten years later the first motor-cars were making their appearance on the Ridgway. But Patrick Fawcett, who lived at number 104 (now Rydons) before the First World War, could not remember any private car owners, except the doctor's "open bright red vehicle with large brass headlamps". Otherwise all the traffic along the road was still "horse-drawn, hand-pushed or foot-pedalled". In particular there were high two-wheeled tradesmen's vans, cabs and occasional private carriages or pony traps. "If we had our hoops with us, we were not allowed to bowl them until we were off the Ridgway, in case they ran off the pavement into the road and entangled the horses' legs."

The last big event in the Ridgway before the War that he recalls, took place at Ridgelands, at the top of Edge Hill. In June 1914 a Red Cross display was held in the large garden, where the eight-year old Patrick saw "splendid uniforms, brilliant white tents containing field-dressing stations and operating theatres, and very clean and tidy 'casualties' played by Boy Scouts". Many of these boys were sadly to become genuine casualties in the years that followed.

RIDGWAY CHURCHES

Emmanuel

This fine red-brick church at the end of Lingfield Road was built in 1888. It originated in a split among the congregation at St Mary's in 1861. For some time the more Evangelical members had been meeting in private houses, like Southside House, the home of the Carfrae family, to pray and study the Bible. Some of them, especially several "holy Colonels", strongly disapproved of Canon Haygarth, his style of services and his reorganisation of the parish with new chapels-of-ease at Christ Church and Holy Trinity in the Broadway. So they "seceded" from St Mary's and put up an iron chapel on a piece of land at the top of Grosvenor Hill.

After ten years as a splinter group, the congregation asked to be readmitted to the Church of England, though outside the jurisdiction of St Mary's. Their numbers then increased so fast that they had to buy a new site for a church, the present one along the Ridgway. First in 1876 a large iron chapel was put up, then twelve years later the permanent church was built. At its opening the preacher was Canon Haygarth!

St John's

This equally fine red-brick church in St John's Road below the Ridgway was built in 1875. Its site is strangely appropriate, the top of a large field known even in the nineteenth century as Lampacre, land which in the Middle Ages had provided the money to keep a lamp burning permanently before the altar at St Mary's. At the Reformation such "superstitions" had been abolished and the land taken over by Sir William Cecil. By the eighteenth century it was part of the Hopkins estates and so passed to Mrs Phillips who sold it to the Church Commissioners.

The new church was designed by Sir Thomas Jackson (before he moved to Wimbledon). He chose a modern Gothic style and intended it to have a tower and spire, but after problems with the foundations, as the church was built on the spring line, the tower had to be abandoned. Instead, Miss Murray of Wimbledon Lodge commissioned Jackson to design a beautiful North Porch with cut-brickwork tracery and a sculpture of the Baptism of Our Lord. The foundation stone was laid in 1873 by Sir Bartle Frere, a distinguished Governor of the Cape, who lived at Wressil Lodge on Parkside. The church was opened in 1875, but has recently been threatened with closure.

The Sacred Heart, Edge Hill

This fourth new church on or near the Ridgway is thought by many good judges to be the finest. The nave was opened in 1887, but the rest of the building was not completed until 1901. It was designed in the late Decorated Gothic style by Frederick

Above: The north porch of St John's Church with the plaque of Our Lord's baptism.

Above right: Edith Arendrup, who was the real founder of the Roman Catholic Church in Wimbledon.

Right: Church of the Sacred Heart.

Walters, a young Roman Catholic architect who was later responsible for Buckfast Abbey.

The real founder of the church was Edith Arendrup, a member of the Courtauld family. She came to live in Cottenham Park in 1877, shortly after her husband, a Danish colonel, had been killed while leading an Egyptian army against the Ethiopians. She found that, since the McEvoys had left the Keir in 1850, there had been no Catholic chapel in Wimbledon, so she built one onto her large house in Cottenham Park Road. (It survives, although no longer used as a chapel, attached to Barkby Close, just above Holland Gardens.) She then persuaded Jesuit priests from

Colonel Llewellyn Longstaff, who was a generous patron of Antarctic explorers, especially Captain Scott.

159

Roehampton to walk across the Common every Sunday to say Mass there. The numbers coming to the chapel soon became so great that in 1884 Edith Arendrup decided to build a large church in a prominent position. So she bought land originally intended for houses in the newly laid out Darlaston Road and there the nave of the new church was built.

Its first parish priest was a Jesuit, Fr. William Kerr. He has been described as "the heart and soul" of the Catholic Church in Wimbledon before the First World War. An essentially humble man, he quickly became the personal friend of all his parishioners. Though his sight was poor and he was no longer a young man, he walked all over the district, south as well as north of the railway, visiting families in their homes. If all was well, he simply made what he called "a boiled egg visit", of four to five minutes. But if there was illness or other trouble, he was ready to stay for hours. He was respected all over Wimbledon by people from all denominations or none. When he died in 1913, the route to the cemetery in Gap Road was lined by large crowds and all the shops were shut.

Marie Reparatrice Convent, once Ridgelands

Like Donhead Lodge a little further down Edge Hill, Ridgelands was probably built in 1867. Eleven years later it was bought by a Yorkshire businessman and Volunteer Colonel, Llewellyn Longstaff.

Longstaff was Director of a Company with interests in steel, coal and ships and a pioneer of profit sharing. He was fond of travel in Europe and America, and a generous patron of explorers. As a Fellow of the Royal Geographic Society, he helped promote the British Antarctic Expedition of 1899 to 1904. Captain Scott was a frequent visitor at Ridgelands and his last expedition to the South Pole was supported by Longstaff.

Ridgelands became the headquarters of the Red Cross in Surrey, hence "the great inspection and display" in June 1914. Another Red Cross demonstration took place in the large garden towards the end of the War, but it must have overtaxed Longstaff's health. He had been unwell for the past year and died at Ridgelands in November 1918, shortly after the Armistice — "one of the best known and most respected men in Wimbledon".

Between the Wars the house became a Bible College for ladies; during the Second World War it was used by Barclays Bank. In the 1950s it was bought by the Sisters of Marie Reparatrice and transformed into a convent. But by the early 1980s it had become too difficult to keep in repair and so was pulled down. A new and much smaller convent was then built. Now the only part of Longstaff's house that survives is the entrance lodge by the corner of Edge Hill.

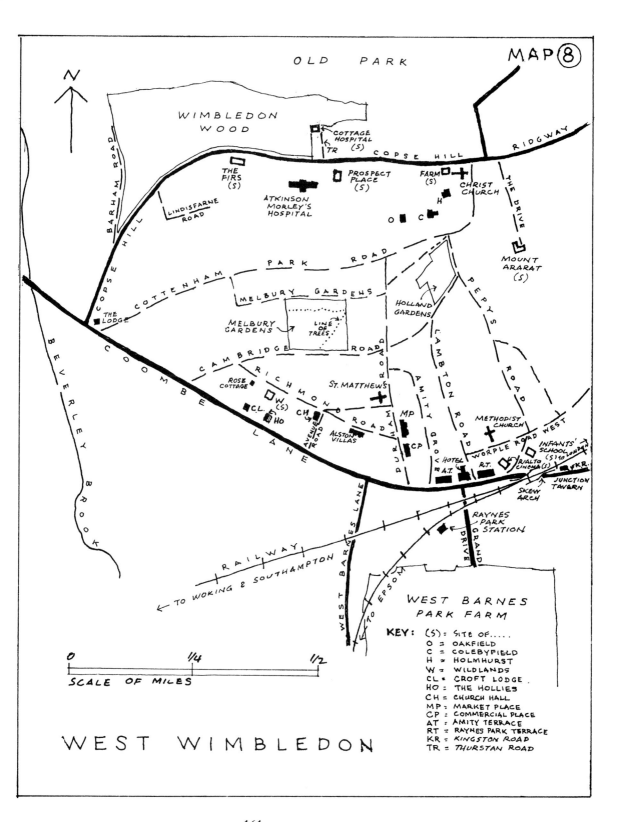

MAP ⑧

OLD PARK

WIMBLEDON WOOD

COTTAGE HOSPITAL (S)

TR

COPSE HILL

RIDGWAY

THE FIRS (S)

PROSPECT PLACE (S)

FARM (S)

CHRIST CHURCH

THE DRIVE

BARHAM ROAD

ATKINSON MORLEY'S HOSPITAL

LINDISFARNE ROAD

H

O C

MOUNT ARARAT (S)

COPSE HILL

PARK ROAD

COTTENHAM

MELBURY GARDENS

HOLLAND GARDENS

PEPYS ROAD

THE LODGE

MELBURY GARDENS

LINE OF TREES

ROAD

LAMBTON ROAD

CAMBRIDGE ROAD

RICHMOND ROAD

St. MATTHEWS

AMITY GROVE

METHODIST CHURCH

BEVERLEY BROOK

COOMBE LANE

ROSE COTTAGE

W (S)

CL HO

CH

AVENUE ROAD

ALSTON VILLAS

DURHAM ROAD

MP

CP

WORPLE ROAD WEST

TO LONDON

INFANTS' SCHOOL

RIALTO CINEMA (S)

JUNCTION TAVERN

KR

HOTEL

A.T.

R.T.

SKEW ARCH

RAYNES PARK STATION

WEST BARNES LANE

RAILWAY

TO WOKING & SOUTHAMPTON

TO EPSOM

GRAND DRIVE

WEST BARNES PARK FARM

KEY: (S) = SITE OF.....
O = OAKFIELD
C = COLEBYFIELD
H = HOLMHURST
W = WILDLANDS
CL = CROFT LODGE
HO = THE HOLLIES
CH = CHURCH HALL
MP = MARKET PLACE
CP = COMMERCIAL PLACE
AT = AMITY TERRACE
RT = RAYNES PARK TERRACE
KR = KINGSTON ROAD
TR = THURSTAN ROAD

WEST WIMBLEDON

SCALE OF MILES
0   1/4   1/2

161

20

Copse Hill

Like the Ridgway, Copse Hill was for centuries only "a very narrow lane". Until the 1850s it ran between woods and meadows with hardly a house in sight. On the south side were fields with evocative names like Broomy Down, Green Coomes and Small Profitts (about where Cottenham Drive is today). Opposite were three meadows, all known as Barn Field. Beyond them was a dense twenty acre wood which began just below the modern Thurstan Road and extended to about the line of Barham Road. In the seventeenth century it was known as Brooms Down Wood; in the eighteenth as Heavon's or Broomfield Wood; only in the late nineteenth century did it get the name Wimbledon Wood. On the southside of the road towards Coombe Lane was another large wood, named after the Pettiwards of Putney who owned the land. This wood extended approximately as far as the line of the modern Cambridge Road; it could be responsible for the wonderful soil in the Cottenham Park allotments.

These woods, which account for the name Copse Hill, were certainly old. The one north of the road was part of the Old Park which had been used for hunting and shooting since the Middle Ages. The other to the south was part of "the Wild Land", a large area mentioned in a document of 1481 as "from ancient time arable, but for many years overgrown with bramble, thorn and furze", a result of the frequent outbreaks of plague in the previous 130 years and the lack of men to till the fields. Parts of the Old Park and the Wild Land were under cultivation by the early seventeenth century, but the full recovery of the land south of Copse Hill took nearly another 200 years.

The first stage began about 1757 when Peter Taylor, a London goldsmith, built a "handsome villa" just to the east of the site of the modern Atkinson Morley's Hospital. He called it Prospect Place because it had "an extensive prospect to the south". Ten years later his son sold the small six acre estate to Moses Isaac Levy. "Mr Levi, the Jew", as he was called in contemporary documents, had recently made a fortune out of Army contracts in the Seven Years' War. He used some of the money to enlarge the house and lay out the garden "judiciously", with a hot-house which "produced the earliest, largest and finest fruits in the county". In 1788 he generously gave a large sum to the fund for rebuilding St Mary's.

His successor four years later, James Meyrick, a Parliamentary agent, had been living on Southside in the house which is now King's College Junior School. He transformed the Prospect Place estate, buying all the Pettiward land and a lot more right down to Coombe Lane and across as far as the line of the modern Pepys Road, in all 250 acres. He then spent a large sum improving the grounds, employing

Humphrey Repton to lay out large "decorative" gardens with a five acre lawn and many fine trees (some in a great avenue from Coombe Lane, which has given the name Avenue Road and a few old trees in Melbury Gardens). The rest of the estate was used to graze cattle (as in a field that later became Holland Gardens) or grow wheat (especially in fields along Coombe Lane). Pettiward Wood seems to have been cut down at this time, but a few of its trees may have survived, notably the two fine oaks just below Lindisfarne Road.

After the death of Meyrick and his widow, the estate was put up for auction. It was bought in 1825 by a rising young politician, John Lambton, later Earl of Durham. A leading Whig reformer and later an important Governor-General of Canada, he seems to have had little effect on the district, apart from the two roads named after him. On becoming Lord Privy Seal in 1831, he sold the estate to a fellow Whig politician who was to have a far greater impact on Wimbledon, Charles Pepys, a descendant of the famous diarist's uncle.

The future Earl of Cottenham was just fifty, a leading barrister, an able judge, but so shy that he made hardly any friends. As the Whig party had few distinguished lawyers, his promotion was rapid: Solicitor-general, Master of the Rolls and in 1836

An engraving made in the 1780s of Prospect Place, "a villa belonging to M.I. Levy Esq". The house faced east with Copse Hill to the right, so it is a puzzle to know how the coach has reached the drive.

Charles Pepys, Earl of
Cottenham and Lord
Chancellor, who lived at
Prospect Place from 1831
until his death in 1851.

Lord Chancellor. He therefore presided at the young Queen Victoria's first Council
of State. His chief interest, however, was his family. He was happily married with
fifteen children. A friend recalled that "his return [from Westminster] was the hour
of peace and joy when he went up to the nursery to sing to the little ones what he
called Chinese songs".

He had bought Prospect Place primarily for his family as a haven from the smells
and disease of London. Yet as soon as he arrived, he found that the London and
Southampton Railway Company proposed to build their new line right across the
southern half of the estate. He refused to sell the land and the Company was forced

to change their route. Once his peace was assured, Pepys began his own improvements: a large model farm on Copse Hill (just to the west of the site of Christ Church), where he experimented with new farming machines; and new entrances to the estate with lodges and private drives, which later became Durham and Cottenham Park Roads.

In his second term as Lord Chancellor after the Corn Law crisis of 1846, he began to show clear signs of age. He dozed on the Bench and his judgments were hard to follow as he had lost all his teeth! Several barristers even suggested presenting him with a set of false teeth. In 1850 his doctors finally persuaded him to resign, but within a year he was dead. His family promptly sold Prospect Place and forty acres of the land to the second Duke of Wellington. He lived there for a few years, but then moved elsewhere and left the house empty. In the end it was purchased in 1863 by a Mr Sims who pulled it down and sold the site and the land to St George's Hospital for a convalescent home they were planning to build with a legacy from Atkinson Morley. All that now remains of the old house is the entrance lodge on Copse Hill, just above the hospital bus stop.

At the same time as the house was sold to the Duke of Wellington, the rest of the estate, now called Cottenham Park, was bought by developers. They laid out a number of wide roads, named after aristocrats connected with the house or the

The Firs, the joint home of the Hughes and Ludlow families, with its two front doors and the common living room in-between.

165

district, and drew up covenants to secure it as a "high-class" neighbourhood with buildings no nearer the road than thirty feet. Their project, however, excited little interest. A map of 1858 shows the new roads, but the only new houses marked in the estate line Copse Hill: the three large Italianate mansions that have recently been renovated to the east of Cottenham Drive. In fact, at least two other houses had already been built on or just off Copse Hill. The earliest was the Firs, put up in 1854 half way down the Hill, a little below Prospect Place. The other, Oakfield, dates from 1857 and survives "down the Avenue", a small side road off Copse Hill leading to Holmhurst (now an Old People's Home, on the site of an earlier house).

The Firs is of particular interest as it was built as an experiment in communal living for the families of two young barristers, Thomas Hughes and John Ludlow. They were leading figures in the Christian Socialist Movement, which aimed at finding a Christian answer to the problems of poverty, ignorance and crime. They thought they had found it in the ideal of fellowship, the better-off helping the "underprivileged" by forming working men's associations for education (like the Working Men's College of which Hughes became the Principal in 1854) and for co-operative production (such as the North London Working Builders' Association). Hughes, the stronger personality, persuaded Ludlow to put their ideals into practice by building two houses side by side and linking them with a common living-room.

So they bought a plot of land in the new Cottenham Park estate, got their North London Working Builders' Association to put the houses up and in 1854 moved in, Hughes with his wife and four children, Ludlow with his mother. At the Firs they kept almost open house. A constant stream of friends and visitors arrived, some by carriage, most on foot, especially the working men from Hughes's College. They were entertained by one of the founders of the Movement, Charles Kingsley, with talks on botany or by Hughes himself, an Oxford blue, with cricket matches or games of leap frog. Other guests included Mrs Gaskell, the novelist, and Alexander Macmillan, a rising young publisher who printed Kingsley's books.

The main claim for the Firs to a place in history is not, however, as a centre for Christian Socialism, but as the place where Thomas Hughes wrote *Tom Brown's Schooldays*. The book originated in concern over his eldest son, Maurice, going off to boarding school for the first time. "Thinking over what I should like to say to him before he went," Hughes told a friend, "I took to writing a story, as the easiest way of bringing out what I wanted." Some months later, discussing childen's books with Ludlow, he took out the manuscript and asked him to have a look at it. Ludlow was gripped by the story and said it must be published. So Hughes sent it to their Christian Socialist colleague, Macmillan, and he agreed to publish it. It came out in April 1857 and was an instant success. Within a year it had gone through six editions and Hughes had made a lot of money.

Only two years later, however, the young Maurice died, aged eleven, and his parents were shattered. Shortly afterwards they left the Firs which now had too many sad associations for them. Hughes later became an M.P. and County Court Judge, and did not die until 1896. Ludlow stayed on in the house with his recently married wife. A small, self-effacing man, he was deeply religious and invited some of his young relatives who had been orphaned to share the house. In 1875 he became Chief Registrar of Friendly Societies, and for years wrote articles for the

CHRIST CHURCH,
COPSE HILL

Thomas Hughes, who wrote *Tom Brown's Schooldays* at the Firs in 1856.

"Spectator". Locally, he was a member of the Wimbledon Board of Health and a trustee of Christ Church and the Village Club. He lived even longer than Hughes, not dying until 1911. His unusual house survived a further fifty years and was demolished in 1967 to make way for the nurses' flats which have kept the name The Firs.

The other early house just off Copse Hill, Oakfield, was the home of another very talented family, the Grensides. The father, Charles, was a London solicitor who wanted a suburban home for his family within reasonable distance of the railway. So in 1856 he bought an acre of land from the Cottenham Park developers and had a large house built, which he called Oakfield after the four oak trees in the garden. In the following summer he brought the family by train to Wimbledon Station, hired one of "Berryman's flys" and drove up to the new house. They soon settled in. His son later wrote: "During our first summers we could roam at will through the woods and grounds of Lord Chancellor Cottenham's old house, then standing empty, though not yet pulled down." Until Raynes Park Station was opened in 1871, the father was not quite so happy on the long walk home from Wimbledon Station on dark winter nights. He always carried a swordstick, kept two revolvers in the house and encouraged his wife to practice shooting at a box in the garden. They never appear to have had to use their weapons; instead, they were able to bring up their family in almost ideal surroundings. Their only son, also Charles and a solicitor like his father, married Harriet Arendrup, who lived nearby in Cottenham Park Road with her step-mother, the foundress of the Sacred Heart Church. Their second daughter, Gerda, was a notable artist, whose water-colours were regularly exhibited at the annual shows of the Wimbledon Art and Benevolent Society.

In 1860, only three years after the Grensides moved into their new house, the next door plot was bought by a Cambridge rowing blue and distinguished architect, Francis Cranmer Penrose. He was Surveyor of the Fabric of St Paul's Cathedral and responsible for hanging the "Great Paul" bell. He was also a keen archaeologist and

Francis Penrose, a distinguished architect, who lived at Colebyfield off Copse Hill from 1862 until his death in 1903.

Sir Arthur Holland, who
lived at Holmhurst from
1874 until he died in 1928.

astronomer. On the small road off Copse Hill, he designed and supervised the
building of his house, named Colebyfield. As well as the usual servants' quarters,
coach-house and stables, he installed a small observatory in the roof. He moved in
with his wife and five children in 1862, and soon made his mark. He took a keen
interest in local affairs and served on the Local Board. He went regularly to services
in Christ Church and was put in charge of the fabric there too, installing a heating
system and a new choir vestry. He was also concerned at earth tremors made by
heavy goods trains travelling on the embankment in the early morning and made

169

observations of their effect on the environment which he sent to Greenwich. One of his daughters, Dame Emily Penrose, was the first woman to get a First-class Honours degree in Greats at Oxford. A formidable character, she became Principal of Bedford College, London, and of Somerville, Oxford.

The Grensides' other neighbours in this little road were equally distinguished and even better known locally — the Hollands. Sir Arthur Holland was head of a shipping firm which traded with the U.S.A. and South America. Yet, after moving to Holmhurst in 1874 with his wife and six children, he found the time to take an active part in local affairs for nearly fifty years. He was a member of the Local Board, the first Chairman of the Urban District Council in 1894 and the Borough's second Mayor in 1906. He was also a J. P., Deputy-Lieutenant for Surrey and unsuccessful Liberal candidate in the election of 1910. He helped to start the Guild of Social Welfare and to get the streets lit by electricity instead of by oil lamps. On top of all that, he was President of Wimbledon Football Club. No wonder that on his death in 1928 at the age of 85, the *Wimbledon Borough News* declared that "his record of lasting achievement is probably unsurpassed in the history of the borough". Yet in 1904 he had been maimed for life in helping to put out a fire at his house. His work for Wimbledon is fittingly commemorated by Holland Gardens, a pleasant recreation ground off Cottenham Park Road, just below Holmhurst, opened by his widow in 1929.

The junction of Pepys and Cottenham Park Roads, about 1900. Behind the boys was an earth track (the bottom half is now Orchard Lane) and a field owned by the Hollands. It is now Holland Gardens.

Holmhurst was recently pulled down to make way for a more up-to-date old people's home. But both Oakfield and Colebyfield survive, along with the two Victorian houses just to the west of Christ Church and built on the site of the Model Farm. Otherwise most of the buildings along Copse Hill date from the late 1920s or 1930s. The road itself was transformed at the same time. In 1925 it was considerably widened and for the first time a footpath was added on the north side. It had at last ceased to be the lane Winifred Whitehead remembered, "fading away into the bluebell woods, full of squirrels, badgers, nightingales and the harsh cry of pheasants".

COPSE HILL HOSPITALS

Thurstan Road

This short road off Copse Hill is named after Edward Thurstan Holland, the first Honorary Secretary and Treasurer of Wimbledon Cottage Hospital which used to exist at the end of the road. It was Wimbledon's first hospital, opened in 1870 after an appeal for money to enable doctors, like the founder Dr Gilbert Love, to treat poorer patients. It existed until 1947 on subscriptions, on gifts like the bath-chair given by Mrs Haygarth, and on innumerable fund-raising activities such as concerts, plays, flower shows and an annual charity cricket match (for long between Jack Hobbs's XI and a Wimbledon and District XVIII).

At first patients had to come with letters of recommendation from subscribers. They were expected to pay at least a token sum, "which only meets a fraction of the cost, but fosters the self-respect and self-dependence of patients, and secures the

171

hospital from the admission of frivolous and improper cases". At the start there were only seven beds for more serious cases, operations were performed on a kitchen table and all hot water had to be boiled in a kettle. But gradually conditions improved. The old hospital was pulled down and a new, large one built in 1912. By 1930 there were seventy-two beds, an operating theatre and an X-Ray unit.

The hospital always remained small. But its closure in the early 1980s was widely regretted. Its site has now been covered by modern houses.

Atkinson Morley's Hospital

Mr Atkinson Morley was a medical student at St George's Hospital, Hyde Park Corner, in the years around 1800. But instead of becoming a doctor, he decided to run a hotel, first the Burlington in Cork Street, then his own in Trafalgar Square. By the time of his death in 1858, he was very wealthy. In his will he remembered his old hospital, leaving it the very large sum of £100,000 "for receiving, maintaining and generally assisting convalescent poor patients".

The Hospital decided to use the money to set up a convalescent home for eighty patients. Just as they were looking round for a suitable site, the Duke of Wellington's house and forty acre estate off Copse Hill came onto the market. It seemed ideal. So they bought twenty-eight acres (after the derelict house had been pulled down) and built a large home in Second Empire style. It was opened in July 1869.

In his *Memories of a Wimbledon Childhood, 1906–1918*, Patrick Fawcett alludes to the "Wednesday Buses": two black closed vehicles which every Wednesday afternoon took patients from St George's to convalesce at Copse Hill and returned with those who had had their week or fortnight's stay. He adds that "These buses were eventually motorised, but up to at least 1915 they were each drawn by two horses and, if we were indoors, it was the clatter of their hooves approaching that would make us rush to the windows to be the first to see them pass."

Atkinson Morley's remained purely a convalescent home until 1939. It was the Second World War that transformed it into one of the most advanced brain surgery centres in the world.

Worple Road

Compared with the Ridgway and Copse Hill, Worple Road was developed late, but quickly made up for lost time. Even in the 1860s it was still a genuine country lane surrounded by fields, with not a single house along it. Indeed, a fine water-colour painted in the early 1870s from a spot at the bottom of Thornton Hill shows a narrow earth track overhung by trees, those on the right forming a small copse which survived behind the houses at the bottom of Darlaston Road until the hurricane of October 1987.

This track was known by a variety of names: in Tudor times as "Warpell Way"; in the eighteenth century as "Middle Worpole Lane"; and as late as the 1860s as "Upper Worple" (with the road now known as Dundonald, "Lower Worple"), Wimbledon does not have a monopoly of this unusual name. At Mortlake there are North and South Worple Way; at Richmond there is another Worple Way, while at both Epsom and Isleworth there are Worple Roads. "Warpelles" were defined in Wimbledon documents of the 1560s as "common ways" or public rights of way across the large open field to the west of Hill Road. Two were especially dignified by the name worple and they were clearly the main rights of way to the fields, especially after the open field was divided into smaller "closes" in the early seventeenth century.

Until about 1870 Worple Road was a quiet cart track, though "often the carts sank into it and were pulled out again with some difficulty". It was an ideal place for children to go "blackberrying from hedges which bordered the lane" — and for huntsmen to chase a fox, as happened at least once in the 1850s. The track petered out at the bottom of the Downs. Beyond was a series of large fields, grazed by cows belonging to the Mount Ararat estate. Their peace was only disturbed after 1838 by the occasional passing of a steam train.

The development of this lane which led nowhere was started by an enterprising builder, Henry Harmer. In 1870 he moved from Lingfield Road and put up a house for himself on the south side of Worple Lane, opposite where the British Telecom building stands today. He was followed by a brick-maker, Joseph Diggle, who developed a large brickfield near the site of Salisbury Road. Their first houses were all on this south side between Harmer's home and the brickfield, and also in Francis Grove, one a children's home, started "to train as servants, girls between the ages of six and fifteen years who from their evil surroundings are likely to fall into vicious ways". Harmer did so well that he was soon employing forty to fifty men and nine boys, and building houses in The Grange.

Aerial view of Worple Road about 1920. In the foreground is the original Centre Court and Nursery Road. In the centre is the Sacred Heart Church, with the playing fields of Wimbledon College above it. On the far left are the houses in the Downs. At the top is the Ridgway. The picture is notable for an almost total absence of traffic.

By the late 1870s other builders were following his example. Soon houses lined both sides of the road, as well as many new side roads, up to just beyond the Downs where a new school, Rokeby, had opened in 1879. Most of them were large, detached, middle-class homes, all with names as well as numbers, with attics for the servants and large front gardens. (The gardens disappeared when the tram lines were laid; the houses have almost all been pulled down and replaced by blocks of flats in the last twenty years.) Yet until Midmoor Road was developed just after 1900, there was still a country atmosphere about the area. Southdown Farm off Albert Grove flourished by supplying "the richest milk and cream" to the new families living near the road. It was run by Messrs. Freeth and Pocock, "Dairymen", who had a "Creamery" at 50 Hill Road. They claimed to have "a superior herd of short horn and Jersey cows, especially selected for their milking qualities" and, showing a very modern outlook, they stressed that their cows were "pasture fed and so have freedom for exercise, so necessary for health".

Most of the men who took part in this rapid development and those who then bought the houses are now only remembered as names in local directories. But two, responsible for roads running north off the middle part of Worple Road, are worthy of special mention. Thornton Road was named after Richard Thornton, the millionaire owner of Cannon Hill House and much land in Wimbledon, including that on which South Place, Hartfield and Pelham Roads were built. About 1860, five years before his death, he also sold the land for Thornton Road, along which some very fine villas were built. One known as Beech House, was bought by Eliza Cook, a very popular, sentimental poet. The self-educated daughter of a Southwark tradesman, she started writing poetry at the age of fifteen and published several volumes of her works, including *Musings in a Wimbledon Churchyard*.

The other notable figure in the development of the Worple Road area was the headmaster of Wimbledon School, Revd John Brackenbury. In 1863 he had bought three fields (two called Great and Little Ladies' Close) below his school grounds from Richard Thornton. Twenty years later and on the point of retiring, he decided to develop them. So he laid out two interconnecting roads, Edge Hill and Darlaston, which he named after his third wife's home, Darlaston Hall in Staffordshire. He then divided the land into building plots and sold them to the highest bidder. One plot on Worple Road was sold for £225 to two Wimbledon builders who then put up a large house and sold it to a Captain Waters of West Kensington for £1,345. The deeds insisted that it could only be "a private or professional dwelling house" and that no other buildings could be put up on the site other than "ornamental stables and a coach house". When the building was pulled down in the early 1970s, a large block of flats was erected on its site.

The Worple Road that men like Thornton and Brackenbury helped to develop remained quiet and almost free of traffic until 1891. On 13 May in that year the Worple Road extension was ceremonially opened and the district was soon transformed. Until then the only way to get to Raynes Park was to climb over a stile at the bottom of Arterberry Road, walk across two fields and so rejoin "Worple Road West" with its few houses near the bottom of Pepys Road. The fields blocking the road were part of a large estate owned by one of the leading Wimbledonians of the second half of the nineteenth century, Thomas Devas.

Like several important families in the area, the Devases were probably descended from Huguenot refugees. Thomas's father had founded a textile firm in 1790 and by the time the son became Managing Director it was prospering. So in 1850 he felt in a position to take out a large mortgage and buy a fifty-five acre estate in Wimbledon which had been carved out of the Phillips lands in 1797. Its two-storeyed mansion, known as Mount Ararat, stood at the end of a long drive from the Ridgway, looking over a magnificent view towards the North Downs. Round it was a collection of other buildings: porter's lodge, coach house, stables, large conservatory and greenhouse, pinehouse, bailiff's house, barns and granary. To the south were the lawns and garden, below which stretched, as far as the railway, fields with unusual names like Upper, Middle and Lower Arterberry. In the fields grazed cows looked after from a small farm halfway down the hill (it survives today as a small bungalow by one of the bends in Arterberry Road).

Devas was very public spirited. He played an important part in the setting up of the Village Club and of Christ Church; he was treasurer of the Cottage Improvement Society; he served on the Local Board. In 1871 he gave £500 towards the cost of building Raynes Park Station. But he also had a large family, four boys and four girls (at least two of them were talented artists). To secure their future and to help pay off his original mortgage, he decided to develop the easternmost part of his estate. So in 1873 he laid out Arterberry Road (with a series of sharp bends to help horses with carts go up and down the hill more easily; at the bottom by Worple Road he also put up a large horse-trough). He then borrowed a further large sum, had a number of sizeable mansions built on the east side of the road (and also along the Drive) and

WORPLE ROAD.

Thomas Devas, who
developed Arterberry
Road and lived at Mount
Ararat from 1850 until his
death in 1900.

The front of Mount
Ararat, facing up the
drive, towards the
Ridgway. From the garden
there was a fine view over
the valley. The house was
pulled down shortly after
Devas died.

leased them to families like that of his son-in-law, Thomas Conway. (The Conways moved in too quickly before the house had dried out and all caught bad colds!) At the bottom, Arterberry was soon linked to Worple Road "East", but to join it to the western part generated a violent controversy.

Many householders in Raynes Park, especially a voluble member of the Board, Bennett Williams, felt isolated and neglected. They claimed that a direct road to Wimbledon would be of great benefit to both communities, would give "a great fillip to building" in the area and would not cost much. Several members of the Local Board, especially the Chairman, John Townsend, a builder, were not convinced. They feared that the purchase of the right of way across the fields would only benefit Devas. After some bitter debates, they were defeated, the road was built at a cost of just over £1,000 and on 13 May 1891 opened amid great popular rejoicing.

The special programme for the occasion shows that it was preceded by the "christening" of a new steam fire-engine, "May Queen", outside the Local Board offices at the top of the Broadway. Then a procession, led by mounted police officers and including members of the Board, three bands, three fire-engines and seventy other vehicles, went "at a slow march" along Worple Road. At the bottom of Arterberry it was met, according to Winifred Whitehead, then a small girl, "by every cart, cab and hansom, all decorated with flags and streamers, and everyone blowing or beating whistles, trumpets and drums, people shouting, singing and waving". After Townsend had declared the extension open, the procession went on up Durham Road, along the Ridgway, Lingfield Road and the High Street, finally going down the Hill back to the Board offices. In the evening the members of the Board held a dinner at the Drill Hall in St George's Road (where the underground car park is now) and doubtless congratulated themselves on a notable achievement.

For the next ten years, until after Thomas Devas died aged 86 in July 1900, the extension produced little real change. Then, as his sons sold off parts of the estate to pay his mortgages, development started. Closely-packed, semi-detached houses, very different in character from those to the east, went up along the Worple Road extension between Arterberry and Pepys. Others were built along new roads like Stanton and Dunmore. But until the early 1920s, as Patrick Fawcett remembered, the land just to the north (on which Montana, Devas, Hunter and Conway roads were later laid out) remained "one huge field, bordered by trees and thick hedges". It was used for "shows" — Wild West Shows or Flower Shows, like the one in 1900, blessed with perfect weather, where the record number of visitors could see a display by the Wimbledon Fire Brigade, while their children enjoyed swings, roundabouts and coconut shies, and "the Manor Club band discoursed sweet music".

Raynes Park clearly took some time to adapt to the new link. At the Wimbledon Hill end of Worple Road, however, there was a major change. In the 1880s it was a road of private houses, rather than shops. By 1900 both sides were lined by shops. On the south (where Sainsbury's Supermarket stands today) there was a fishmonger, dressmaker, plumber, watchmaker, dairy, bootmaker and hairdresser. Opposite (on the site of McDonalds) were the Public Swimming Baths with a Baths Arcade by their side. These baths were soon to be superseded by the Latimer Road Baths, opened in 1901. They were then covered over, renamed Worple Hall and used for public meetings.

177

The Wimbledon end of Worple Road about 1910. On the right are Ely's, a fish shop and barber's. The Worple Hall is off to the left behind the roller skating rink. In the background is the Alexandra public house.

The most famous meeting held there took place during a by-election in 1907. Wimbledon had been a safe Conservative seat since it first gained an M.P. of its own in 1885. But at the time of the Liberal landslide in 1906, the Conservative majority slumped to barely two thousand. So when their M.P., Charles Hambro, suddenly resigned the next year, they feared defeat and chose a well-known ex-Cabinet minister, Henry Chaplin, as their candidate. To their surprise the Liberals decided not to oppose him. They wanted Arthur Holland (of Holmhurst, Copse Hill) to stand, but he was then Mayor of Wimbledon. With only a fortnight to go before polling day, the Women's Suffrage Society decided to put up a candidate, the philosopher Bertrand Russell. Russell was a good speaker and a strong supporter of women's right to have the vote. But he had little time to put over his case and he antagonised many Liberals by drawing support from the new Labour party.

The meeting he held in Worple Hall drew a noisy crowd of about two thousand. Russell was greeted with both loud applause and frequent interruptions. Eggs were thrown at him and two large black rats were let loose from a bag. These caused "a great commotion". Ladies jumped on the chairs, while some of the men hunted and killed the rats. The Chairman finally got some quiet by remarking: "Surely this is not the way that Wimbledon men and women greet a stranger." Russell made an effective speech and at the end a resolution supporting his views was carried "by an overwhelming majority". It was all to no avail. When the votes were counted a few days later, Chaplin had gained 10,263, Russell only 3,299, the largest Conservative majority until then.

178

1907 was the year not merely of the by-election, but of the end of Worple Road's peace with the coming of the trams. A tram service from Vauxhall to Kingston via Wimbledon had first been proposed in 1871, but it came to nothing. In 1902, however, the London United Tramways Company was given the right to extend its line at Tooting to Wimbledon, Kingston and Hampton Court. It took five years to lay the tracks, which involved widening the roads, including Worple (and compensating house-owners for loss of their gardens, which helped to spoil the appearance of the road). At last in 1907 the first tram arrived, to be greeted by large crowds at Ely's Corner. From then on the pace of change — and of the traffic — became ever faster, until the road has sadly become one of the least interesting and most dangerous in Wimbledon.

THE DOWNS

The Ursuline Convent

For centuries the Downs had been a right of way linking the Commons at Wimbledon and Merton. So it is hardly surprising that it was developed in the 1870s as soon as houses began to go up along Worple Road. Wealthy businessmen bought large plots of land and built sizeable mansions on the slopes of the hill. Few of these houses survive. Of these that do, two are notable.

The first is the Ursuline Convent. It was built in 1877 by Francis Lambert of Tunbridge Wells for his son Richard, a coal merchant. It was a magnificent home,

The arrival of the first tram at Ely's Corner in August 1906, a trial run by Board of Trade inspectors. The fronts of the shops on the right have been moved back to widen the road.

179

built in Italian style, with some fine rooms, large servants' quarters and a beautiful garden. Unfortunately, little seems to be known about the life of the Lambert family or the reason why they sold the house in 1894.

It was bought by Roman Catholic nuns (of the Ursuline order). They had come to Wimbledon two years earlier to set up a girls' school and had first leased a house in Worple Road. But the Lamberts' mansion on the Downs was far more suitable and they moved there. Like the Jesuit Wimbledon College, their Convent School has grown out of all recognition, but the nuns have been more successful both in preserving the old buildings and in commissioning new ones which blend well with the old.

Rokeby

The other notable house is Rokeby, which in 1879 gave its name to a well-known local Preparatory School. The school had been started two years earlier in a large red-brick house called Helmsley in Woodhayes Road, opposite Gothic Lodge. Its founder, a young man not long down from Oxford, was Charles Olive who had been advised to start a school in the Wimbledon area as it "swarmed with boys".

The beginning was not too promising. In the first term not a single pupil appeared; in the Easter term there was one boy, Charles Saunders. But by the end of the summer

A tram and horse bus meeting in Worple Road near the bottom of Spencer Hill about 1910. In the background is a Methodist church.

there were fifteen. After a further year there were too many boys and Olive had to look for a larger house. He found it in the Downs and the school took on the name Rokeby, which it still retains, although it has now moved to Coombe Hill.

Horse-Troughs

The Downs was probably too steep for horse-drawn carts to climb. So it was never given a horse-trough. But one was installed in 1887 at the bottom of Arterberry Road by Thomas Devas.

It was one of seven erected in Wimbledon by the Metropolitan Drinking Fountain and Cattle Trough Association. This organisation had been founded in 1859 "for the amelioration of animal suffering and the promotion of habits of temperance amongst our itinerant and working population". It claimed to be "the only Society which provides free supplies of water for man and beast in the streets of London". It proved its value by stating that "More than 1,800 horses, besides oxen, sheep and dogs, frequently drink at a single trough in one day" and that "more than 8,000 people have been known to drink at one fountain in a single day, many of whom are working men, who would otherwise be compelled to resort to the public house to quench their thirst."

The first such fountain in Wimbledon was put up in 1868 at the top of Hill Road not by the Association but by "working men" of the area. It was a memorial to the distinguished ear specialist, Joseph Toynbee, who had died two years earlier at the age of fifty. The first Horse Trough was erected in 1879 in South Park Road and is now in the Gardens there. Others followed at the top of Cottenham Park Road, near Christ Church, in 1886 (now in the Museum of London); at the bottom of Arterberry Road, 1887 (recently removed by the Council); at the top of Wimbledon Hill, 1893 (now at the corner of Belvedere Grove); in Haydons Road, at the corner of Gap Road, 1900 (now disappeared); at the end of Parkside near the Pound, 1904; and at the bottom of Copse Hill, 1905 (now at the bottom of Cottenham Park Road).

Drinking fountains were erected in many of the Council's recreation grounds. In 1904 three were put up in Dundonald Gardens, South Park Gardens and Melbury Gardens, Cottenham Park.

181

*Wimbledon in the
Twentieth Century*

22

Raynes Park

While Victorian Wimbledon below the hill developed around the railway, Raynes Park virtually rose along tram lines laid in the early years of the twentieth century. As late as 1863 there were only thirteen houses in the whole of the district just north of the railway, most of them along Richmond Road; twenty years later there were still less than one hundred. Yet the name Raynes Park had been chosen in 1871 for the new station to try and attract families to settle along the many deserted roads newly laid out north of the station in the 1850s and given drains and even footpaths.

Strictly speaking Raynes Park is the land to the south of the line, on either side of Grand Drive. Between 1823 and 1847 it had been farmed by a man from Durham, Edward Rayne. He had inherited the 200 acre West Barnes Farm (the site of the farmhouse is near the bottom of Blenheim Road) and made it very prosperous. He used three "Parks" or very large fields for grazing his many sheep — and also for the steeplechases that he enjoyed with neighbouring farmers. On his death his widow kept the farm going for another twenty years, but in 1867 ill-health forced her to sell it to Sir Richard Garth.

Garth wanted to develop the land along a grand drive to the railway. At the same time, on the other side of the line, Cottenham Park was beginning to be developed and Devas was thinking of building houses on Arterberry Road. All three developers needed a station as a focus to attract people to the district. Garth offered the railway company £4,000 to pay for it; Devas gave £500. The station was built and opened as Raynes Park, the name perhaps chosen by Garth. This name has remained and spread to the area immediately north of the line — Pepys, Lambton, Durham and Cambridge Roads, along with Coombe Lane, all strictly in Cottenham Park. In 1937 a campaign was started to rename the station West Wimbledon as, it was claimed, this would be "a good letting title" and would prevent goods being misdirected. But the Southern Railway refused and the name Raynes Park has stayed.

For over twenty years the station remained isolated with few buildings near it, apart from the station-master's house and two "railway cottages". On the south side of the Skew Arch, the Junction Tavern had been built in 1864, its name commemorating the opening of the branch line to Epsom and Dorking three years earlier. On the other side the small Raynes Park Hotel opened about 1873 (the date 1904 on its tower alludes to later additions); it was managed by a Samuel Tebutt, perhaps a descendant of the Mr Tebutt who looked after Earl Spencer's lodge on the Portsmouth Road in the 1800s. There was also an even smaller Church of England Infants' and Sunday School in a corrugated iron hut just north of the Skew Arch. It opened in 1867, run by a Miss Crump who was paid twelve pounds a year — and could not have had many children to teach.

Otherwise, until the opening of the Worple Road extension in 1891, the main focus of the small settlement seems to have been to the west of the station. There houses were being built along Amity Grove, Durham and Richmond Roads, and Coombe Lane. The oldest of these roads was clearly Coombe Lane. For centuries it had been known as "the Lane from Merton to Kingston" or "the Highway to Coome Bridge", and had run beside woods. By the mid-nineteenth century, as the road began to be called Coombe Lane, the woods had been cleared and replaced by fields. Those to the south (which had once belonged to Merton Priory) were known as East, Middle and Barn Close and there grazed the cattle from Hoppingwood Farm (near modern New Malden). Between the fields and the lane ran a wide ditch, "the common sewer parting Wimbledon and Merton", which went right down to Beverley Brook. It was covered over when the wide grass verge was laid in Coombe Lane.

The earliest houses in the road, in fact in the whole of Raynes Park, were on the north side, a pair of stucco semi-detached homes (now numbers 194 and 196). They were built about 1855, shortly after the sale of the Cottenham Estate, and were first known as the Hollies and York Villa. They originally had large gardens extending right back to Richmond Road and were lived in by a secretary to a building society and a "hosiery houseman". In the 1880s they were joined by a larger gabled house, built of white brick, with two stone lions guarding the front door. It was known as Croft Lodge (now number 206). Otherwise the road was then little more than a narrow country lane.

Coombe Lane about 1900, taken from near the bottom of Avenue Road, looking towards the station. To the right are fields and in the background is West Barnes Lane.

The first of the new streets to have any buildings along it was Richmond Road, just to the north of Coombe Lane. Towards the eastern end near Durham Road was a line of workmen's cottages built about 1860 and known as Alston Villas (they survive as very desirable residences). Several were owned by a leading Methodist, Henry Palmer, who lived opposite in a small terrace, known as Melbourne Villas (it too is still there). Nearby stood Cottenham Park Farm surrounded by a large orchard — and several pigsties. When the Tilling buses started to run from the Junction Tavern to London in the 1890s, a large stable was built here for the horses and Ben Carpenter, "Shoeing Smith", set up a smithy.

In the same street, on the other side of Avenue Road, lived two of the more interesting characters in Victorian Raynes Park. The first was Bennett Williams, a Welsh gentleman, member of the Local Board and voluble supporter of the interests of the district he always called Cottenham Park. He named his house Wildlands. The reason is implicit in an amusing letter he wrote to the local paper in January 1886. After alluding to "this pretty, rural end of the parish", and to "the woodland music of this bird-frequented spot", he got down to the main point: "[a list of] our many grievous afflictions".

RAYNES PARK.

First among these was the claim that "the place has become a perfect paradise of stray cattle". Mr Williams maintained that "it is no uncommon thing to wake up in a morning and find a small herd of cows dotted picturesquely about your lawn, philosophically chewing the cud — your early spring greens — sublimely indifferent to your most frantic imprecations, and even to the hair brush and shaving pot." He added that occasionally he had seen "a horse or two in the background industriously browsing off the choice young fruit trees or choicer rosebuds".

His next complaint concerned "the gentleman in blue" who "is supposed to perambulate the district, when not otherwise engaged". In fact, Mr Williams commented, he did little to stop burglaries, which were not more numerous because of "the well-known fact that the rate and tax collectors give us no chance of accumulating a sufficiently tempting hoard". In addition, "The state of our roads hereabouts is such that Mr William Sykes, if encountered with even a moderate amount of swag, would inevitably stick in the mud and hereby become an easy captive to the morning postman."

As if these "afflictions" were not "grievous" enough, Mr Williams finished by asserting that "the almost impassable roads are insufficiently marked out — I cannot call it lighted — by the feeble glimmer of the wretched oil lamps which, like the visits of the Local Board members, are few and far between". As a result he maintained that people were leaving the neighbourhood because of "the difficulty and danger attending the journey from the railway station to their homes".

Whether the Board made any improvements to "this unhappy district" after reading the letter is not known, but the contemporary troubles of the householders in Lambton Road suggest that they took a long time to do so. In 1886 the Cottenham Ratepayers' Association wrote to the Board asking for the road to be "put in repair" as the houses were "untenantable" and also for street lamps to be installed. The Board refused both requests on the ground that there were only six houses in the road. When it was pointed out to them that there were in fact double that number, they reluctantly agreed to put up three lamps, but claimed that the road was a "private" one and must be repaired by the householders. Soon after, however, they relented and made up the road.

The other interesting personality living in Richmond Road in the 1880s was a farmer, whose cows were probably the ones chewing the cud in Bennett Williams's garden. He was Benjamin Richardson and his farmhouse was known as Rose Cottage (now number 30 Richmond Road, where the brick floor of the cowshed was recently unearthed in the back garden). Richardson's father had come to Wimbledon about 1850 as bailiff to the Earl of Cottenham. After the Earl's death he settled down at the lodge situated at the bottom of Cottenham Park Road. He farmed forty-eight acres and on the side acted as a beer retailer. He was a good shot and was reputedly very strong. His great feat apparently was to jump across the wide ditch along Coombe Lane with a full sack of corn under each arm. When his grandson tried to copy him, he promptly fell in the water!

In the early 1880s, Benjamin, the youngest of the eight children, was set up by his father in a dairy farm of his own in Richmond Road. He kept a small herd of six cows, which grazed in nearby fields and supplied milk to the large houses on Copse Hill. His children, also eight in all, used to mind the cows after school and delivered the milk

Shakespeare Villas, Amity Grove, built in 1885.

in large cans. Benjamin also kept a few pigs, which when fattened he sold to Lintott, a local butcher, and several "heavy horses". These he used to pull a large farm cart, which carried sand and gravel from "Coombe Gravel Pits" (apparently at the top of Richmond Road) to new building sites. Houses around Melbury Gardens, Durham and Lambton Roads were therefore constructed with local mortar. The farm survived at least to the middle 1920s, but later became a private house.

At about the same time as Benjamin Richardson was settling in at his farm, a line of small houses was going up along Amity Grove to the east of Durham Road. The Amity Investment Company was responsible for laying out the road, putting in the drains and building the terraces of houses. But an unknown individual who was keen on English literature was responsible for the largest block, Shakespeare Villas, which still displays its date, 1885.

The new houses were served by two parades of shops that were built at the same time in Durham Road. The one nearest Coombe Lane was known as Commercial Place; the other, further up the road, was called The Market Place. By 1888 they contained a wide variety of shops: three grocers, two boot-makers (the Victorian equivalent of our shoe-repairer), a butcher, carpenter, dairy, greengrocer and tobacconist, as well as a coffee room and "fancy repository". The greengrocer was E. Warner, whose family continued to provide good fresh fruit and vegetables at very reasonable prices until well after the Second World War.

Such development, however, was on a relatively small scale. Nothing bigger could be expected until communications improved. In 1886 it was pointed out that tradesmen in Wimbledon could only deliver orders in Raynes Park by sending their

The junction of Amity Grove and Coombe Lane before the First World War. The shops on the right were demolished in the 1970s to make way for Liptons Supermarket.

189

carts round by the Ridgway or Kingston Road. The next year Bennett Williams presented a petition to the Board from the inhabitants of Cottenham Park asking for a direct link to Wimbledon through the extension of Worple Road. To support his case he cited a recent fire in the district where the fire-engine from Kingston had reached the blaze quicker than the one from Wimbledon. It took the Board four years to act, but in 1891 the extension was opened and Raynes Park was at last linked to Wimbledon.

The immediate effect showed in the building during the 1890s of two new parades of shops on the opposite side of the road to Raynes Park Station. The one nearer the Skew Arch — Raynes Park Terrace — contained a grocer (now Boots the chemist), baker, chemist and tobacconist in the same shop, dairyman and milliner. Beyond was a separate shop, a butcher's, the latest in a chain of shops belonging to Mr Way, who owned others in Hartfield and Durham Roads, and in Merton. (The shop is still a butcher's, known by its pre-war name, Hartshorns, and one of the few local shops to have kept the same trade for nearly a hundred years.) In the days before refrigerators, the animals were killed on the spot: at Way's the slaughterhouse, which was in the passage by the side of the shop.

The second parade of shops — Amity Terrace — was directly opposite the station. This included the West Barnes Farm Dairy, with Mr Prewett as manager, Mr Chapman's Bakery (now Coombes Bakery) and Hawes, estate agents. But despite the extra shops, few houses seem to have been built until the news spread in 1902 that tram lines were to be laid between Kingston and Wimbledon. Then at last a mass of small, relatively cheap terraced houses and flats went up, above all in the streets between Lambton and Pepys Roads. "Maisonettes" in Durham Road, complete with the latest luxuries, electric light and a fitted bath, could now be rented for under three pounds a month. So for the first time people began to flock into the district.

The arrival of the first tram in May 1907 was greeted as joyfully in Raynes Park as it was in Wimbledon. The children at the Primary School were given the morning off to watch it go by and were told by their teachers to look carefully as they were going to see an historic event. The trams reached Raynes Park from Kingston along the new Burlington Road and West Barnes Lane where the street had to be almost doubled in width and an avenue of a hundred elms felled. Beyond Raynes Park, where "their comings and goings were eagerly watched by curious crowds", the trams at first only went as far as Hill Road; the remaining track to Tooting was not opened until the end of June. There was a ten-minute service with a fare of four pence for the long ride between Hampton Court and Tooting. The trams proved so popular that many passengers deserted the trains which did not regain their business until the line was electrified during the First World War.

By then two of the major buildings in Raynes Park, St Matthews Church in Durham Road and the Worple Road Methodist Church, had been built. Church of England services had first been held at the Primary School in 1880. Four years later they were transferred to the hall at the top of Avenue Road (since 1914 the home of the West Wimbledon Society). The hall was also used for mothers' meetings, concerts, lectures, talks on temperance and as the headquarters of a Provident Club. By the 1890s, with the population of Raynes Park growing fast, a temporary iron church was erected at the corner of Richmond and Durham Roads (on the site of a modern block of flats). In 1903 the services became very "high" with a sung Eucharist, vestments and incense. There were noisy protests and some of the congregation, including the men in the choir, refused to attend any more. The vicar, Revd Charles Fynes-Clinton, however, persisted and commissioned Ernest Shearman to design a permanent church to be built on a new site at the corner of Spencer and Durham Roads. St Matthews was opened in 1909, a fine building notable for its

A tram passing Raynes Park Station about 1910.

A luxury covered-top tram, full of passengers, turning from West Barnes Lane into Coombe Lane about 1910.

191

beautiful rose window, known as "The Bishop's Eye". Sadly it was wrecked by a flying bomb in June 1944, but has since been rebuilt.

The Methodists were probably even more influential in Raynes Park. Their founder was Henry Palmer, "a hay and wood dealer", who lived in Richmond Road. He had first come to Wimbledon Village in 1849 and, along with John Oakman, a butcher, and Edwin Trim, a printer, had opened the first Methodist chapel in Denmark Road in 1865. He then moved to Melbourne Villas, Richmond Road, and held the first services in the farm opposite. In 1887 he was joined by a Mr and Mrs Bond, and together they took over a "Mission Hall" in Durham Road. (It survives as a warehouse, next to Jefferys, where fish has been sold since 1900.) Services were held there until March 1914 when a fine new church was opened in Worple Road. The foundation stone had been laid the previous year by Lady Holland and the money raised by contributions from the congregation, sales of work and similar activities. After the war the minister was provided with a house in Pepys Road by the church trustees — a gardener, a slate and tile merchant, a glass cutter, a civil servant, a builder and a lock manufacturer (Charles Chubb). Their occupations show the wide appeal of the Methodist movement and of the varied backgrounds of the new inhabitants of Raynes Park in the first quarter of the twentieth century.

THE STATION

Strictly speaking, neither the station nor the Skew Arch are in Wimbledon. The old parish boundary between Wimbledon and Merton runs along the middle of Coombe Lane right up to Beverley Brook. But both places are so well-known to people living north of the railway that they deserve a place in a book on Wimbledon.

Appropriately it was the Rayne family who first put forward the idea of a station. In the early 1860s Edward Rayne junior suggested one on the Epsom line by the West Barnes crossing near their farmhouse. In 1868 the idea was taken up by Richard Garth as soon as he bought West Barnes Park, but he wanted one on the main line and was prepared not merely to pay £4,000 towards its cost, but to build an "approach" to the Kingston Road from the farm drive. His scheme was accepted by the railway company, but it took three years to build the station, which finally opened on 30 October 1871.

Only thirteen years later it had to be altered when the Epsom line to Waterloo was brought into the station on a long loop. As a result the platforms had to be staggered, not placed opposite each other as at most stations, and a new booking-office built on the north side. In 1935 the station was modernised and took on its present appearance. A new exit was made on the Approach Road side. Until then the exit from the down line had been through the old tunnel under the railway (this had been built in 1838 over Rayne's drive from his farm to Coombe Lane).

THE SKEW ARCH

"The Merton Arch", as it should properly be called, probably caused more traffic problems than any other railway tunnel in the district. It was originally built by the London and Southampton Railway Company in 1838 to carry their line over the

highway to Kingston. Its angled arch was not unique and the fact that it was only eighteen feet wide did not at first cause any serious trouble.

When the track was widened in the 1850s and 1860s to take extra lines to Epsom and Kingston, the arch turned into a dark tunnel. This became very awkward when traffic on the roads increased after the opening of the Worple Road extension. As with the tunnel at Lower Downs, carts, and later cars and vans, could only go through from one direction at a time, while unfortunate pedestrians were hemmed in to the wall on a very narrow pavement.

In the 1920s plans were made to build a new, straight tunnel, but they came to nothing. Instead, traffic lights were installed and after the Second World War the tunnel was heightened and widened. Finally, in 1973, the straight tunnel was built through the embankment a little to the west and the old tunnel became a pedestrian route to Kingston Road.

23

The Theatre

In 1909, the year that saw Raynes Park's first church, Wimbledon's first cinema opened, followed the next year by its first theatre. Both proved great successes — until the 1960s. Then, while most cinemas closed, the theatre continued through crisis after crisis.

Before its opening, plays were certainly performed in Wimbledon, but they have left few traces in the records. The earliest "entertainment" mentioned in any local document was given by Sir Thomas Cecil to Queen Elizabeth I when she visited his new manor house in July 1599. The only part to survive is the opening speech in verse by the "Porter" called John Joye:

> "That your Highness may not stay to knock,
> "Take this double key and open every lock."

It sounds as if the stage was the front courtyard of the great house with its magnificent drop down two flights of steps to the park, a fine setting for the entertainment of a Queen.

Equally fine was "a glade on the Warren" (now the Royal Wimbledon Golf Course) chosen in the 1880s and the 1890s by Lady Campbell when she put on "pastoral plays" in the grounds of Cannizaro for the owner, Mrs Schuster. She used a number of amateur actors, charged high prices (for charity) and attracted a very fashionable audience, including the Prince and Princess of Wales (the future Edward VII and Queen Alexandra). "The entrance" according to Mrs Schuster's daughter, "was at the side gate opening on to Caesar's Camp and we cut narrow lanes, just wide enough for one person to pass through the bracken — often seven and eight feet high — for the audience to walk down to the sylvan theatre."

The first indoor plays seem to have been staged in local halls. At Christmas 1897, for instance, the Drill Hall in St George's Road was used by an amateur company to put on a pantomime, *Humpty Dumpty*. It was a great success. The two Baths Halls in Latimer and Worple Roads were also hired by touring companies. But clearly there was need for a permanent theatre in the new Borough.

The man who both saw the need and in 1909 determined to fill it was John Mulholland. Then in his early fifties, he had wide experience of the stage as actor, playwright, manager and above all pioneer in founding suburban playhouses. In 1894 he had opened the Metropole Theatre in Camberwell and it had proved so successful that his example was followed by other managers who built fourteen suburban

THE THEATRE

194

Merton Road before the Theatre was built. On the left is the turning into King's Road; on the right is the doctor's house which was pulled down in 1909 to provide a site for the Theatre.

theatres in the next six years. He himself opened a second in 1903, the King's Theatre, Hammersmith. This too proved a success, so "the man of vision", who believed that a theatre was essential to the life of a town, decided six years later to found another in Wimbledon.

He chose a site on the busy road linking Wimbledon and Merton, still known as Merton Road, but soon to become the Broadway. It had been occupied for the previous thirty years by a large house and garden, owned by a doctor. But for at least six centuries before that it had been part of a twenty acre field known as The Blacklands. The name is interesting. A leading expert on local history, Prof. Hoskins, says that it refers to the darkening of the soil caused either by long-continued human occupation of the site (which here is very unlikely) or by the burning of a building, often a Roman one. Whatever the origin of the name, the field is first mentioned in a document of the thirteenth century. In 1458 it was claimed by both St Thomas's Hospital and Merton Priory; a judge decided in favour of the Priory. By the eighteenth century it had become part of the large estates of the Hopkins family and, in the next century, of Mrs Phillips and her sons. They leased it to successive Watneys who grew wheat there — until Russell and Palmerston Roads were laid out about 1870.

So it was on an historic site that John Mulholland started building his "Theatre Royal" in 1909. He commissioned two architects, Cecil Masey and Roy Young, to draw up the plans. They certainly provided an impressive building. One expert has described the front as "Georgian Renaissance", whatever that may mean. It had a dome and above that eight columns, supporting a platform on which was a large globe and carved wooden "angel" (more likely a muse) eleven feet high, which dominated the sky-line of South Wimbledon. Inside, the auditorium (described as "Italian Renaissance" by one writer; as "eclectic Adamish" by Prof. Pevsner) thrilled at least one small boy. In later life Patrick Fawcett vividly remembered "the pillared entrance hall and marble staircases; the white and gold walls and ceiling of the auditorium; the crimson curtains, carpets and seats, the rich grandeur of it all". The

Mulholland's "Theatre Royal" in the 1930s with the "angel" on its globe.

theatre critic of *The Times* agreed: "For beauty and size, Wimbledon Theatre would not disgrace Shaftesbury Avenue." The stage was one of the largest in the country and therefore wonderful scenic effects could be produced. The batteries of lights were run off the theatre's own power supply. At the rear, in a special basement, there were Turkish Baths, from which heat could, if necessary, be wafted to the auditorium through ducts (the Baths are still there, under a men's outfitter).

The Theatre opened on Boxing Day 1910 with a pantomime, *Jack and Jill*. The enthusiastic audience was charged six pence for a seat in the gallery, a shilling for the pit, two shillings and six pence for the pit-stalls and three guineas for a box. In that audience was the four-year-old Patrick Fawcett. He had looked forward eagerly to seeing his first Christmas pantomime and he was not disappointed — "three hours of brilliant spectacle, music and humour". Unfortunately, the leading local paper, the *Wimbledon Borough News*, deliberately did not send a reporter to cover the historic occasion. Instead, in the issue of 31 December, the editor briefly reported the event in a tiny notice hidden half way down page five. Apparently, six years earlier he had annoyed Mulholland by campaigning for strict safety regulations in local theatres at the time the King's, Hammersmith, was opened. So "Mr Mulholland left out us alone of all the local papers in giving the announcements and advertisements by which he prefaced the opening of his theatre." In return, the editor decided not to give "free

196

advertisement to what is after all a commercial enterprise". The feud never seems to have been resolved. When John Mulholland died in June 1925, the *News* only gave him the briefest of obituaries and barely alluded to the success of his theatre in Wimbledon.

Despite this boycott, the new theatre was a great success under Mulholland's management. During its first fourteen years there was a series of "big shows" and "popular entertainers", who attracted "packed houses". Famous actors like F. R. Benson in *Hamlet*, Martin Harvey in *Tale of Two Cities* and Laurence Irving in *Typhoon*

A theatre programme of August 1920 — cover.

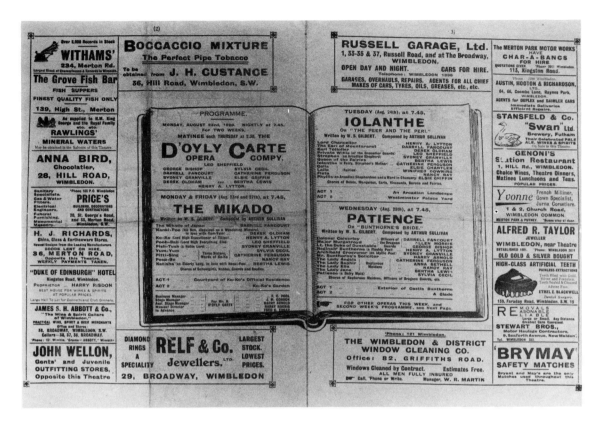

A theatre programme of
August 1920 — inside.

(just before he set out to cross the Atlantic on the maiden voyage of the Titanic);
leading companies such as the D'Oyly Carte in *Iolanthe*, the Carl Rosa Opera in
Carmen and the Imperial Russian Ballet (not long before the Revolution); well-known
variety artists — Vesta Tilley, Marie Lloyd, Harry Tate — all appeared in successive
seasons at Wimbledon, along with a special Bioscope Week of film "in glorious
colour" showing King George V's Coronation Durbar at Delhi. But of all the shows
the greatest success was the appearance of Gracie Fields in the early 1920s. She drew
such crowds that all the staff at the theatre had their wages doubled for the week.

On Mulholland's sudden death in 1925 after an operation, his widow took over the
management. The following year she achieved a further success when Sybil
Thorndike appeared as St Joan in Shaw's play. In the early 1930s, however, the
Theatre faced its first major crisis — falling attendances. The blame was laid at the
doors of the neighbouring cinemas which had been screening the new talkies. But the
economic depression and growing unemployment in South Wimbledon probably
played a part.

In fact, attendances at local cinemas in the early 1930s were equally poor. In
addition, the first of these cinemas, the Queen's, Worple Road, had been burnt down
in April 1930, fortunately when empty. The Queen's had started at the Worple Hall
in 1909 as The Electric Theatre, alongside a skating rink and a public hall. It attracted
relatively small audiences until film of Edward VII's funeral in 1910 drew record

crowds. Many who then came to a cinema for the first time returned to see normal programmes.

The Queen's, however, soon had a rival — the King's Palace, "adjoining the new Theatre Royal" in the Broadway. Its manager placed a large advertisement every week in the local paper proclaiming it "luxurious" with four hundred tip-up seats, "a complete change" of programme on Mondays and Thursdays, with "thrilling drama, uproarious comedy, beautiful travel programmes". He added that "the management have spared no effort or expense to provide a high-class entertainment and to ensure the comfort of their patrons". He even offered free teas and light refreshments to those who bought six penny or one shilling seats.

Faced with such strong competition, the Queen's retorted by proclaiming: "Continuous performances from 3 p.m. Pictures changed daily. We rely on our pictures, not on cheap gifts to the audience." Its manager went one better than the King's by taking half-page advertisements in the *Borough News*. He claimed to have made extensive improvements, so that it was now "cool in summer, warm in winter" and provided "fun without vulgarity". He even succeeded in screening up-to-date newsreels, once showing the Derby within two hours of the race finishing.

The entrance of the King's Palace Cinema, just below the Theatre. The photograph was taken about 1914.

After the end of the First World War, two more cinemas were opened: the Elite Picture Palace in the Broadway, nearly opposite the King's, and the Raynes Park Cinema (later renamed the Rialto) opposite the Skew Arch. In 1928 they began to show the new "talkies". Yet, like the Theatre, their takings were hit by the slump and by the Entertainment Tax which had first been imposed in 1916, but now seemed more of a burden. They therefore began to campaign for Sunday opening; the King's and the Elite even announced that they were losing money and would have to close unless allowed to open seven days a week. They were opposed by many who feared the secularisation of Sunday, and a poll in 1933 produced a small majority against Sunday opening. But two years later a second poll decisively reversed this vote and cinemas started showing films on Sunday 28 July 1935.

By then, however, the immediate problems of both cinemas and the Theatre seemed to be over, helped by the revival of the economy, at least in the South of England. One sign was the opening of two more cinemas in Wimbledon. In November 1933 the Regal was opened in the Broadway, just below the King's, by the Mayor with the Coldstream Guards' trumpeters and string orchestra. It was designed by a well-known cinema architect, Robert Cromie, in Art Deco style and had a grand organ and café (renamed the Odeon, it is now Wimbledon's one surviving cinema). Three years later the original Odeon was put up a short distance from the site of the old Queen's (where Bejams stands today). It also was opened by the Mayor, this time accompanied by the Band of the Scots Guards. Meanwhile, in 1935 the Theatre had found a new lease of life with Vivien Leigh playing her first great part in *The Mask of Virtue*. She was followed in the years before the Second World War by a further string of successes, above all the amazing achievement of Donald Wolfit who in one week with his Shakespeare Company played the parts of Hamlet, Macbeth, Shylock, Petruchio and Malvolio.

The First World War had not had any dramatic effect on the Theatre, beyond a notice which stated: "Soldiers in uniform admitted free and those accompanying them at half price." The Second World War, however, was very different. The threat of aerial attack persuaded the management to remove both "the angel" and the globe. Without them, the theatre was less of a sighting point for German airmen, but the dome now had, in Patrick Fawcett's words, "a sad truncated look". During the Blitz bombs came down all around the building, but none fell on it. For a time the theatre had to close, but for most of the War it continued to put on shows which helped to take people's minds off the trials of daily life.

Since 1945 Wimbledon Theatre has been in almost constant crisis. Often it has seemed on the point of closing for good, above all in 1962 when it was threatened with redevelopment. Every time so far it has been saved, largely by public support which in 1965 persuaded the Council to buy it and hand over control to Merton Civic Theatre Trust Ltd. Yet, despite all its troubles, it has attracted almost every post-war performer or company of any eminence, while many future West End comedies, thrillers and musicals, like *Oliver*, were given their premières there. Even Gracie Field's record attendances were broken by Marlene Dietrich in 1973. So Wimbledon has managed to retain one of the few theatres remaining in the London suburbs and the only one, according to an expert, "of architectural merit".

Under half a mile up the Broadway and across the railway bridge there still stands a hall which between 1929 and the 1970s also saw the production of many excellent plays. Now the Reference Department of Wimbledon Library in Compton Road, it used to be known as Marlborough Hall and was the home of the Wimbledon Repertory Company. Its founder, Eric Ward, had been one of the first pupils at Wimbledon College in the early 1890s and later returned to his old school as art master. His chief interest, however, was drama. He had started as assistant stage-manager at the Globe Theatre in London; toured with Beerbohm Tree's Company before 1914 and became an actor-manager after the War. He lived in Wimbledon and with a number of friends formed the Repertory Company in 1929 to put on regular plays at Marlborough Hall. Ward insisted on high standards both in acting and in production: he designed the sets himself; his wife designed the costumes. Over the next eleven years until another war finally forced a halt, the Company performed over forty plays, many highly praised by good judges. In 1946 Eric Ward managed to revive the Company, but he soon became seriously ill and within four years had died. The plays, however, continued until the 1970s when competition from television drama proved too strong and Marlborough Hall disappeared inside the Library.

A VERY DIFFERENT ENTERTAINMENT:
PLOUGH LANE

The road to the old Plough Inn beyond the Wandle only dates from the 1840s. It was laid out by the Copper Company to divert the road to Tooting that until then had run just to the north, through the middle of their works. Until about 1900 the new road was lined by meadows, though one on the north side was "a piece of swampland used as a refuse dump".

Immediately before the First World War the dump was cleared and the ground laid out for Wimbledon Football Club. The Club had originated in 1889 as the Old Centrals, the Old Boys of the National School in Camp Road. Their early matches

Plough Lane before the football ground was built in 1914.

201

were played on the Common, but they later moved to a ground off Worple Road West (near the bottom of Pepys Road). Plough Lane was their first real home and has remained their ground to the present day.

By this time they had played in a variety of South London Leagues. Shortly after the end of the First World War they were invited to join one of the leading amateur leagues, the Isthmian, as a Club "which is giving much promise of making a mark in the football world". In the next forty-three years they came top of the league eight times, and won the Amateur Cup in 1963. The next year the players turned professional and in 1978 earned promotion to the Football League. Only eight years later they were playing in the First Division and in 1988 astonished the country by defeating Liverpool to win the F.A. Cup. They were given an ecstatic welcome when they returned to Wimbledon and a civic reception at the Town Hall.

Wimbledon Theatre.

The Town Hall

If Merton Council had had a free hand, there would have been no Town Hall in May 1988 as a centre for the Mayor to welcome home Wimbledon Football Club in triumph. A majority of the councillors had supported a scheme to replace it with multi-storey offices and a large shopping-precinct. Just in time, however, they had been forced to modify their plan by strong local opposition, supported by the Secretary of State for the Environment.

Wimbledon Town Hall is the third building to occupy the site in the past 150 years. Until 1838 the land had been the westernmost edge of Cowdrey Farm, part of a large arable field, known as Cox's Close, across which the London and Southampton Railway Company then laid its tracks. The rest of the field was left to grow corn, except for a small plot below the railway line where the Company put up a house for the Station Master, Mr Bradford (with a garden and large pond), as well as a small cottage for a railway policeman. There they lived with their families, out in the country with only occasional trains to disturb their peace. Then in the late 1850s the first houses began to go up at the top of Hartfield Road and within twenty years, as Wimbledon became a railway junction, a new suburb sprang up south of the Broadway.

This dramatic growth presented the local authority with serious new problems. The Vestry, the regular meeting of leading ratepayers, which had governed Wimbledon reasonably well for the past three hundred years proved quite unable to deal with them effectively. So, though they continued to meet until 1885, their powers were increasingly given to a Local Board of Health of fifteen members, elected by the ratepayers. Set up in 1866 primarily to deal with sanitation and infectious disease, it was soon supervising the laying out of roads, plans for new houses, provision of a good water supply and the creation of a fire-brigade. It therefore began to employ a growing number of paid officials — a treasurer, a medical officer, a surveyor of roads, a rate-collector and a clerk, as well as road-menders and six "scavengers" to collect refuse. A proper headquarters was urgently needed.

For the first twelve years the Board's office had been a house in the Village, number 8 High Street, next door to Standen's Bakery (later Gravestock's). It was quite inadequate and too far from the main source of its problems, New Wimbledon. So in 1878 the Board bought the Station Master's property from the railway company, pulled down the house and on the site built new offices, a surveyor's residence and a fire station. The building was hardly one of great architectural merit.

Wimbledon's first Town Hall, built as Local Board offices in 1878 and pulled down in 1929.

Right: Voting paper for the election of members of the Local Board in 1883. Electors could vote for up to six people on the list and some were clearly still expected to be unable to write their names.

Fifty years later an editorial in the *Borough News* described it as "not only mean and insignificant, but hideously ugly, an eyesore which lets down the whole town". Yet it provided the new suburb with a focus for its growing civic pride. In front of its balcony, large crowds gathered to celebrate Queen Victoria's two Jubilees in 1887 and 1897, the accession of King Edward VII in 1901 and above all the granting of a Borough Charter in 1905.

Charter Day, 26 July 1905, was described by one of the people taking part in it as "a day never to be forgotten". It was the climax of seven years of debate and violent disagreement. In 1894 the Local Board had been transformed into an Urban District Council, with the same officials and largely the same members, although chosen by a wider number of electors, for the first time grouped in wards. Many of the new Councillors felt that, as Wimbledon was now a parliamentary constituency, it should have the higher dignity of a borough with its own charter and in 1898 they passed a resolution in favour of one. But this provoked strong opposition among some ratepayers who were sure it would mean "freer scope for extravagance" and claimed that the scheme was being imposed on them. At a public meeting in the Worple Hall, they secured its defeat. The Council waited six years, then canvassed each district of Wimbledon and declared that a majority now favoured the idea, except in Cottenham Park. So a petition was sent to the Privy Council asking for a charter. In July 1905 the charter received the royal assent and the first Mayor, Alderman Hamshaw and Town Clerk, Mr Butterworth, drove in a carriage to Westminster to receive it.

ELECTION OF MEMBERS OF LOCAL BOARD, 1883.

VOTING PAPER.
District of WIMBLEDON.

NO. OF VOTING PAPER.	NAME AND ADDRESS OF VOTER.	NUMBER OF VOTES.	
		As Owner.	As Ratepayer.

Initials of the Voter against the Names of the Persons for whom he intends to Vote	NAMES OF THE PERSONS NOMINATED.	RESIDENCE OF THE PERSONS NOMINATED.	QUALITY OR CALLING OF THE PERSONS NOMINATED.	NAME OF THE NOMINATOR, OR OF ONE OF THE NOMINATORS.	ADDRESS OF THE NOMINATOR.
	Belham, Stephen	Osborne House, Griffith Road	Builder	Paxton, James	Wandle Bank Villa, South Wimbledon
	Chatterton, George	Linton, Grosvenor Hill	Civil Engineer	Holland, E. Thurstan / Norcott, William B.	Cotswold, Lansdowne Road, Grosvenor Hill [Wimbledon
	Cole, Arthur Lowry	12, Lansdowne Road, Wimbledon	Colonel	Gore, Charles / Norcott, William B.	Wimbledon Common / Grosvenor Hill
	Diggens, J. G. A.	30, Griffith Road	Civil Service	Wilcock, John E.	Ardincaple, Worple Road
	Fenton, Charles	18, Courthope Villas, Wimbledon	Gentleman	Arnold, C. T.	2, Thornton Hill, Wimbledon
	Hellier, Henry James	Seymour House, Merton Road, S. Wimbledon	Home Office	Crickmay, Herbert John / Stride, Edward Ernest	66, Merton Road, S. Wimbledon / Highbury, 31, Lingfield Road, Wimbledon
	Little, Edward	South Wimbledon	Doctor of Medicine	Norcott, William B.	Grosvenor Hill
	Mason, Thomas	50, The Broadway, South Wimbledon	Land and Estate Agent	Croft, Henry C.	The Common, Wimbledon
	Mellin, Joseph Phillips	Brompton House, High Street, Wimbledon	Chemist	Cousens, George / Norcott, William B. / Palmer, Henry A.	5, Hartfield Road, Wimbledon / Grosvenor Hill / 1, Melbourn Villa, Cottenham Park, Wimbledon
	Olley, Alfred	Berkeley Terrace, Ridgway, Wimbledon	Surveyor, etc.	Ward, Alfred	The Elms, 69, Hartfield Road
	Townsend, John	Lingfield Road	House and Estate Agent	Norcott, William B. / Paxton, James	Grosvenor Hill / Wandle Bank Villa, South Wimbledon
	Welsford, Henry G.	9, Southey Road	Schoolmaster	Walker, Henry Burtwell	17, Southey Road
	Wright, William James	The Homestead, Herbert Road, Wimbledon	Merchant	Gowan, J. G.	Woodlands, 36, Crooked Billet

I vote for the Persons in the above LIST (not exceeding SIX) against whose Names my Initials are placed.

Signed _____

Or the Mark of _____

Witness to the Mark _____

Or _____ *Proxy for* _____

DIRECTIONS TO THE VOTER.

The Voter must write his Initials against the name of every Person for whom he votes, not exceeding SIX, and must subscribe his Name and Address at full length.

If the Voter cannot write, he must make his Mark instead of Initials, but such mark must be attested by a Witness, and such Witness must write the Initials of the Voter against the name of every Person for whom the Voter intends to vote.

If a Proxy votes he must in like manner write his Initials, subscribe his own name and address, and add after his signature the name of the body of Persons for whom he is Proxy.

This paper will be collected on the 7th day of April, between the hours of 8 a.m. and 10 p.m.

(Copyright.)
Election Form.
PUBLIC HEALTH ACT, 1875.

Printed by Edwin Trim, 30, Homefield Road, Wimbledon.

Their return with the charter was greeted by huge crowds in glorious summer weather. They were followed up the gaily decorated Broadway by a procession of nearly fifty carriages, escorted by the Surrey Yeomanry and a Volunteer Band. At the Council Offices, now the Town Hall, which had been covered with bunting, the charter was read to an assembly of distinguished guests who included the Lord Mayor of London, the Lord-Lieutenant of Surrey, local M.P.s and many Mayors. The procession then went on up Hill Road under a series of floral arches, bearing such inscriptions as "Prosperity to Wimbledon" and "Success to our Borough". It finally reached King's College School where the guests were treated to a large lunch in the hall and a long selection of speeches.

Meantime, on the Common the ordinary people of Wimbledon were having their own celebrations. They were first entertained with a "Grand Military Display and Tournament" by the Imperial Surrey Yeomanry. Then nearly seven thousand school children from South Wimbledon, fortified with ginger beer, cake, sweets and four tickets "of the value of a half-penny each to be used on the Common for refreshments or roundabouts as they might wish", were marched there "in regular and orderly formation", accompanied by a Salvation Army Band. At the same time, five hundred old people enjoyed a high tea in the Drill Hall, St George's Road. Next came two great processions to the Common. First a Carnival Procession started from Queens Road; it was two miles long and consisted of decorated tradesmen's carts and people in fancy dress riding on bicycles or on horseback. Then at nightfall a torchlight procession went up the hill, now lit by hundreds of Chinese lanterns. At last came the grand finale when the Mayor set light to a huge bonfire on the Common, which became the signal for fireworks and further illuminations all over Wimbledon.

The great day was over. It had cost just under seven hundred pounds and the editor of the local paper, under its new title *Wimbledon Borough News*, thought on balance that it had been well worthwhile. "We do not expect to see in the new form of government any great improvement on the old. But never yet was a borough launched under happier auspices."

The new borough was fortunate in the dedication of at least two of its permanent officials, the Medical Officer of Health, Dr Pocklington, and the Surveyor, Charles Cooper. Pocklington was Wimbledon's first Medical Officer and remained responsible for the health of the district for nearly forty years until he was compulsorily retired in 1909 when in his early seventies. He presided over an amazing improvement in public health. His establishment in 1876 of a Fever Hospital for infectious diseases like scarlet fever, diphtheria and typhoid, once prevalent in the suburb, played a major part in keeping epidemics under control. He also did his best to improve the bad condition of drains, dirty overcrowded houses with drinking-water cisterns which were "the last resting place of mice, birds, etc. and these decomposing", the poor state of workshops and the wrong feeding of children. In 1901 he even had to take precautions "in the unfortunate event of the outbreak of plague". Yet, by the time of his retirement, the Borough's death rate was just over half the national average and better than any but two of the chief towns in England.

Charles Hamlet Cooper worked in the Surveyor's Department for exactly forty years. He started as Assistant Surveyor in 1878, took full control in 1890, officially retired in 1918, but was then made Consulting Borough Engineer, a post he held until

Above: A large crowd of people outside the Town Hall listening to speeches, probably to mark the accession of King George V in May 1910.

Left: Charter Day, 26 July 1905. The charter is being read to the crowd outside the Town Hall.

his death in 1932. A hard working and very knowledgeable man, who was said to have "beneath a rugged exterior a large and sympathetic heart", he played as crucial a part as Dr Pocklington in helping to make Wimbledon a pleasant place in which to live. The extent of his concerns is shown by the detailed reports and papers he wrote both for the Council and for learned Societies. Vital topics like the treatment of sewage, the collection and disposal of house refuse, water supply, flooding, burials, footways, trees, flowers and seats by the side of roads, the adaptation of highways for modern traffic, all aroused his interest and keen mind. The solutions that he found to such problems, notably the fine pathway that he designed on the east side of Hill Road, left a lasting mark on the Borough, of which he was rightly made a Freeman in 1919.

In that same year the total inadequacy of the old Board Offices for the work of the new Borough was starkly revealed. Until then the Council had been able to use a large hall in Queens Road for its more important meetings. But when this ceased to be available, the Town Hall could not provide a suitable room. The Mayor complained that he sometimes found it difficult to distinguish councillors from members of the public, who themselves often joined in the debates. In addition, the council offices were scattered in different buildings all over Wimbledon.

So in 1923 a Town Hall Committee was formed to draw up a scheme for an entirely new civic centre. Straight away they encountered a major snag: the Minister of Health in Ramsay Macdonald's first Labour Government of 1924 would not allow them to borrow the necessary money, saying it was needed for more houses. But the return to power of Stanley Baldwin and the Conservatives, along with a revival in the economy, allowed the Council to go ahead with their scheme. In 1927 their Committee invited architects "of British nationality" to submit designs for the new Town Hall, with a prize of two hundred pounds for the best. One hundred and fourteen did so and, after long consideration, A. J. Hope, a Lancastrian, was declared the winner as his plans showed "architectural quality of no mean order" and most nearly fulfilled the council's conditions for the building: "It should be dignified and indicate its purpose; it should rely on good proportions and a fitting architectural setting rather than an elaborate decoration and detail."

When the winning design was published in 1928, it seems to have been generally praised as "a fine building". Only later, once building started just as the Wall Street Crash of 1929 hit the world economies, did critics claim that it was wrong to spend money on a large public building at a time of slump. In fact, the building provided work and the Council borrowed the money (estimated to be just over £150,000 at the start and found to be less than £50,000 more when the work had been completed). The building, carried out by a firm from Camberwell, took little more than eighteen months. The foundation stone was laid in February 1930 and the finished Town Hall was opened on 5 November 1931 by Prince George, later Duke of Kent, President of the All-England Lawn Tennis Club. There followed a week of celebrations, presided over by the Mayor, Alderman Bathgate (who was elected Mayor three times and is commemorated by a road off Parkside which was renamed in his honour). There was a baby show and pram contest in South Park Gardens, a display by the Fire Brigade and a grand firework finale.

For the next thirty-four years the Town Hall provided a dignified and practical centre for grand civic occasions, the regular meetings of the Council and the day-today administration of the Borough. The Civic Hall, which was built on extra land acquired from the railway, played a central part in its success. It could seat 1,500 people and had excellent acoustics. It was therefore ideal for large public meetings, for concerts and for school prize-days.

In 1963, however, not long after the Golden Jubilee of the Borough Charter, the Government of London Act was passed by Parliament. Under it Wimbledon was merged with Merton, Morden and Mitcham to form the new London Borough of Merton. The idea of a merger was not new. In 1918 Wimbledon, Merton and Morden had been linked in a single parliamentary constituency. So in 1919 Wimbledon Council proposed the amalgamation of the three districts under a single local authority. The idea was rejected by Merton and Morden Urban District Council, doubtless fearing domination by their much larger neighbour. Had this proposal, which had both history and common interests to support it, been revived in 1963 the future of the new London Borough might have been happier. Instead, Mitcham, which had had few links with Wimbledon throughout its long history, was added, seemingly in the interests of administrative convenience.

As a result, the launch of the London Borough of Merton on 1 April 1965 was not welcomed in Wimbledon. The town had governed itself competently for just four hundred years. Now it was powerless to stop what the *Wimbledon News* (ostentatiously dropping the "Borough" in its title) referred to as "The Big Take-Over". The Conservative M.P. for Wimbledon, Sir Cyril Black, who alone of his party had voted against the new Act, summed up the feelings of many when he declared: "We are going into the new venture hoping for the best, but fearing the worst." At a dinner he gave in the House of Commons to honour prominent citizens of the old borough, he rightly predicted that "Wimbledon will live on and retain its unique character which has signally evoked the love and loyalty of its people." Another speaker, Sir James Cassels, Chairman of the Commons' Conservators, remarked that he had never seen a funeral gathering at which the mourners tried so hard to look cheerful.

Since 1965 Wimbledon has certainly remained "a well-defined community within the boundaries of the larger borough". Its citizens too have remained cheerful, although often very critical of the policies of their new Council. The Town Hall, however, has inevitably followed the fate of the previous Local Board Offices in becoming totally inadequate for the work of a large Council and its vastly increased number of officials. So in 1985 Merton's headquarters were transferred to Crown House, Morden, and the Town Hall became redundant.

MUNICIPAL BUILDINGS

Professor Pevsner, who dismissed the Town Hall as "stone-faced, symmetrical and dull", rather liked "the jollier municipal buildings" just behind it in Queens Road, as they are "in the stripy style of the turn of the century". Both the Magistrates' Court of 1895 and the Fire Station of 1904 are now out of use, but like the exterior of the Town Hall, their facades have been saved by the Secretary of State for the Environment and have to be embodied in any future development.

The work of the Magistrates' Court is often unexciting, but the Justices and their Clerks have a crucial role in maintaining order and protecting ordinary people and

THE TOWN HALL

their property. The cases that come before them used to be fully reported in the pages of the *Wimbledon News*. Two old issues selected at random show the Court at work.

In the last week of December 1897 four J.P.s, including John Townsend, had to deal with a labourer from Mitcham "drunk and disorderly", a man from Hartfield Road "driving a carriage without a light" and another from Queens Road "allowing his dog to be at large without a muzzle" (presumably during a rabies scare). Then in July 1905 a far more dramatic case, reported almost verbatim, came up before Mr C. Tyrrell Giles and Surgeon-Major McSheehy. The *News* printed it under the headline: "Rowdyism at Cottenham Park: Police Attacked." A young labourer and his brother who lived in Amity Grove had been lying in a field in Durham Road drinking beer, bought at a neighbouring off-licence. A policeman walked by and knowing the pair made some remark. The labourer replied with a string of "obscene language" and followed the policeman down the road and into Coombe Lane. There, in front of

The old Fire Station in the High Street. Built in 1890, it was closed in 1907 and is now used as shops.

Dunmore House, just beyond Avenue Road, he caught up with him, shouted: "You have always been onto me and now I am going to finish you", and hit him in the chest. The policeman grappled him to the ground and tried to blow his whistle for help, but his opponent pulled it out of his mouth. Fortunately, Miss Bertha Ediss, who lived at Dunmore, saw what was happening, rushed out, picked up the whistle and blew it. Two other policemen soon arrived and with a liberal use of their truncheons finally overpowered the labourer, who was "kicking and plunging all over the road". They took him to Wimbledon Police Station which had recently been transferred to Queens Road from the Broadway (it had to move in 1900 when Victoria Crescent was built over its site). When the case came up in court, Mr Tyrell Giles sentenced the man to three months' hard labour, because "when a severe assault is committed on the police, it must be visited by severe punishment".

The Fire Station was built in 1904 in a determined attempt to improve the performance of the Volunteer Fire Brigade. The Brigade had been formed in 1869, primarily to deal with fires in South Wimbledon (the Village had had its own small fire-engine, kept in the High Street since the early years of the century). Until 1884 it only had a manual fire-engine, drawn by horses and manned by firemen dressed in gleaming brass helmets. But then they received their first steam fire-engine named "Perseverance" and celebrated its arrival with a big parade through the decorated

Wimbledon Fire Brigade parading at Wimbledon House, Parkside with their two steamer fire-engines in May 1894.

211

streets, followed by a huge banquet. Another "steamer", called "May Queen", arrived in 1890 and this was kept in a new fire-station built in the High Street (it survives, opposite the Dog and Fox, with the old village clock above it). Five years later the Brigade opened a third station in Raynes Park at the top of Amity Grove, where they kept a pony-driven hose cart, known as "Victoria". They also set up six "telephone call-points" for quick warning of fires. Their efficiency, however, was called into question in 1900 when the old Cannizaro House was burnt down. The firemen blamed its destruction on an inadequate supply of water, but many Councillors felt that the fire-fighting system needed improving.

So first the old Fire Station by the side of the Local Board Offices was replaced by a new one at the rear in Queens Road. Then in 1907 Captain H. J. Butler was put in charge and told to reorganise the Brigade. He closed the substations and concentrated all the appliances at Queens Road. To man them, he insisted on having full-time, paid firemen, as well as some part-timers. Above all, he aimed to speed up the arrival of the engines at a fire, helped by the replacement in 1913 of the horses by motors. The Brigade proved its new efficiency during the First World War, when it had to deal with air-raid damage, especially from dud anti-aircraft shells. When Captain Butler retired in 1937, he had transformed not only the Wimbledon fire-service, but the status of firemen. He was also able to claim that once his Brigade arrived on the scene of a fire, no life had ever been lost.

13 QUEENS ROAD

For long the local office of the Metropolitan Water Board, this shop opposite the Town Hall became the offices of the *Wimbledon News* in the early 1970s. Until then the paper had been produced in St George's Road in a parade of shops on the site of the underground car park.

The *News* was not Wimbledon's first newspaper. That honour goes to *The Surrey Independent and Mid-Surrey Standard; Wimbledon, Merton and Tooting Mercury; Putney, Barnes, Mortlake, Roehampton and Wandsworth News*, which had been founded in 1876 to cover that large area. In fact, it soon concentrated on Wimbledon and Merton, and provided a good coverage of local news (until it ceased publication in 1905 on the death of its proprietor). In the 1880s and early 1890s it was followed by several rivals, but all quickly failed except the *Wimbledon Gazette* which lasted for twenty-five years between 1892 and 1917, and the *Wimbledon News* which started two years later in 1894 and is now nearing its century.

The secret of its success lay in the personality of W. H. Stoakley who took over as editor in 1895 and remained in charge for over thirty years. He had worked as a journalist on *The Surrey Independent* and showed great enterprise in taking over the *News* with little capital to back him. He had a long struggle to keep the paper going, but succeeded through his determination to be both fair and frank. He had strong views on local issues, but was never afraid to let those who thought differently have their say and, as Sir Tyrrell Giles J.P. commented on the paper's thirtieth anniversary in 1924: "You seldom fail to give all the news that is going." Stoakley reported everything of importance in Wimbledon — council debates, local meetings, shows, court cases, deaths — and he did not sensationalise the news. To readers of today, his tightly printed pages with very few illustrations and small headlines might appear uninteresting, but to anyone interested in the past they are now "a wonderful budget of Wimbledon's history".

One thing the old issues show is that problems seldom change in Wimbledon. In the thirtieth anniversary issue of 1924, there is a letter from the great Baptist preacher, Charles Ingrem, asking Stoakley to continue to campaign on urgently-needed local reforms: the infrequent emptying of dustbins, the poor state of the roads, the need to build more houses for young families and the over-large size of classes in the schools. He finished: "Wimbledon yet needs what it has now had these thirty years — a forward-moving paper, with a forward-looking Editor in the chair."

THE RAILWAY STATION

The present Station, not far from the Town Hall, dates from 1930, the fifth to be built in less than a hundred years.

The original Wimbledon and Merton Station of 1838 lay on the opposite side of the road (about where Dixons is now). It only had two platforms, which were reached down a steep narrow staircase. When the Croydon line was built in 1855, its station was on the opposite side of the line, reached from Hartfield Road. In the early 1880s, after the opening of new lines to Kingston and Tooting, a new booking office for all the lines was built on the London side of the bridge with a cab-rank for hansoms and four-wheelers on a road in front. Finally in 1889, down a sloping ramp, a separate District Line Station was added just to the north of the main line.

The forecourt of Wimbledon Station about 1910 with horse-cabs waiting for hire. The booking office for the London and South Western Railway is in the centre of the photograph, that for the District Railway is to the left.

In the early years of the present century Patrick Fawcett often used the station. He later recalled that the bridge over the railway had no shops on it, but was "just a road bridge with a brick and iron parapet wall, over which, if one was tall enough, one could see the railway track and trains". The station, he remembered, was made "of brick, grey with age and smoke" with "the platforms connected by an enclosed wooden foot-bridge". Until 1915 when the line was electrified, all the trains were "steam, with light green engines and brown carriages". A railway guide of 1909 shows that Patrick could have reached Waterloo in fourteen minutes, that on average he rarely had to wait longer than ten minutes for a train to London and that his father could buy a yearly first-class season ticket to Waterloo for £14.

West Wimbledon Society Mace
Plaque "1881"

25

The Wimbledon Society Museum

The special trowel used to lay the foundation stone of the Town Hall in 1930, as well as the programme printed to celebrate its opening eighteen months later can both be seen in the Wimbledon Society Museum at the corner of the Ridgway and Lingfield Road. They are just two of the innumerable items exhibited or stored there which are of interest to the casual visitor and of real value to a local historian.

The first brief account of the history of Wimbledon, however, is not to be found in the Museum. It was written in the late eighteenth century by Revd Daniel Lysons, a curate first at Mortlake and then at Putney. He had become interested in the history. of the two parishes; his interest extended to neighbouring villages, including Wimbledon, and in the end to all the country places around the capital. He visited each, walked around notebook in hand, studying particularly the church with all its monuments, and the great houses and their families. He then wrote to the parsons and the chief landowners for further information and spent hours researching in libraries. Finally in 1792 he produced the first volume of his *Environs of London* (four more volumes appeared in the next eight years, with a supplement in 1811). His account inevitably concentrated on the parson and the squire, but it was the work of a pioneer and all later historians of the places in the London area have been in his debt, whether or not they acknowledged it. At Wimbledon he had obviously liked the "spacious and beautiful" grounds of Wimbledon House, Parkside; he had noticed that the parish church had been rebuilt in 1788 "with grey stock bricks"; and he recorded that horse races "for the King's Plate" had been held on the Common in 1718.

Lysons' book was one of the sources used by the Wimbledon curate, William Bartlett, when he came to write his far more detailed *History and Antiquities* in the early 1860s. He also made use of two large Histories of Surrey which had come out after Lysons: Manning and Bray (1814) and Brayley and Britton (1841). It was the publication of such massive works that aroused interest in Wimbledon's past among the professional and businessmen who came to live there in the 1850s and 1860s.

Among them the most influential was Joseph Toynbee, the ear and throat specialist, who lived on Parkside. He was fascinated by "the common objects of nature which surround us", as well as by "rare and curious objects" from the past. In 1862 he proposed at a meeting of the Committee of the Village Club that they should "foster" such interests by setting up a local museum. There had been one previous museum in Wimbledon — the collection of antiquities (statues, urns, busts, sarcophagi) which Lyde Browne had displayed at Cannizaro in the 1770s — but it had contained no local exhibits. Toynbee's idea was very different. He wanted a museum

WIMBLEDON
SOCIETY MUSEUM

215

"for the reception of specimens in natural history or in antiquities found within the radius of six miles from the parish church". He hoped that this would create such interest that in time every house in the parish would have its own museum collection. His scheme interested his fellow members and he was promptly appointed Treasurer of the Wimbledon Museum Committee. Sadly, the scheme went no further. In 1866 Toynbee died while conducting an experiment with chloroform, and without his enthusiasm to drive them on the Club shelved the project.

It was not taken up again until the early years of the present century. Then in 1903 a leader writer on the *Pall Mall Gazette*, Richardson Evans a man in his late fifties, was shown a copy of Toynbee's little book, *Hints for the Formation of Local Museums*. He had lived in Wimbledon for over twenty-five years and had already started to make his own collection of local objects of interest. His chief interest was neither antiquarian nor scholarly, but "to protect and improve the grace, dignity and picturesque

Joseph Toynbee, the distinguished ear and throat specialist, who lived on Parkside. He put forward the first idea for a Wimbledon Museum in 1862.

Richardson Evans, who founded the John Evelyn Club (now the Wimbledon Society) in 1903. He lived at the Keir.

amenities of the area". He had already founded a National Society for Checking the Abuses of Public Advertising (S.C.A.P.A). He was now hard at work starting one of the first local conservation societies, the John Evelyn Club.

Ten years earlier, in 1893, he had found little support for such a society. But when he made a second attempt in 1902, he roused considerable interest among leading Wimbledonians, notably the architects Sir Thomas Jackson and Francis Penrose, the barrister George Edwards-Jones, the patron of explorers Llewellyn Longstaff, and the electrical engineer Sir William Preece. So early the next year he held a public meeting at which he explained his choice of title: "I use the word Club as I aim to bring people together in a friendly way to talk over common interests, not to frighten

Sir Thomas Jackson, a leading architect, who lived at Eagle House from 1888 until his death in 1924. He was the first President of the John Evelyn Club.

them with the notion that they are radical reformers. I suggest the John Evelyn Club as the name because I know no other character in English History who showed so delicate a love of nature, such cultivated taste in art and such genial familiarity with the ways of man as the author of *Sylva* and *The Memoirs*." He won general support for the title and for the aims he set the new Club: to safeguard the amenities of the district; to promote an interest in local history and wildlife; and to preserve objects of historical and natural interest.

Over the next twenty-five years, until Richardson Evans's death in 1928, his Club achieved considerable success in these aims. Campaigns by its members helped to preserve part of the old Village Green, parts of Wimbledon Park as an open space, all Wandle Park as a public recreation ground and above all the "Common Extension" or Beverley Meads which was saved from development just before the Kingston By-Pass was built in the 1920s. Lectures on local history and guided walks

218

on the Common helped to spread interest in Wimbledon's past and concern about its present condition. Above all, a local museum was at last set up and now serves as the ideal memorial to a man about whom the Vicar of St Mary's commented at the time of his death: "Wimbledon would have been a less attractive place had it not been for the indefatigable efforts of Richardson Evans."

The Museum was opened on 19 October 1916, in the middle of the First World War. But it had been talked about for the previous eleven years both by members of the Club and the Borough Council. The Council had its own exhibits stored in the Public Library and for a time thought of opening a Museum and Art Gallery in Wandlebank House. Nothing practical was done, however, until October 1915 when the committee of the Village Club, anxious to improve their finances, asked

A notice of November 1917, announcing the days on which the Museum was open.

THE

WIMBLEDON MUSEUM

of the JOHN EVELYN CLUB

Is now installed in the Reading Room of the Village Club, and the entrance to it is by the door in the Lingfield Road only.

Members of the John Evelyn Club with their friends are admitted free during all hours when the Reading Room is open, other visitors are admitted between the hours of 11 a.m. and 4 p.m., on the introduction of any Member of the John Evelyn Club, or on application to the Hall-keeper.

All Visitors are requested to enter their names and addresses in the Visitors' Book.

The Secretary to the Museum Committee acts as Curator and attends on SATURDAYS from 2.30 to 4.30 p.m. Visitors who wish to examine objects not placed on exhibition should apply to the Curator during that time.

Communications intended for the Museum Committee should be addressed to its Secretary, at the Lecture Hall.

November, 1917. MARGARET GRANT,
Lecture Hall,   Secretary to the Museum Committee.
    Wimbledon.   E. CLAPHAM,
                 Hon. Secretary to the Village Club.

Richardson Evans if he was interested in leasing their Reading room as a meeting place and museum. An agreement was soon reached and by the summer of 1916 the Richardson Evans collection had been installed at a cost of only thirty pounds, as "no new furniture was to be ordered or new work done", so as to avoid "any diversion of labour from national purposes of prime importance". The formal opening, at which all were expected to wear "morning dress", was accompanied by a reception and tea in the Lecture Hall, a display of "objects of special interest" in the new Museum and a talk by the first Chairman of the Museum Committee, Dr Bather, a Deputy-Keeper at the British Museum.

A few days before the opening, Margaret Grant had been appointed the first Curator. Miss Grant, rather a formidable Scottish lady, was Almoner at Wimbledon Hospital. She was a tireless worker who loved Wimbledon and its past, and was determined to make the Museum an outstanding success. For the next thirty years, until she retired just after the end of the Second World War, she presided in the room almost every Saturday afternoon from 3 p.m. to 6 p.m. and often at other times during the week. She organised talks and exhibitions there; she wrote many short articles for the *Borough News*; she secured numerous items for the Museum, above all the massive mahogany table (bought in 1927 for £3.10.0) and the Hope collection of Hassell water-colours and drawings of houses in Wimbledon and Merton (bought in 1922 for £32); she even suggested popularising the Museum by holding tea parties there. She rightly won praise for "the enthusiastic and expert way" she carried out her duties.

Her years at the Museum, however, were far from easy. Within two years of its opening, the room had to be cleared in October 1918 as the Village Club and Lecture Hall had been "commandeered for military use". Fortunately, the President of the John Evelyn Club, Sir Thomas Jackson, allowed the collection to be stored in his home, Eagle House — except for the cases of stuffed birds and animals, which were taken to the Public Library. Not for a year could the collection be returned and the Museum (now known officially as "the John Evelyn Club Museum for Wimbledon") be reopened. Then in 1924 the Village Club decided that they wanted their old Reading Room back and offered to exchange it for "two adjacent rooms which could be made into one, not so pretty and not so well lighted, but they could be locked up". This final advantage led the Museum Committee to agree to the move, but first they had to whitewash the walls which had been in two different colours. The new room was soon "abused". People referred to as "strangers" (i.e. non-members of the John Evelyn Club) were said to be using it to shelter from the weather or to meet friends; they were leaving the door unlocked, scattering books on the floor and tearing pages out of the Visitors' Book; some even smoked! The Museum Committee promptly tightened the rules for admission and decreed that the room would be closed to the public except on Saturday afternoons when the Curator would be there.

Miss Grant faced her worst moments during the Second World War. In November 1939 she was told that the "irreplaceable" part of the collection could be stored in "a place of safety" — the cellars of the Town Hall. So she carefully packed all the water-colours, engravings, prints, maps, documents, photographs, slides and books in special cases, loaded them into a van and drove them down the hill to the Town Hall. There she was met by the Mayor, Councillor Crowe, who took one look at the serried ranks of boxes, condemned the lot as "worthless" and refused to allow

The Museum in 1926.

even one into his cellars. Apparently he had thought "the Club's records" meant only "a small packet of papers that could be laid on a shelf". Miss Grant's immediate reaction is not recorded, but she was forced to bring everything back up the hill and store the collection temporarily in the Lecture Hall. She concluded her report on the incident with the telling sentence: "The Museum Room is all upset, the work of months having been upset in a day"—and promptly asked for three months' leave of absence to recover!

When she returned in February 1940, she found that the collection had already been stored in two "excellent cellars" under the Clock House, Windmill Road and Grangemuir, Southside. So she tried to reopen the Museum, only to be forced to close it again during the Battle of Britain and to obliterate its notice-board, presumably to prevent enemy parachutists realising that they had reached the Ridgway. That October, during the Blitz, the roof was damaged by an unexploded anti-aircraft shell. So the Museum remained closed for the rest of the War. The "irreplaceable" part of the collection, now all together again in the Clock House, nearly disappeared in one of the "tip and run" raids by an isolated German bomber in March 1944. A bomb fell on Windmill Road, seriously damaging the Clock House. Almost miraculously the Museum collection "escaped injury" and had to be moved yet again

— to two strong rooms in the old Council offices, Kingston Road. There it remained in safety for the rest of the War.

The Museum reopened in September 1945. An association, Friends of the Museum, was set up to help Miss Grant catalogue and arrange the exhibits, as well as to look after the room on Saturday afternoons. In the spring of the following year most of the stored collection was returned to the Museum, although a number of "irreplaceable" items, especially eighteenth century field-maps of Wimbledon and documents about the Janssen family, had somehow disappeared. Miss Grant now felt that with the Museum back in working order her duty was done and in the summer of 1946 she resigned as Curator. She was thanked for her "outstanding work" and presented with a silver salver and cheque in recognition of her thirty years' service. She continued to attend meetings of the Museum Committee until just before her death in 1954.

In her last years she nearly saw the achievement of the goal Richardson Evans had dreamed of — the creation of a permanent Wimbledon Museum. Negotiations seem to have been started with the Council in 1937 and just before the War councillors were "invited to tea to see the collection". As this move led nowhere, the John Evelyn Club set up its own special committee in November 1944 "to acquire a house suitable for use as a Museum". They advised the purchase of Eagle House both because of its character and the fact that it was on the 93 bus route and so "easily available" from South Wimbledon. Shortly after the end of the War they discovered that the Council too had chosen the house as a Borough Museum and Art Gallery. So negotiations were reopened and in 1947 the club agreed to transfer its collection to the Council on permanent loan, so long as it was adequately cared for and exhibited in Eagle House on at least three afternoons a week. The Council in return agreed to prepare three rooms on the first floor of the house for a Museum and Art Gallery, under the care of a part-time Curator.

Within four years the Club's hopes had been dashed. Repair work started on Eagle House, but the builders discovered that there was far more wrong with the brick-work than they had expected and the cost began to mount. In 1949 the repairs were suspended. The following year the Club suggested they should be restarted and the Museum installed as the ideal way for Wimbledon to celebrate the Festival of Britain. Instead, "because of financial stringency", the Council finally decided in 1951 to give up the idea of creating a Museum and Art Gallery, a sad end to an imaginative scheme.

So the recently renamed John Evelyn Society had to continue housing and supporting a small and quite inadequate Museum out of their own resources. They tried opening it on Sunday afternoons instead of Saturdays to attract more visitors, but this was not a success and in 1956 they returned to the traditional Saturday. They published their first local history pamphlet in 1947, Guy Boas's *Wimbledon, Has it a History?*, which sold well. In 1950 they at last found a new Curator, Herbert Warren, who made a number of models for the Museum and gave many talks on local history. As a result, the number of visitors, including parties of school children, passed the thousand mark every year in the late 1960s.

Several Committee members, however felt that the Museum had become almost a relic itself and was in need of a major overhaul. Led by Guy Parsloe, a distinguished historian and leading figure in the Institute of Welding, they set up a new Museum

The Museum in 1989.

Committee in 1973. First they tried to secure larger premises either in the White House, Hill Road, or in the Windmill, but once again they found no support from the Council (as was to be the case ten years later with Cannizaro, which instead became a hotel). So they appealed to the members of the Society for £6,000 to clean and restore the collections, redecorate and refurnish the Museum and compile a new and complete catalogue.

Their appeal met with a very generous response. As a result, the Museum Room was transformed and became much lighter, with a more up-to-date display of part of the Society's collection. At the same time the deeds of Nelson's house, Merton Place, were bought for the Society and a start was made on the long task of conserving the water-colours and engravings which mainly have to be kept in store for lack of adequate space to show them. Finally, in 1982 the Society itself was brought up-to-date when the misleading "John Evelyn" was dropped and the name was changed to The Wimbledon Society.

THE LECTURE HALL

For over sixty years the hall attached to the Village Club was used for John Evelyn Society lectures. Originally built in 1859 at the same time as the Club, it has been put to many other uses. In its first twenty years, Toynbee's lectures and penny readings were held there, as well as Earl Spencer's public meeting in 1864 to announce his plan to enclose the Common. In addition the hall was used for Scripture classes for servants, dancing, fencing and boxing lessons, and even drill for men of the Rifle Corps.

In 1878 it was enlarged and central heating was installed. Now it could be used for dinners, concerts, exhibitions and even political debates. During the Second World War it was requisitioned and put to an entirely new use: the temporary housing of families who had been bombed out of their homes. The hall was partitioned into a number of "rooms", each for one family. Only in 1949 was the last family moved out and the Hall returned to the Club.

THE WAR MEMORIAL

This Memorial to nearly 200 men from Wimbledon killed in action during the First World War was unveiled by the M.P. for Wimbledon, Sir Joseph Hood, on 5 November 1921. It had been designed by Sir Thomas Jackson who lived less than a hundred yards away at Eagle House (he was also responsible for the Warrior Chapel in the parish church). Since then it has been the focus for the services on every Armistice Day or Remembrance Sunday.

The Memorial seems to have been placed on the last surviving piece of the old Village Green, rather than near the Town Hall, because the Common was used as an Army training ground in the First World War. In 1915 a huge camp was set up to the west of Windmill Road and was used first for Kitchener's Volunteers and later for conscripts. It did not disappear until 1921, along with a large Y.M.C.A. hut for the soldiers' recreation, situated on the edge of the Common, near the site of the Memorial.

The Air Force also used the Common. For a short time early in the War a few fighter planes were based on the open ground between the Windmill and Parkside; one struck the roof of a house in Parkside on take-off and crashed. There were many air-raid warnings, especially in 1916 and 1917, when both Zeppelins and Gotha heavy bombers appeared near or over Wimbledon. But only one bomb (an unexploded one near Rydons on the Ridgway) seems to have fallen in the district. It was a very different story in the Second World War, as can be seen from Norman Plastow's excellent account, *Safe as Houses*.

QUEEN ALEXANDRA'S COURT

This fine collection of brick mansions, built in Georgian style, stand near the bottom of St Mary's Road. Officially the Royal Homes for the Widows and Unmarried Daughters of Army, Navy and Air Force Officers, the Court was built in 1904 to the designs of the firm of Ernest George and Yeates. It was opened on 15 July 1905 by King Edward VII and Queen Alexandra. The Queen had taken great interest in the scheme from its start and had subscribed £5,000 from her War Fund, set up to help soldiers' families during the Boer War. Queen Alexandra's Court is therefore Wimbledon's memorial to the first war of the twentieth century.

26

The Centre Court

The origin of the Centre Court, like that of the Museum, lies in the 1860s, the decade when Wimbledon began to change from village to suburb. In 1868 John Walsh, the editor of *The Field*, and five young sportsmen decided to start a croquet club, which they grandiloquently named the All-England Croquet Club. They needed a ground, but had little money and found all the promising sites near London much too expensive. They were on the point of giving up when in September 1869 they heard of a four acre field on a country lane by the side of the railway in Wimbledon, which was considerably cheaper. A solicitor acting for the owners, the Mansel-Phillips family, was prepared to lease it to them for only £50 the first year, rising to £100 in the third. The offer was accepted and in the autumn the Club took over their new home.

For centuries the field had been used to grow corn and for at least the past hundred years it had been farmed by successive members of the Watney family. Just beyond its western boundary lay the relatively new Southdown Farm with its herd of Jersey cows. Its situation could not have been more rural. In 1869 the country lane, still known as Upper Worple, was nothing more than a rutted cart track, quite unsuitable for carriages. The nearest houses were in St George's Road, near the Station, and the only practical way to reach the ground from that station was to walk along a narrow path, owned by the Railway Company, that ran at the side of their line. So the club paid the Company one pound for the right to use the path and to make a gate in their fence giving access to it.

They then had to improve the ground. The field sloped towards the railway line and was rather boggy. A lot of soil had to be removed, after which three terraces were created and on them twelve croquet lawns were laid out. Paths were made between them, along with a number of round, thatched summer houses from which ladies could watch the games. A small club-house was built in the north-east corner (it is the one feature of the club that survives in its original place). And the fences had to be repaired to keep the neighbouring cows from trespassing. Finally, John Walsh presented the Club with a roller to keep the lawns even (it is still in use, though now on the Centre Court, Church Road).

The Club held its first All-England Croquet Championship in 1870. It seems to have been a success, but the popularity of the game was already declining and the Club was soon in danger of bankruptcy. Then in 1875 one of the Committee suggested allowing the new game of Lawn Tennis to be played on one of the croquet lawns and it proved so big an attraction that the next year four more courts were

Tennis at the Worple Road ground in 1880. The club house is in the background to the left. Behind is the slope of Darlaston Road with one of its new houses on the top; to the right is the railway; in the centre are two of the thatched summer houses for the ladies.

added. In 1877 the Club was renamed the All-England Croquet and Lawn Tennis Club and the Committee decided to hold its first Tennis Championship.

By this time Upper Worple had become Worple Road. Its surface had been made up by the Local Board and houses had begun to appear along its eastern end. Private carriages could now drive up to the ground, while spectators coming by train could hire a "fly" outside the station. So, on 9 June a notice was put in *The Field*:

"The All-England Croquet and Lawn Tennis Club, Wimbledon, propose to hold a lawn tennis meeting, open to all amateurs, on Monday July 9th and following days. Entrance fee £1.1.0. Two prizes will be given — one gold champion prize to the winner, one silver to the second player. Players must provide their own rackets and must wear shoes without heels."

Twenty-two men entered (ladies were not allowed to compete until 1884). They wore white shirts and trousers, kept up by a belt, with a small necktie and hat, and used pear-shaped real tennis rackets. The matches were played on all the twelve croquet lawns, instead of the worst four which had previously been used for tennis. They were umpired by men in top hats sitting on small platforms, with ball boys provided for each court. The first four rounds were played without special incident, but the final was held over to the second Monday so that players and spectators could watch the Eton and Harrow cricket match. It then rained hard and the final was only played on the Thursday in damp, overcast conditions so as not to disappoint the two hundred or so people who had come some distance and paid a shilling to watch.

The finalists were Spencer Gore and William Marshall, both real tennis players. Marshall had played for Cambridge; Gore was an Old Harrovian and "a natural genius for all games". His parents, one a senior civil servant, the other a relation of the Spencers, lived at Westside House on the Common. Gore had been born there in 1850, but after his recent marriage had moved to Wandsworth. He is said to have cycled from there each day of the championships to Worple Road, although he would have had to use a penny-farthing, none too pleasant for a journey down Wimbledon Hill. Tall, well-built and sporting a fine red beard, he proved much too good for Marshall. Between the showers, he served and volleyed his way to a quick victory 6-1, 6-2, 6-4 and so won both the twelve guinea gold prize and the silver challenge cup, presented by *The Field*.

The next year Gore returned to defend his title, but only had to play in the final or "challenge round". This time he lost, in three close sets, to a fellow Old Harrovian, P. F. Haddow. He did not play at Wimbledon again, regarding lawn tennis as rather an inferior game, and preferred to play club cricket at which he excelled. He became a successful surveyor and died in 1906.

Meanwhile, the Centre Court had been born. The first final was probably played on the court in front of the club house. By 1880 with over a thousand spectators arriving to watch the Challenge Round, two movable stands and score boards had to be provided around the most central of the courts. Four years later the stands were made permanent and soon afterwards the first tarpaulin covers were provided to protect the court against the almost inevitable rain. (In 1911 they were first raised, "on two poles so that the rain runs down into gullies on each side of the arena".) The Railway Company acknowledged the growing number of passengers travelling to the tennis by stopping their trains at a special platform opposite the ground during the Championships. But after a few years the concession had to be withdrawn as the number of trains on the line increased. Players and spectators on courts six to nine nearest to the railway then began to object to the growing noise and smoke from the engines.

By the Edwardian era "Wimbledon" had become an important event in the London social calendar, alongside Lords, Ascot and Henley. Tickets for seats on the Centre Court were much in demand, while tea on the lawn in front of the club house gave the Championships the atmosphere of a garden party. Photographs of the period show the ladies and gentlemen, all well-dressed, all wearing hats (many of the men in boaters) and seated at white tables where they were served by an army of waitresses. Plenty of Wimbledonians used to go to the ground, as well as an ever-growing number of visitors, but none seem to have left any memories of the tennis, except for two small boys. One regularly played truant from his school in Haydons Lane to stand in Nursery Road and open the doors of cabs in the hope of being given

Spectators walking down Nursery Road towards the entrance turnstiles in 1912. Cabs, probably from Wimbledon Station, wait to put down their passengers. Behind the hoarding on the left was the site of the old covered courts. The railway lies behind the trees in the background.

a few pennies. The other, the six year old Patrick Fawcett, used to go to tea in Worple Road with friends whose back windows overlooked the grounds. He later remembered "the gaily summer-clad spectators", especially the ladies whose dresses, according to the tennis correspondent of the *Borough News*, were "of rainbow hues" and whose "flower or plume-decked hats" made "an extremely pleasing picture".

By 1914 the ground had reached saturation point. The stands around the Centre Court could now seat 3,500 spectators and had been enlarged to the limit of available space. People began waiting outside the ground all night for the gates to open and the queues often stretched far down Worple Road. They were now brought by trams which since 1907 made special journeys from Wimbledon Station, or by motor taxis which began to operate in 1912 — or even by private cars. The 1913 Championships were particularly crowded. The weather was perfect and a record number of spectators turned up, above all on Men's Final's Day when about 10,000 got into the ground. To make matters worse, some suffragettes tried to burn down the Centre Court stands. Just in time they were spotted by a guard who captured one of them. For the rest of the meeting all bags and parcels were closely scrutinised. But this did not solve the traffic problem. Worple Road was blocked with traffic; local residents complained; the police confessed that they had no answer. The next year the club tried to solve the congestion by buying two houses overlooking the ground and using their gardens as an extra tea lawn and car park.

The real answer, however, was to move. After failing to buy other neighbouring properties, the club decided to look for a new ground. The First World War broke out before any could be found, So the change had to be postponed until after the Armistice. In 1920 a much larger ground was bought — just over thirteen acres in Wimbledon Park, a triangle of land between Church and Somerset Roads. Over half the area, where the main courts were to be laid out, had been owned by John Augustus Beaumont's daughter, Lady Lane. It had been a part of the dairy farm established by the Spencers in their park and had long been used for grazing cows and horses. Early in 1922 it was the scene of vast construction work as a new "Centre Court" made of reinforced concrete was built to the designs of Captain Stanley Peach. It was to hold three times as many spectators as the old Centre Court and kept the traditional name despite being at one end of the new ground.

The courts were declared open by King George V on 26 June 1922. He gave three blows on a gong, the tarpaulins were removed, the first match started — and the rain came down. The first championships in Wimbledon Park were the wettest on record and could not be finished until the third Wednesday. But huge crowds came to watch,

A familiar sight, even in Worple Road: the Centre Court in 1914 with spectators waiting for the rain to stop. To the right, the court lies under a large tarpaulin, raised "on two poles" so that the rain runs off.

THE CENTRE COURT

despite the price for admission going up from 2s.6d. to 3s.6d. Meanwhile, Worple Road settled back to its normal quiet. The old Centre Court was dismantled and the wood used in the construction of stands around the new Courts 2 and 3. The ground was put up for sale. For some years it was used by a private tennis club, but ultimately it was bought by Wimbledon High School and used as a sports field.

The new Centre Court became the focus of international attention for the fortnight of the Championships every year up to 1939. During the Second World War its buildings and concourse were used by the Red Cross, Civil Defence and Home Guard, and its roof was badly damaged by a bomb in October 1940. Yet the Championships were able to restart in the summer of 1946 and they have continued without a break ever since. They are not universally popular among the residents, particularly the shop-keepers in the Village whose trade is ruined for the fortnight by no-parking signs. Householders in Church, Somerset and Arthur Roads also object to the never-ending queues which leave piles of litter and even more to the hospitality tents which have sprung up in private gardens and ruin their peace.

Nonetheless, the Championships make the name Wimbledon known in every country of the world. While even well-informed people are reputed to have asked: "Merton, where is that?" few who watch televison can be in any doubt about the location of the Centre Court. Wimbledon may have started as the site of an obscure Bronze Age Camp, and certainly now has to continue as part of an overlarge London Borough. But it has a secure niche in history as the place chosen by some of our greatest families in which to live, as the centre of one of the finest Commons in the London area, and as the town where lawn tennis first became a great international game.

ROADS AROUND THE CENTRE COURTS

Nursery Road

The short street leading from Worple Road to the ornamental gates (put up in 1935 to commemorate the sixtieth anniversary of tennis at the original All-England ground) takes its name from the Worple Nursery which once existed on its western side. Established about 1880 by G. Legg, "Florist", it had become by the First World War a flourishing business. Run by his son Ernest, a Fellow of the Royal Horticultural Society, from a house (which still exists) on the corner of Worple Road, it had a large greenhouse at one side and a line of smaller greenhouses in the garden behind. An advertisement of 1912 described Mr Legg as "nurseryman, seedsman and florist" and declared that he could provide "wreaths, crosses, all kinds of floral designs and bouquets to order". He also "laid out, planted and attended to gardens". After the war, the shop passed through several hands and finally closed in 1938.

On the opposite side of Nursery Road a roller-skating rink was put up in the late 1870s, but the craze soon passed. In 1880 it was offered to the All-England Club. The Committee turned it down, but four members took it over and converted it into two indoor tennis courts. Unfortunately, it was not really large enough and the roof was too low. So by the early 1890s it was again disused. Jesuit priests came to the rescue. They had just founded a school for Catholic boys in a house near the bottom of Darlaston Road, but with numbers soon rising into double figures they needed extra

room. So in September 1892 the Headmaster, Fr. Nicholson, decided to lease the covered courts. He arranged for the boys' lunches to be brought from Darlaston Road by an odd-job man. One day the man tripped and the lunches spilled all over Nursery Road, "to the intense dismay of the hungry, waiting school". The boys were pacified, however, when they were sent to the Jesuit house, "where a fresh lunch had been hurriedly prepared". Nine months later the school, now twenty-two strong, moved to its present buildings in Edge Hill, and the covered courts were again without a use. They were next taken over by Patmore's "Rocket Cycle and Riding School", about which unfortunately nothing is known. Finally, they were turned into a factory.

Church Road

Originally known as Wimbledon Park Road, it is now a continuation down the hill of the old Church Road, the lane that for centuries linked the Village to the Parish Church. It was laid out in the 1760s by Capability Brown for the first Earl Spencer and (along with Victoria Drive) was part of a new carriage-way through the park from the Portsmouth Road.

Apart from the All-England Courts, it passes two places of historic interest. The first lies just below the turning into Burghley Road: a broken turnstile and a short footpath which now leads only to some new houses. For many years it used to be known as the Dairy Walk and was a right of way between the Church and the Dairy Farm, whose cows and horses grazed in the surrounding fields. Parts at least of the farm seem to survive in houses in Burghley Road, opposite the end of Calonne Road.

The other place is a little further down on the same side of the road. It is now

An abrupt end to a road in Wimbledon Park about 1910 with the lake in the background. The site appears to be Marryat Road, just beyond the junction with Burghley Road. If it is so, the tracks going across the picture from left to right would be Somerset and Church Roads. Between them, therefore, is one of the fields of the Dairy Farm, which in 1920 was bought as part of the new All England Ground.

William Stead, on the right, with two friends in the garden of Cambridge House, Church Road.

covered by the modern town houses of Welford Place, but a hundred years ago it was the site of a large mansion known as Cambridge House, the home of one of the most "notorious" of all Victorian journalists, W. T. Stead. The son of a Yorkshire Congregationalist minister, he settled in Church Road with his wife and six children in 1880, when appointed Assistant and then full Editor of the *Pall Mall Gazette*. Five years later he made his name by exposing the extent of criminal vice in England, under the heading "The Maiden Tribute of Modern Babylon". A year later he found himself in Holloway Prison for three months through "a lack of precaution" in gaining some of his evidence. On his release a large crowd waited at Wimbledon Station to greet him, but he was delayed and only a few were still there when he finally arrived. Two days later he conducted a service at the Congregational Church which, the local paper said, was "filled to overflowing"; it even printed his long sermon in full.

Stead often talked at local meetings, particularly those held by the Radical

Association, but as a pacifist he was not very popular in Wimbledon. In 1884 he was hanged in effigy at his own gate. Sixteen years later, as one of the strongest opponents of the Boer War, he had his windows broken and his flower beds trampled on by crowds celebrating the relief of Mafeking. In 1912 he sailed for New York on the Titanic to attend a peace congress and lost his life trying to save women and children from drowning.

Many tributes were paid to his courage and generosity. Lord Esher even claimed that "no events happened to the country since the year 1880 which had not been influenced by the personality of Mr Stead". All that time he had been living in Cambridge House, Church Road. He certainly deserves to be remembered as a great Wimbledonian.

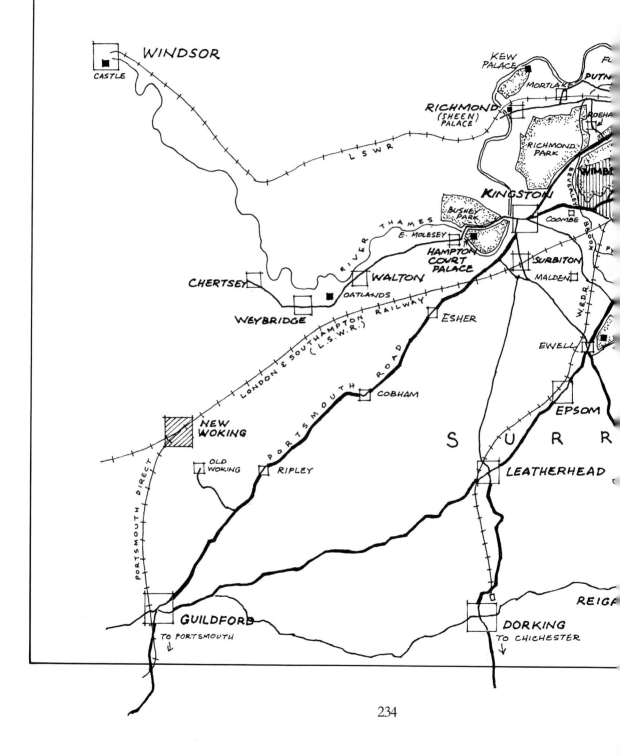

WIMBLEDON'S NEIGHBOURS

MIDDLESE

WINDSOR

CASTLE

L S W R

KEW PALACE

MORTLAKE

PUTN

RICHMOND (SHEEN) PALACE

ROEHA

RICHMOND PARK

BEVERLEY BROOK

WIMB

KINGSTON

RIVER THAMES

BUSHEY PARK

COOMBE

E. MOLESEY

HAMPTON COURT PALACE

MALDEN

SURBITON

W.E.D.R.

CHERTSEY

WALTON

OATLANDS

WEYBRIDGE

LONDON & SOUTHAMPTON RAILWAY (L.S.W.R.)

ESHER

EWELL

PORTSMOUTH ROAD

COBHAM

EPSOM

NEW WOKING

S U R

S U R R

PORTSMOUTH DIRECT

OLD WOKING

RIPLEY

LEATHERHEAD

REIGA

GUILDFORD

TO PORTSMOUTH

DORKING

TO CHICHESTER

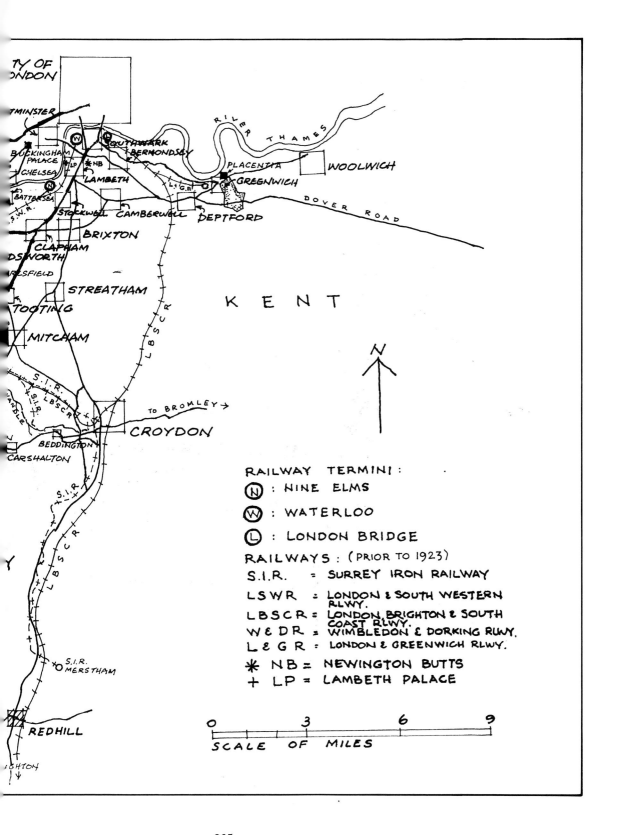

RAILWAY TERMINI:
(N) : NINE ELMS
(W) : WATERLOO
(L) : LONDON BRIDGE
RAILWAYS : (PRIOR TO 1923)
S.I.R.   = SURREY IRON RAILWAY
LSWR = LONDON & SOUTH WESTERN RLWY.
LBSCR = LONDON, BRIGHTON & SOUTH COAST RLWY.
W&DR = WIMBLEDON & DORKING RLWY.
L&GR = LONDON & GREENWICH RLWY.
✱ NB = NEWINGTON BUTTS
+ LP = LAMBETH PALACE

SCALE OF MILES

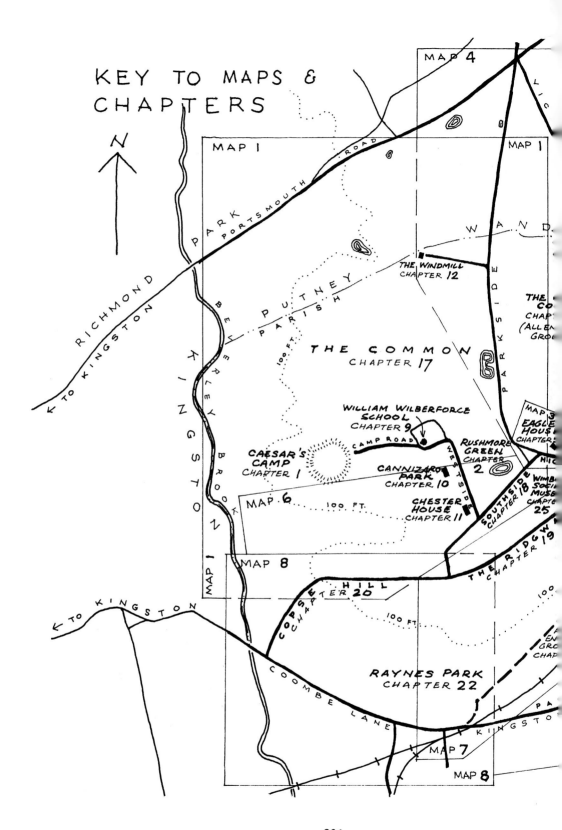

KEY TO MAPS &
CHAPTERS

MAP 4

MAP 1

MAP 1

N

RICHMOND

K TO KINGSTON

PARK

PORTSMOUTH

ROAD

PUTNEY

PARISH

KINGSTON

BEVERLEY BROOK

THE WINDMILL
CHAPTER 12

WAND

PARK SIDE

THE
CO
CHAP
(ALLE
GRO

THE COMMON
CHAPTER 17

WILLIAM WILBERFORCE
SCHOOL
CHAPTER 9

MAP
EAGLE
HOUS
CHAPTER

CAMP ROAD

WEST SIDE

RUSHMORE
GREEN
CHAPTER
2

HIG

CAESAR'S
CAMP
CHAPTER 1

CANNIZARO
PARK
CHAPTER 10

WIMBL
SOCIE
MUSE
CHAPTE
25

100 FT.

CHESTER
HOUSE
CHAPTER 11

SOUTHSIDE
CHAPTER 18

MAP 6

MAP 1

MAP 8

COPSE HILL
CHAPTER 20

THE RIDGWA
CHAPTER 19

K TO KINGSTON

COOMBE LANE

100 FT.

RAYNES PARK
CHAPTER 22

E
EN
GRO
CHAP

KINGSTO

PA

MAP 7

MAP 8

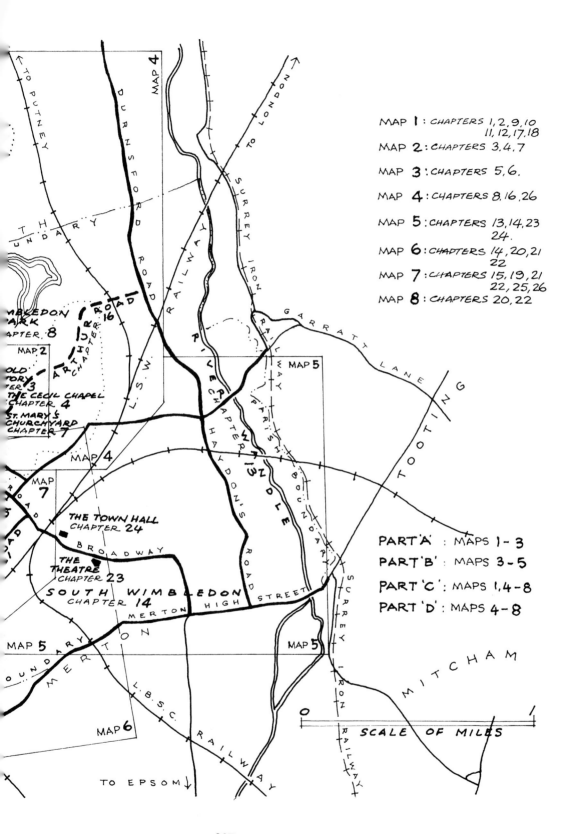

MAP 1 : CHAPTERS 1,2,9,10 11,12,17,18

MAP 2 : CHAPTERS 3,4,7

MAP 3 : CHAPTERS 5,6.

MAP 4 : CHAPTERS 8,16,26

MAP 5 : CHAPTERS 13,14,23 24.

MAP 6 : CHAPTERS 14,20,21 22

MAP 7 : CHAPTERS 15,19,21 22,25,26

MAP 8 : CHAPTERS 20,22

PART 'A' : MAPS 1-3

PART 'B' : MAPS 3-5

PART 'C' : MAPS 1,4-8

PART 'D' : MAPS 4-8

SCALE OF MILES

TO EPSOM↓

237

Acknowledgements

To the Wimbledon Society for permission to use many pictures from their Photographic Survey and Albums of Famous Wimbledonians; to the Wimbledon Reference Librarian, Charles Toase, for the use of three fine photographs by Johns, as well as much other help; to James Russell, of St Mark's Place, Wimbledon, for a number of interesting old photographs from the firm's archives; to the ex-editor of the *Wimbledon News*, Peter Miller, for giving me many of the other pictures, first used in 1973 to illustrate a series of articles, "The Merton Story"; to the Keeper of Manuscripts at the British Library for allowing me to do research in the Spencer Papers, so making possible the chapter on Wimbledon Park; to Aerofilms for several of the excellent aerial photographs; and to Pip Atkinson for typing the manuscript.

R.J.M.

Further Reading

General Histories

Revd W Bartlett	History and Antiquities of Wimbledon (1865; 2nd edition 1971).
G Boas	Wimbledon, Has it a History? (1947).
A A Cooke	Old Wimbledon (1927).
H Copeland (Editor)	Wimbledon and Merton Annual; four volumes (1903–1910) Articles on Eagle House (Vol.1); Canon Haygarth (Vol.3); Joseph Marryat (Vol.4); Old Folks' Memories (Vol.4); Old Rectory (Vol.2); Water Supply (Vol.3); River Wandle (Vol.4); Wimbledon House (Vol.3); Wimbledon at the Accession of Queen Victoria (Vol.1).
J Harvey	History of St Mary the Virgin (1972).
W Johnson	Wimbledon Common (1912).
R J Milward	A New Short History of Wimbledon (1989).
N Plastow (Editor)	A History of Wimbledon and Putney Commons (1986).
R Twill and N Wilks (Editors)	The River Wandle (1974).

Early Wimbledon

C S Higham	Wimbledon Manor House under the Cecils (1962).
A W Lowther	Caesar's Camp — Archaeological Journal, Vol 102 (1945).
R J Milward	Early and Medieval Wimbledon (1984). Tudor Wimbledon (1972). Wimbledon in the Time of the Civil War (1976). Wimbledon's Manor Houses (1982).

Georgian Wimbledon

C Arnold	Wimbledon's National Schools, 1733–1912 (1912).

P Bridgwater	Arthur Schopenhauer's English Schooling (1988).
F M Cowe (Editor)	Wimbledon Vestry Minutes, 1743–88 (1964).
R J Milward	A Georgian Village: Wimbledon, 1724–65 (1986).
W Myson and J Berry	Cannizaro House (1972).

Victorian Wimbledon

E C Baker	Sir William Preece (1976).
J Barrett	A Hundred Wimbledon Championships (1986).
M Bentley	Guiding Light: the Baptist Church in Wimbledon (1972).
F Bonham	Notes on Wimbledon Methodism, 1849–1943 (1943).
B Cook and C Riggs	History of Ricards Lodge (1975).
S Cornfield	The Queen's Prize: the Story of the N.R.A. (1987).
C Cruickshank	History of the Royal Wimbledon Golf Club, 1865–1986 (1986).
A Elliot	Wimbledon's Railways (1982).
E M Jowett	Raynes Park, a Social History (1987).
R J Milward	Portrait of a Church: the Sacred Heart, Wimbledon, 1887–1987 (1987).
D and B Norman-Smith	The Grange: a Centenary Portrait (1984).
G Parsloe	Wimbledon Village Club and Village Hall, 1858–1958 (1958).
N Plastow	The Wimbledon Windmill (1977).
M Rands	The Church in Cottenham Park (1958).
T Todd	The Tennis Players (1979).
W Whitehead	Wimbledon, 1885–1965 (1965).
R Willis	History and Guidebook of Christ Church (1972).

Wimbledon in the Twentieth Century

C Curry	Memories of my Side of the Common (1988).
V Ellacott	Wimbledon Theatre, a Brief History — Friends of Wimbledon Theatre Quarterly Review (1974).
V Ely	Fifty Years Hard (1976).
P Fawcett	Memories of a Wimbledon Childhood, 1906–18 (1981).
L Moore	Wimbledon Common Golf Club: the First 75 Years (1986).
F Miles and G Cranch	Kings College School; The First 150 Years (1979).
N Plastow	Safe as Houses, Wimbledon, 1939–45 (1972).
M Smith	Short History of Wimbledon Cinemas (1988).
J Spencer	Chronicles of the Wimbledon Literary and Scientific Society (1988).
G Wilson	London United Tramways (1971).

Index

241

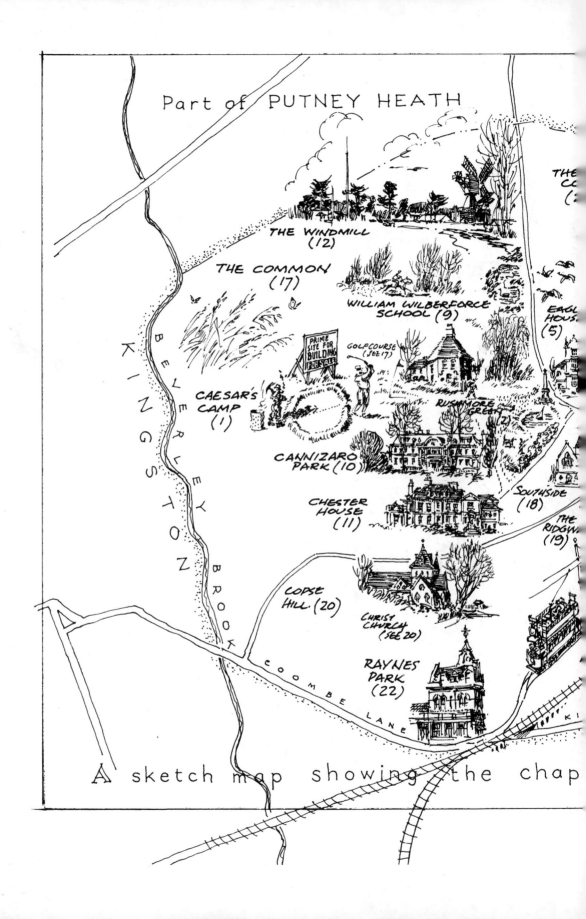

Part of PUTNEY HEATH

THE WINDMILL (12)

THE COMMON (17)

WILLIAM WILBERFORCE SCHOOL (9)

THE CL (:

EAGL HOUS. (5)

PRIME SITE FOR BUILDING FOR SALE

GOLF COURSE (see 17)

CAESAR'S CAMP (1)

RUSHMORE GREEN (2)

CANNIZARO PARK (10)

SOUTHSIDE (18)

CHESTER HOUSE (11)

THE RIDGW (19)

COPSE HILL (20)

CHRIST CHURCH (SEE 20)

RAYNES PARK (22)

KINGSTON

BEVERLEY BROOK

COOMBE LANE

KI

A sketch map showing the chap